Forex Essentials in 15 Trades

Founded in 1807, John Wiley & Sons is the oldest independent publishing company in the United States. With offices in North America, Europe, Australia and Asia, Wiley is globally committed to developing and marketing print and electronic products and services for our customers' professional and personal knowledge and understanding.

The Wiley Trading series features books by traders who have survived the market's ever changing temperament and have prospered—some by reinventing systems, others by getting back to basics. Whether a novice trader, professional or somewhere in-between, these books will provide the advice and strategies needed to prosper today and well into the future.

For a list of available titles, visit our Web site at www.WileyFinance.com.

Forex Essentials in 15 Trades

The Global-View.com Guide to Successful Currency Trading

JOHN M. BLAND

JAY M. MEISLER

MICHAEL D. ARCHER

WILEY

John Wiley & Sons, Inc.

Published by John Wiley & Sons, Inc., Hoboken, New Jersey.
Published simultaneously in Canada.

For general information on our other products and services or for technical support, please contact our Customer Care Department within the United States at (800) 762-2974, outside the United States at (317) 572-3993 or fax (317) 572-4002.

Wiley also publishes its books in a variety of electronic formats. Some content that appears in print may not be available in electronic books. For more information about Wiley products, visit our web site at www.wiley.com.

Library of Congress Cataloging-in-Publication Data:

Bland, John M., 1946–
  Forex essentials in 15 trades : the global-view.com guide to successful currency trading / John M. Bland, Jay M. Meisler, Michael D. Archer.
      p. cm. – (Wiley trading series)
  Includes index.
  ISBN 978-0-470-29263-1 (cloth)
  1. Foreign exchange market.   2. Foreign exchange futures.   I. Meisler, Jay M., 1948–
II. Archer, Michael D. (Michael Duane)   III. Title.
  HG3851.B53 2009
  332.4′5–dc22

                                                                    2008047042

Printed in the United States of America.

10 9 8 7 6 5 4 3 2 1

To all the members of the worldwide
global-view.com community

Contents

Preface

*F*orex Essentials in 15 Trades takes a new and different approach to teaching the basics of currency trading. The three authors combined have nearly 100 years of experience in the markets; our experiences are from different perspectives and vantage points. What we have in common is that our insights come from the perspective of a trader. Many books are available on learning the mechanics and language of FOREX, but reading this book along with the resources on the Global-View.com web site will give you a unique, in-depth perspective on currency trading.

HOW THIS BOOK IS ORGANIZED

This book is divided into three parts. Part One provides a substantive background in FOREX basics, money management, fundamentals, technical analysis, and what it takes to be a successful trader. Part Two details 15 of author Mike Archer's trades, showing how theory might be translated into practice. Part Three is a compendium of articles written by the authors to supplement Parts One and Two.

Part Two analyzes 15 FOREX trades to let the reader see the book's concepts in action and to get inside a trader's mind as he sifts information, seeks candidate trades, makes a trade, monitors it, and finally conducts a postmortem of the trade. These are all real trades made by author Mike Archer. Part Two begins with his Snowflake heuristic for finding trades (Chapter 8) and describes his two primary trading methods, the Goodman Swing Count System and market environments (ME).

Part Three is a compendium of readings primarily from the Global-View web site. These articles supplement the Part One and Part Two chapters. For example, you may even wish to skim Chapter 27 (GSCS basics) and Chapter 28 (ME applications) *before* reading Part Two. Appendix A, GVI's "Common Sense for Traders Checklist," provides more perspective to the reader for both the FOREX basics and the money management chapters in Part One.

This book also offers two unique learning tools: "The Inside Scoop" and GVI Snippets. Most traders never know or learn more about the markets than they see on their broker-dealer's trading platform or hear from a news squawk box. The professional's edge is in seeing the hidden structures behind market movements; herein we attempt to peer through that window with "The Inside Scoop." Following is an example:

THE INSIDE SCOOP (MIKE ARCHER)

As a newbie in 1973 I was struggling with some of the syntax and intricacies of the futures market. The meaning of the important concept of a "carrying charge" was eluding me. I read several explanations of it, and two brokers attempted to explain it to me. No luck. Finally, I stumbled across a discussion of hedging where the term was used twice in context. I had a eureka moment, and suddenly the other explanations all fell nicely into place. Looking at the same subject or concept from different perspectives is almost always worthwhile to the beginner.

Global-View has been in operation for about a dozen years. The amount of useful material archived in just its forums is enormous. By becoming a GVI member (it is free!) you can participate in the current, ongoing forums—which run seven days a week, 24 hours a day—and access the wealth of materials and insights in the archives. A simple keyword search on the GVI forums of a term or concept can be illuminating by virtue of the many contexts in which you will see the word or phrase. The back-and-forth, theory-and-practice approach is both an easier and a more effective method for learning FOREX. It is also more entertaining and enjoyable than a straight description. You have the opportunity to learn most FOREX subjects by viewing them from a range of perspectives and contexts. Following is an example of a GVI Snippet, which will appear throughout the book (this is a typical market comment from a U.S. trader):

I expect a slight dollar pullback on some pairs, though the euro should remain weak. I expect some spec buying starting @ 1.4327. Until this level I don't expect major moves. Cable (British pound) might firm up a little. For a good yielder it may be time to scale in a micro lot in gbpusd. GL/GTs to ALL.

Or (from a trader in Shanghai):

Oil has been leading Dollar for the last few years and Dollar's medium-term direction may depend on it as well. Oil may correct some more in coming weeks. Expecting Dx to range in 75-78 range for a few weeks. Medium-term, it may test DX 80 region but that may be as far as it can bounce. Dollar's long-term trend is still down. It never had any medium-term bounce since 2006 and having one now and that is all. All the best.

Or (also Shanghai):

For medium-term traders, the combination of Spot and Option positions is the way to go to take advantage of the whole move lasting for weeks and months. For example, when Eur/Usd and Usd/Jpy moved some 1,000 pips it is always advisable to use Option strategies to lock in the profits and also cover the future advances as well. In that way, you will keep your original positions and still be able to take advantage of future moves at little or no cost. Study of Option strategies will help a lot for medium-term traders to avoid the pitfalls when the market retraces some or most of its advances. Spot and Options must be used together as two weapons in the whole strategy and that may enhance your performance as a position trader a great deal. But at the end of the day, not all traders can have those nerves of steel and patience which can stand months of holding positions. So, a trader can adjust some suitable strategy for his own personality as well.

Each chapter offers highlights and excerpts from the Global-View web site on the topic at hand via the GVI Snippets. In the Summary sections we provide Global-View web site links with supplemental material for study.

BEYOND THE BOOK: THE GLOBAL-VIEW WEB SITE

The goal of the Global-View.com web site is to support traders of all levels of experience. It offers a broad range of content and tools to support traders. It is a web site designed by traders for traders.

The centerpiece of the Global-View community is its trader forums. The forums, which operate 24 hours a day, seven days a week, include members from over 160 countries. The forums are not chat rooms. They are nonintimidating places where traders can come at any time to exchange ideas and follow the news and flows that are driving the FOREX and financial markets.

Global-View offers a wealth of free content and products to support trading activities. They include free charts, FOREX rates, chart points, signal services, selected FOREX blogs, and a Jobs Center. The free FOREX broker listing service is one of the most popular pages.

A key feature of the web site for new traders is the extensive Learning Center. The Learning Center features a free Learning/Help Forum that is manned by experienced FOREX professionals. The Learning Center is a place where a trader of any level of experience can benefit, and is a good place to get started. We suggest reading through the various articles, watching the video trading courses, and checking out the dynamic FOREX trading handbook.

We also encourage the reader to open a demo FOREX trading account (Chapter 7 includes a list of brokers you might choose from). Practice doesn't necessarily make perfect, but it provides yet another perspective for learning the information and acquiring the knowledge you will need for a reasonable chance of long-term success as a FOREX trader.

READY TO GO

We hope readers who are new or recently new to FOREX will find *Forex Essentials in 15 Trades* instructive and entertaining. Our goal is for you to come away with a more rounded and, especially, deeper understanding of what makes the currency markets tick than most traders acquire.

JOHN BLAND
Co-Founder, Global-View.com

JAY MEISLER
Co-Founder, Global-View.com

MICHAEL ARCHER
CEO, FXPraxis.com

Introduction

This is a book designed by traders for traders. The unique opportunity with *Forex Essentials in 15 Trades: The Global-View.com Guide to Successful Currency Trading* is in the ability to use the book in conjunction with the Global-View web site at www.global-view.com (GVI). This Introduction gives you a brief history of that web site and the people involved and its popular forums, which have made it a unique FOREX experience.

ORIGINS OF GLOBAL-VIEW

The Global-View.com web site is a trading community designed by FOREX traders *for* FOREX traders. It was conceptualized in the early days of the commercialization of the Internet (1996) and launched in 1997 by two FOREX market professionals, John Bland and Jay Meisler, each of whom had been in the FOREX markets in various capacities for decades. They continue to manage the site.

Originally the two felt their audience would be institutional bank traders, but they quickly discovered a fledgling FOREX trading world of retail speculators, fund managers, and former bank traders. Global-View arrived on the scene in the early days of online foreign exchange (FOREX) trading for the individual retail investor. Before this time there had been only wholesale institutional (interbank) trading and currency futures markets for individual FOREX traders. These were the very early years of the impersonal world of electronic trading. The two founders realized that many traders entering the new online FOREX community would require assistance in getting started.

The gift of the Internet was interactivity, so Jay suggested that the Global-View web site could be built around an interactive trader forum. Just as in a bank dealing room, new market participants could learn best from one another. Initially, Jay and John provided guidance and took an active contributory role in the forums. They posted a great deal of market analysis to establish a professional tone in the forum conversation. It was surprising in those days how quickly people found the web site. It was not long before Jay and John were able to retreat to the background. This allowed the forum to evolve along the lines of what worked best for its members. The Global-View FOREX Forum had become a community. The forums are free and registration is not required to view them. However, only registered members are permitted to post. Posters are required to include a location (initials or name optional) to provide an added geographical perspective on who is posting.

THE INSIDE SCOOP (JAY MEISLER)

In the summer of 1997, the manager of a small fund in Hong Kong had joined the community and was posting under the name "HK Vic." Vic revealed that he had just attended a meeting with Japanese insurance company executives who had indicated that they were required to achieve a 7 percent return on their managed assets just to cover their liabilities to investors. With the Nikkei mired in a long-term slump, interest rates at ultralow levels, and the Japanese property market depressed, the logical conclusion was that they would need to look to overseas opportunities to secure those returns (i.e., sell Japanese yen). Japanese insurance companies began selling JPY for U.S. dollars (USD), and this selling lasted for months. The USD/JPY was trading at around 115.00 in August 1997 and it eventually rose to almost 148.00 before collapsing under the weight of the Long-Term Capital Management (LTCM) carry trade meltdown. We never saw the information that had been posted by HK Vic published elsewhere. It was at that point we realized that Global-View had the potential to become a clearinghouse for market information for the retail and institutional foreign exchange market.

After this episode, the importance of encouraging *all* forum members to post even the smallest of informational items was recognized, as it is impossible to predict what information might spark an idea for a trade.

GOAL OF GLOBAL-VIEW

From its inception, the goal of the Global-View web site has been to support traders of all levels of experience: from novice to professional. With members from over 160 countries, Global-View is a true global community. It is the home of the original FOREX Forum, which is active 24 hours a day and seven days a week. *The primary objective of the Global-View forums is to generate trading ideas.*

Following is a typical trading ideas post:

Sell AUDUSD
   Entry: 8740 Target: 8520 Stop: 8778

In addition to the centerpiece FOREX Forum, Global-View also hosts active Futures, Learning/Help, and Political forums. The various Global-View forums have evolved to meet the varied needs of the community. The Futures Forum focuses on related markets, such as metals, bonds, and energy.

The Political Forum provides an outlet for political discussions, and the Learning/Help Forum is at the core of the new Global-View Learning Center. The Learning Center is designed to provide learning materials for market participants of all levels of experience, but especially new and less experienced traders. No question on the Learning/Help Forum is too basic or too sophisticated, and each will be answered by a member of the community. Thus the replies come from other traders. This is in keeping with the Global-View objective of a "site designed by traders for traders."

WHY AN OPEN FOREX FORUM?

An initial idea of Jay and John was to re-create online the atmosphere of an institutional FOREX dealing room, where traders could talk to one another to exchange views, monitor trading flows, and analyze news to handicap the market. Since it is impossible to foresee when or from where a good trading idea will develop, the forum has not been fragmented into threads, although it can be viewed in an alternative threads format for those who want to browse by subject.

Following are examples of typical rumor mill posts:

Some earlier chatter that [name omitted] had an "emergency meeting" over the weekend. Company reports later this week, so rumors being circulated of a bigger write-down in subprime securities.
   Rumors of Fed emergency meeting
   Market rumors of a large Asian name protecting an option at the 1.3250 level at the moment

The Global-View community has become a clearinghouse of market information and analysis flow for the FOREX market. This includes news and rumors as well as trading ideas. The FOREX Forum is now being exported to a number of outside broker web sites. This has enlarged its universe and allowed it to become a backbone of the industry.

A typical news post goes something like this:

BOE unchanged at 5.5%
   US Jul Durable Goods Orders +5.9%; Consensus +1.0%
   Data event on deck on the half-hour:
   July Challenger Layoffs. Previous: –21.6%

FORUM RULES OF BEHAVIOR

There must be a set of rules for behavior on the forums, and adherence to the rules determines the success of this trading community. The Global-View forum rules are simple and primarily try to encourage polite and professional behavior. Aside from trying to curb spam and any content that might be inappropriate for a global audience, it was determined Global-View should not become a chat room. The goal was to prevent cliques from developing and to make all community members feel welcome and at ease. This objective has been achieved even beyond initial expectations. The rules are designed to keep the flow on topic and to avoid distractions. Occasionally, the webmasters have to step in to enforce the eight rules.

Global-View Forum Rules

1. The forums are meant to be places where traders from around the globe can relay information and ideas. Their purpose is to *generate trading ideas.*

2. Include location (initials are optional) when posting a message. Only one identity is permitted.

3. These are not chat rooms. They are forums that are directed to all viewers. Please direct updates to the general forum and avoid two-way chats.

4. No form of direct or indirect advertising is permitted without permission.

5. To protect the privacy of participants, posting e-mail addresses is not permitted. From time to time, the webmaster may, at its sole discretion, act as an intermediary to pass messages between contributors.

6. Profanity or disruptive behavior on the forums is not permitted.

7. Personal attacks on individual participants are not permitted. Readers are encouraged to respect the ideas of those who have been kind enough to contribute to the forum and treat one another with civility and respect.

8. Discussions of brokers are not permitted.

HOW TO USE THE FORUMS

Some new traders make the mistake of thinking the community will tell them what trades to make. While there is a constant flow of trading ideas, traders are solely responsible for the consequences of their trading decisions and cannot shift that responsibility to the Global-View trading community or anyone else. Novices to FOREX speculation must understand FOREX trading is usually highly leveraged and thus a risky endeavor. Losses (or gains) can exceed the initial margins demanded by the broker for trading. FOREX trading is not for the faint of heart. This topic is discussed in detail in Chapter 2 on money management.

Remember that this is a global community. Manners and good taste know no nationality or culture. It may be best to sit in the background for a while and see how the forums operate before jumping in. As in many other fields, foreign exchange has its own terminology and ways of doing business. Many answers about what something means can be found in the Global-View Trading Handbook in the Learning Center. If that topic is not covered, ask a question on the Learning/Help Forum. That is why it exists. The FOREX Forum is for live trading discussions, not for technical market questions. There is probably no better vehicle for learning FOREX terminology than spending some time on the forums, in the background and observing.

A regular tells the tale:

As always I only post comments for criticism and comments, and in response to your postings on this forum—from hard-earned personal experience.

Keep in mind also that participants in the community are voluntarily offering their advice, so the words "please" and "thank you" cannot be used too frequently. Also, it is not considered polite just to be a taker. Everyone is expected to contribute to the discussions. One advantage to an open forum is that it provides posters the opportunity to tap into the collective wisdom of the community. Thus it is best to pose questions or offer opinions the community at large will be able to understand. The reasoning behind a trading recommendation can be more important than the idea itself. Do not be surprised or offended if someone on a forum challenges a post. The community can be helpful only if it probes the logical underpinnings of a proposed market outlook. If the entire forum agrees with a view (a rare event), that should be cause for concern, because when the entire market is leaning in one direction, prices almost invariably will move in the opposite one (contrary opinion). Criticism and counterplay are important components of the forums' effectiveness. You will take many hits trading FOREX; learn to take them in the forums, also.

Here is a typical FOREX Forum thread (chronological order). There has been some minor editing done for the sake of clarity. Note the way the community steps forward with ideas to help a fellow community member.

Original Post: Could somebody help me as to where the usd/jpy might stop—I am currently long and need a stop area for if it drops further. Thanks.

Reply: If you can afford it the best level to stop for a long USD/YEN position would be below 120.20.

Original Poster: I could do 120.30 but not much more below— am looking for a bounce to get out of this trade. What do you think my chances are for a bounce outta here? Or conversely would 120.20 area produce a bounce? Thanks for help.

Reply: IMHO the only real support is 120.20 which held very well the other day. If you can't afford that far then cut the position size to what you can afford.

Original Poster: Yes sorry, that was a typo—I can afford to go to 120.20 but would like to know what the chances of a bounce from here are. Thanks for help.

Reply: Well if you look at the daily, it's bounced off the 21dma, what five time so far this year, but today it's after it again and it may be determined to stay below this time ... the sixth attempt ... hasn't done that yet on a daily basis though, but the day isn't over yet.

Reply: This trade is not meant to re-enter the triangle as it is doing.

Reply: Asian session signals are more likely to fail imo. OUT.

Original Poster: Thanks to both of you for giving your valued opinions—I am hoping this current bounce will see me out ... thanks again.

Reply: You could set a stop now below the day's low if you wanted to reduce your risk.

This exchange is typical and illustrates how the collective wisdom of the trading community is brought to bear to help a member decide on what to do with a difficult trading situation.

GVI FOREX: A SPECIAL FORUM

The founders believe strongly in an open trading community but understand that many retail traders often do not approach FOREX trading the way the professional market participants do. Whereas retail traders rely primarily on technical analysis and accept market movements as they occur, institutional and more experienced dealers often try to figure out the reasons for price movements. Many rely on fundamental analysis to supplement their technical studies.

A separate home, Global-View Forex (GVI), exists for institutional and more experienced traders because of their reliance on fundamental analysis. Global-View set up a split forum format for its traders with an institutional bias so that the FOREX Forum and the Professional Forum could run simultaneously side by side. This format permits GVI participants to participate on the FOREX Forum while following the fundamentals simultaneously. Professional Global-View market analysis is also provided on this forum. GVI is a fee-based service and open to traders of all levels of experience. Only more experienced traders are permitted to post on GVI, while less experienced traders are granted read-only access.

ADDITIONAL TRADER SUPPORT

In addition to the forums, Global-View generates a considerable amount of unique content to support traders: a research blog, live news, real-time rates and charts, a data calendar, exclusive calculators, an extensive FOREX database, and other items.

AS YOU GO FORWARD

By using this book in conjunction with the Global View web site, the student is in a position to learn subjects from varying perspectives and understand the real action behind the trading platform screen. Spend some time observing the forums before participating, and follow the commonsense rules for posting. The forums and Learning Center are the heart of the web site.

Forex Essentials in 15 Trades

PART ONE

The Basics of FOREX

CHAPTER 1

An Introduction to FOREX

W e assume you are relatively new to FOREX or even new to trading. Perhaps you have dabbled with a demo account or you have some experience in other markets—stocks, futures, or options. This chapter offers a brief overview of FOREX. Our goal is not to give you an extensive primer on FOREX. Several books currently offer that information, such as *Getting Started in Currency Trading*, by Michael Duane Archer (John Wiley & Sons, 2008). The information in this chapter is intended as a brief primer of FOREX trading essentials and mechanics.

Supplementing study with actual practice is the best and fastest way to learn your way around FOREX. If you haven't done so already, we recommend opening a demo account. Consult Chapter 7 for information on brokers with robust demo platforms.

More important to you in the long term is to chart a course of study, personalized to meet your own specific requirements and incorporating the key elements of a successful trading plan. Most new traders shoot from the hip when they begin. Without at least a basic trade plan, they are doomed from the start and thereafter are quick to disparage FOREX trading. Getting started correctly is tremendously important in FOREX. The leverage involved in trading currencies is significant, and small missteps can be fatal. The following GVI snippet is some guidance from a North American trader:

> *How many traders these days take the time to print a chart and annotate a trading plan? Probably the only ones are guys who are held accountable to themselves, their boards, or managing body.*

Even if you are a short term trader, keeping a file with charts and annotations of reasons for entry, trade management, and results is a wonderful teaching tool.

The mechanics of FOREX are not difficult; serious students can learn what they need to know in a week or two of reading and another week or two working with a demo account. The real task is to get started correctly, with a well-thought-out plan. *Forex Essentials in 15 Trades* combines the trading and instructional experiences of three professionals who have a combined century of experience in the market. Following our advice might not make you an instant winner, but it is our hope it will keep you from the fate of most new traders—instant losing.

Along with the text, diagrams, charts, and tables you will find two learning devices that distill our collective experience: "The Inside Scoop" and GVI Snippets, relevant material taken directly from the Global-View web site forums and Learning Center. As a trader you will spend most of your time in front of a computer monitor, watching and studying charts and indicators. "The Inside Scoop" shows you the life behind that screen: the pulsating and vibrating world of professional FOREX trading. Interspersed throughout the book are GVI Snippets from the Global-View web site, providing an inside look and unique perspective you will not find elsewhere. Taken together, they comprise a compendium of advice and maxims that most new traders learn only over many years—if they last so long. They will give you the perspective of experience even if you haven't yet made a single trade.

THE INSIDE SCOOP (MIKE ARCHER)

I first traded commodity futures at the Denver office of Peavey & Company in 1973. It was a modern office then but would be a dinosaur now. There were a dozen or so chairs for traders, a small open room for high rollers, and a private office in the back for the charmed few. The entire front wall of the office was a large mechanical "clacker board" displaying the open, high, low, and close for 20 different commodities and delivery months. It was called a clacker board because of the sound it made when prices changed. New high prices elicited a green light; new lows, a red light.

In the high rollers' area sat a grain trader from Eads, Colorado: Charles B. (Charlie) Goodman. For a reason I never knew, Charlie took a liking to me and offered his informal services as a mentor. The techniques I learned—the Goodman Swing Count System and Market Environment (ME) charting—I still use today, although I have developed them much more deeply on my own. His money management style of "the Belgian dentist"—a very conservative approach to trading—has stood the test of time.

What works for one person might be poison to another—but it is useful to study others' attitudes and approaches to trading, their money management techniques, and their trading heuristics. If you can find an experienced and successful trader to assist you for the first year of your trading career, you will benefit greatly. A mentor can at the very least keep you from making the many common mistakes of the beginning trader. Most new traders are shown the door quickly because of the mistakes they make. By avoiding them, you greatly enhance your chances of at least staying in the game long enough to learn the game—and eventually succeed. Much of winning in FOREX, as in any business venture, is about staying power.

If a mentor is unavailable, the Global-View forums can act as a useful substitute. A U.S. Global-View member posted:

> *This [FOREX] forum and better yet, the GVI pro forum are great places to learn different techniques and styles, and learn much of the basics if you pay attention and study.*

Most new traders spend too much time and effort on devising a trading method. The hundreds of books on such methods, systems, and technical analysis attest to this misplaced interest. Keep your initial trading method a simple trend-following one. The markets can only go up or down—do not make things more complex than they are in reality. Devote most of your time to managing your money, improving your trading attitude, and getting a true feel for how the markets move and operate: their pace, characteristics, and rhythm.

A successful North American FOREX money manager advises:

> *Before trading ... spend time and money on your FX education—it boggles my mind that so many "traders" have never pursued a mentor, developed a method, kept a journal of results, etc. So many beginning traders think for some reason that they can come into a very sophisticated and massively well funded market and compete "off the hip." They've learned to read a few charts, read a book or two, and it's off to the races. This is a professional career choice ... much like securities analysts/brokers, doctors, lawyers, and so on.*
>
> *Does anyone think for a second that these career choices get handed to them? ... Not in your life! It takes years of study, cost of tuition, and in the case of FX, should come with a mentor or a few mentors of choice, to shortcut the learning curve.*

Here is a perspective on the same topic from an Aussie dealer:

To learn any profession, one has to go through a period of learning. This is through various stages, which can be defined as: certificate, diploma, degree, masters, . . . etc.

As an example—How many years (and the hours involved) does it take to obtain a degree in any subject? This is the starting point to trade. From there you continue to learn and refine. . . .

An example—Medical doctors in their training don't get to see anyone before they have their degree—after "x" years of training. Then they have to learn more by practical experience, based on previous knowledge. That is just the basics. Then how long does it take to become a specialist?

Just an analogy, as trading is not as simple as many would like to portray it.

FOREX FIRST STEPS: WHAT IS IT?

FOREX, which stands for FOReign EXchange, is the global trading of currencies. More than $3.0 trillion in foreign exchange transactions take place each business day, and the volume is increasing steadily. Until the mid-1990s the arena was the domain of large banks (the interbank market), governments, and corporations. Now it is possible for small speculators to trade online with any of a large number of retail FOREX broker-dealers using an online trading platform.

It is important to remember that a currency trade is between two currencies—a pair if one of them is the U.S. dollar (USD) and a cross otherwise—and not a buy or sell of something such as a security (e.g., General Motors) or a commodity (e.g., gold) against the dollar.

The most popular currency pair is the EUR/USD—the Eurozone euro against the U.S. dollar. To be long this pair is to want the EUR to go up and the USD to go down. To be short this pair is to want the USD to go up and the EUR to go down.

There is no central clearinghouse for currency trading as there is for stocks or commodity futures. It is the closest thing there is to a pure laissez-faire market. That cuts both ways: The opportunities are enormous but it is a largely unregulated and often cutthroat enterprise.

In the United States, retail FOREX is partially regulated by the Commodity Futures Trading Commission (CFTC) and the National Futures Association (NFA). But, with no central clearinghouse, regulation is by definition less robust and effective than in stocks or commodity futures. Regulation is largely limited to seeing that retail brokers meet certain capital requirements and follow good-practice guidelines. Caveat emptor is the watchword in FOREX.

WHY TRADE FOREX?

Despite the risks, the retail market is growing by leaps and bounds. Obviously, many traders have concluded that the opportunities outweigh those risks. Here is a short list of why people are attracted to currency trading.

No commissions. There are typically no clearing fees, no exchange fees, no government fees, and no commissions. FOREX works off a bid/ask spread and the costs are contained therein. Some brokers who use the electronic communications network (ECN) transaction model, however, also may charge a small lot fee.

High liquidity. With an average of over $3 trillion in transactions daily, it is easy to execute even very large orders in foreign exchange. Online brokers most often offer instantaneous fills on retail orders.

No fixed lot size. The standard lot size in retail FOREX is 100,000 units. Most brokers offer mini-lots of 10,000, and some let you trade as few as 100 units! The variable lot size can be an excellent money management tool for the trader. It also allows the new trader to gradually increase trade size as his or her knowledge and profits rise.

A 24-hour market. There is no opening bell in FOREX! You may trade from late Sunday afternoon (U.S. time) to late Friday evening. You may come and go as you like, and trade for as long a time or as short a time as you wish.

Online access. All retail FOREX is conducted online, via the Internet. You will trade from a broker's trading platform, which typically includes not only real-time prices and the ability to place buy and sell orders but also a variety of trading tools such as charts and indicators. Most brokers allow clients to call in orders by phone if the need arises.

Low margin, high leverage. Perhaps the most attractive element to FOREX trading is the ability to trade leverage ratios of from 10:1 up to 400:1! This means that you may control 100,000 USD with from $10,000 to as little as $250. With high leverage, a very small move may result in a 100 percent profit—or loss. Gradually increasing leverage can also be an effective money management tool.

Volatility. The FOREX markets can move quickly and sharply; profits can be large if you are correct in your price forecast.

Variety. There are more than 30 currency pairs and crosses traded, although most of the volume is concentrated in about half of those. Many traders claim individual pairs and crosses have personalities that help them make forecasts. There is enough variety to keep opportunities plentiful, but not so much as to be bewildering and confusing.

Not related to the stock market. Currencies most often move independently of the stock market, although there has been a close correlation during the 2008 financial crisis as equities are used as a measure of risk aversion. From an investment perspective it is said that currency prices are *noncorrelated* with stock prices. For this reason FOREX may be an attractive hedge to a larger stock market account.

Limited regulation. Because FOREX is a global interbank enterprise, regulation is necessarily limited. This, of course, can cut both ways, as mentioned earlier.

No insider trading. It is difficult to get useful inside information on currencies. Even if you did know in advance a key government statistic, the markets are so unpredictable that it is not often easy to foretell which way the market will go after a news release.

Countries with popularly traded currencies include:

- United States
- European Union
- Switzerland
- Great Britain
- Japan
- Canada
- Australia
- New Zealand

FOREX TERMS

Here are the most important FOREX terms. To a large extent, learning the syntax or lingo of FOREX is learning FOREX itself.

Ask price. The price at which the market is prepared to sell a specific currency in a foreign exchange contract or cross currency contract. At this price, the trader can buy the base currency. In the quotation, the ask price is shown on the right-hand side. For example, in the quote USD/CHF 1.4527/32, the ask price is 1.4532, meaning you can buy one U.S. dollar for 1.4532 Swiss francs.

Base currency. The first currency in a currency pair (for example, USD is the base currency in the currency pair USD/CHF). The rate shows how much one unit of the base currency is worth as measured against the second currency. For example, if the USD/CHF rate equals 1.6215, then one USD is worth CHF 1.6215. In the foreign exchange markets, the U.S. dollar is normally considered the base currency for quotes, meaning that quotes are expressed as a unit of $1 U.S. per the other currency quoted in the pair. The primary exceptions to this rule are the British pound, the Eurozone euro, and the Australian and New Zealand dollars.

Bid price. The price at which the market is prepared to buy a specific currency in a foreign exchange contract or cross currency contract. At this price, the trader can sell the base currency. It is shown on the left-hand side of the quotation. For example, in the quote USD/CHF 1.4527/32, the bid price is 1.4527, meaning you can sell one U.S. dollar for 1.4527 Swiss francs.

Bid/ask spread. The difference between the bid and ask (offer) price.

Big figure quote. Dealer expression referring to the first few digits of an exchange rate. These digits are often omitted in dealer quotes. For example, a USD/JPY rate might be 117.30/117.35, but would be quoted verbally without the first three digits, that is, as "30/35."

Closed position. A foreign currency position that no longer exists. The process to close a position is to sell or buy a certain amount of currency to offset an equal amount of the open position. This will square the position.

Correlation to the stock market. At the time of this writing currencies are moving in close correlation with the stock market. This is not always the case, however. Professional traders do watch for changes in correlation as an aid to decision making in placing FX orders. The switch between being correlated and non-correlated happens slowly over longer periods of time.

Counter currency. The second listed currency in a currency pair.

Cross currency pair. A foreign exchange transaction in which one foreign currency is traded against a second foreign currency. For example, EUR/GBP is the euro versus the British pound.

Currency pair. The two currencies that make up a foreign exchange rate, for example, EUR/USD.

Electronic communications network (ECN). A system wherein orders to buy and sell are matched through a network of banks and/or dealers. *See also* market maker; no dealing desk (NDD) broker.

Flat/square. Refers to a trader on the sidelines with no position.

Foreign exchange (FOREX, FX). The simultaneous buying of one currency and selling of another.

FOREX (FX). Foreign exchange.

Going long. The purchase of a stock, commodity, or currency for investment or speculation.

Going short. The selling of a currency or instrument not owned by the seller.

Leverage. The ratio of the amount used in a transaction to the required security deposit, otherwise known as margin. Leverage is typically quoted as a ratio. For example, 100:1 means one dollar controls one hundred dollars of a currency. A 1 percent move of the currency is equal to a 100 percent gain or loss of margin.

Long position. A position that appreciates in value if market prices increase. When the base currency in the currency pair is bought, the position is said to be long.

Lot. A unit used to measure the amount of the deal. The value of the deal always corresponds to an integer number of lots.

Major currency. Any of the following: Eurozone euro, British pound sterling, Australian dollar, New Zealand dollar, U.S. dollar, Canadian dollar, Swiss franc, Japanese yen. *See also* minor currency.

Margin. The required equity that an investor must deposit to collateralize a position.

Market maker. A dealer who regularly quotes both bid and ask prices and is ready to make a two-sided market for any financial instrument. Most retail FOREX dealers are market makers. A market maker is said to have a dealing desk and is the effective counterparty to your trade.

Minor currency. Any of the currencies between a major currency and an exotic. The South African rand and Swedish krona are minor currencies.

Mundo. A synthetic global currency devised by James L. Bickford, calculated as the average of multiple ISO currency pairs. See Michael Archer and James Bickford, *Forex Chartist Companion* (John Wiley & Sons, 2006).

No dealing desk (NDD) broker. Provides a platform to which liquidity providers such as banks can offer prices. Incoming orders are routed to the best available bid or offer. *See also* market maker; electronic communications network (ECN).

Short position. A position that appreciates in value if the market price decreases. When the base currency in the pair is sold, the position is said to be short.

Trading platform. The online set of tools used to trade FOREX. Trading platforms provide real-time prices of currencies, order entry mechanisms, accounting logs, and a variety of trading tools such as calculators, charts, and indicators.

The Glossary offers a comprehensive FOREX lexicon.

FOREX CALCULATIONS

The calculations in FOREX can be confusing, although they are not inherently difficult. Study will get you only so far; practice is the key. Use an online FOREX calculator to see how the various calculations work, then practice with a demo account from one of the brokers we highlight in Chapter 7. More on calculations used in FOREX is provided in Chapter 2 on money management.

You'll eventually need to be able to make these calculations instantaneously; the FOREX markets move quickly, real-time, and you'll need to concentrate on trading, not calculations. But don't worry if they don't come to you right away.

Most broker trading platforms have FOREX calculators you can use to become familiar with how the various values and units interact.

Remember that a currency transaction is between two currencies, not a single currency and a product as is true in stocks and commodity futures. You may either buy or sell a currency, profiting if it goes up or down. If you buy a currency, you are said to be long and an offsetting transaction is to sell. If you sell a currency, you are said to be short and an offsetting transaction is to buy.

EUR/USD is the symbol for the euro-to-U.S. dollar currency pair. If you buy, you are going long the front or base currency and effectively short the back or counter currency. If you sell, you are going short the base currency and effectively long the counter currency.

The basic calculations you will want to learn are the following:

Leverage and Margin Percent

Leverage = 100 ÷ Margin Percent
Margin Percent = 100 ÷ Leverage

Leverage is typically quoted as a ratio of X:1, where 1 is the margin for the position and X is the value of the position. For example, 100:1 means you control 100 times the margin amount. Typically anything under 50:1 is considered low leverage, whereas over 100:1 is very high. New traders should begin with low leverage (e.g., 10:1) and increase by 10:1 units as their confidence increases and until they maximize their money management parameters.

Pips

A pip is typically the smallest increment that any currency pair can move in either direction, up or down. In FOREX, profits and losses are calculated in terms of pips first, dollars second. The pip is very much the basic FOREX value. Some brokers now offer fractional pips on the more popular pairs. The pip is typically $10 on a 100,000 currency lot, $1 on a 10,000 lot, and $25 on a 250,000 "bank" lot.

Profit and Loss

Very basically, profit or loss is price change, which in turn is exit price minus entry price. If the value is positive, you made a profit; if it is negative, you lost.

$$\text{Profit in Pips} = \text{Price Change} \times \text{Pips}$$
$$\text{Profit in USD} = \text{Price Change} \times \text{Units Traded}$$

Trading Units

You will always want to know how many units of a pair you can buy or sell. Again, almost all broker-dealer trading platforms offer this information—but you should know how to calculate it on your own, also.

$$\text{Units Available} = 100 \times \text{Margin Available} \times \text{Rate} \div \text{Current Price}$$
$$\times \text{Margin Percent}$$

If the USD is the base currency:

$$\text{Units Available} = 100 \times \text{Margin Available} \div \text{Margin Percent}$$

Standard trading units are 10,000, 100,000, and 1,000,000.

Margin

$$\text{Margin Requirement} = \text{Current Price} \times \text{Units Traded}$$
$$\times \text{Margin Percent} \div 100$$

Most retail broker-dealers now limit how much of your total account value may be committed to active trades.

Transaction Cost

In FOREX, cost is a function of the bid/ask spread.

$$\text{Spread} = \text{Ask Price} - \text{Bid Price}$$
$$\text{Transaction Cost} = \text{Spread} \times \text{Units Traded}$$

Typical pip spreads run between one and three pips for active markets such as the EUR/USD and four to five pips for less active markets. You pay the pip spread both when you enter (buy/sell) and when you exit (sell/buy).

Pip spreads may vary widely in fast markets, slow markets, and before and after a news announcement. Market makers use this—in principle at least—to maintain an orderly market.

All broker-dealer platforms automatically calculate these figures. Nevertheless, the complete FOREX trader will want to be able to do them on his or her own. At the minimum it will add confidence to your knowledge of the business—and provide a check against any calculations made on your broker's platform.

A few hours with a demo trading account will be an invaluable tool in becoming familiar with the basic FOREX calculations. A picture or an example is worth a thousand words. We suggest you work with only the most popular pair initially, the EUR/USD. After you have mastered the calculations therein, proceed to the other popular pairs and crosses.

USD/CHF
USD/JPY
GBP/USD
EUR/JPY
EUR/CHF
EUR/GBP

GBP/JPY
GBP/CHF
AUD/USD

Orders

The palette of FOREX orders—to enter a market, protect a trade, and exit a market—is large and varied. Some broker-dealers support their own unique order types, as well. The new trader can manage everything comfortably with three basic order types: market, limit, and stop orders.

Market Orders   A market order is an order to buy or sell at the market price. The buy may be to initiate a new position or liquidate a previous sell position. The sell may be to initiate a new position or liquidate a previous buy position. A market order may not be filled at the current price, though, since, like a river, prices are always flowing. Most market makers show you the price you will receive before you execute the order. In requoting, you do not get that price. Large orders and slow, fast, and illiquid (thin) markets affect the price you will receive on a market order.

A buy adds to aggregate demand and pushes prices up, if only slightly; a sell adds to aggregate supply and has the opposite effect. The bid/ask spread in FOREX reflects this, as well as protecting your broker and helping him maintain an orderly book—and make a fair profit by serving you.

Limit Orders   A limit order specifies a certain price to execute your order. It may also specify duration—how long you wish to keep the order active. A limit order is filled at your price or better.

Stop-Limit Orders   There is also a stop-limit order. You specify a price and also a maximum range beyond that price for which the order can be executed. The advantage of a stop-limit order is that you will get the price you want if that price is reached. The disadvantage is that if prices do not trade in your specified range, your order remains unexecuted. In a fast market, a stop-limit order may be a complete waste of effort; they simply will not be executed.

A suggested rule of thumb: Use market orders in normal markets, and use limit orders for large orders and in fast, slow, and thin markets. A market order in a fast market, such as after the release of a news item, can be a disaster because of ballooning pip spreads and other dealer-intervention actions.

Time-Based Orders A good till canceled (GTC) order remains active until the trader cancels it.

A good for the day (GFD) order remains in the market for the duration of the trading day. Inasmuch as FOREX is a continuous market, the end of the day must be for a set hour.

Be sure to keep track of all open orders you have in every market. It is your responsibility to cancel them, not the broker's.

Stop Orders A stop order is the terminology used for a limit order that liquidates or offsets an open position.

An automatic trailing stop is offered by several broker-dealers. This raises or lowers your stop by a fixed value as the market goes in the direction of your position, thus protecting some of your profits. You can, of course, mechanically apply trailing stops. They are great in theory, but not quite so great in practice. They work better with some trading methods than with others.

A major debate has raged for years as to whether traders should use stop loss orders in the market or simply keep them to themselves (mental stops), wait for the market to reach that price, and then use a market order. Many traders believe brokers use stops entered in the market to balance their books, a practice referred to as "harvesting stops." Brokers are occasionally accused of running or harvesting stops—moving the data feed specifically to execute the stop order. This does happen; how often is very difficult to say.

Beginners should use stops. Once you have some experience in the market—and if and only if you have good discipline—keep mental stops. It is very easy to ignore a mental stop and hope the market turns back in your favor—and it usually does not. Yes, by using stops you let the broker see your order; and yes, stops may be harvested; and yes, stop fills—especially without limits—may be poor. But we still recommend the new trader use them.

We reiterate: *Never leave a position open without a stop! Yes, brokers will occasionally harvest your stop and, yes, you will occasionally be whipsawed—but neither is as bad as coming back and finding that a nice profit has turned into a large loss. Remember: The markets can do anything, anytime. Don't get lulled to sleep by a slow market. Don't think you are sure what a market will do at any time. From any price you see, it is possible for the next price to be up or down.*

MARKET CONVENTIONS

Following is a summary of common FOREX conventions.

Nomenclature

Currency symbols have evolved over the years and predate the computer era. Over the past few decades, dealers increasingly have come to accept the Society for Worldwide Interbank Financial Telecommunication (SWIFT) codes as a standard, although many older codes remain. The SWIFT foreign currency symbols are the international standard for currency codes established by the International Organization for Standardization (ISO). Each currency symbol has a three-letter code. The ISO 4217 currency codes list is the standard in banking and business all over the world.

Since there is no universal standard of value for currency valuation (e.g., the price of oil or wheat is usually expressed in U.S. dollars), the value of a currency has meaning only when it is expressed in terms of another currency. One wag has said that the FOREX market is the largest barter market in the world.

Selected Currency Codes

USD—U.S. dollar

EUR—Eurozone euro

CHF—Swiss franc

GBP—British pound

JPY—Japanese yen

CAD—Canadian dollar

AUD—Australian dollar

NZD—New Zealand dollar

See Appendix C for additional currency codes. A comprehensive list also is available in the Global-View Learning Center at www.global-view.com/forex-trading-tools/swifta.html.

QUOTING CONVENTIONS

As noted, the value of a currency has meaning only when it is expressed in terms of another currency. Thus the EUR/USD rate is the price of one euro in terms of U.S. dollars. The quoting convention is that the first symbol indicated (e.g., EUR) is one unit of the currency being measured in terms of the second currency indicated (e.g., USD).

Example: EUR/USD = 1.4535 means one euro is worth $1.4535.

The markets do not have a consistent rule for how any currency is quoted, including the USD. Thus some currencies are quoted in terms of their USD valuations, while other pairs see the USD quoted as its foreign currency value. Which pair uses which convention has been determined by historical precedent.

Selected Pairs

In some pairs, USD value is calculated in terms of one unit of the opposite currency. Thus as the value rises, the opposite currency gains and the USD weakens; and when the value falls, the USD strengthens.

> EUR/USD = 1.4535
> GBP/USD = 1.9525
> AUD/USD = 0.9060
> NZD/USD = 0.7930

In other pairs, the opposite currency value is calculated in terms of one USD. Thus as the value rises, the opposite currency weakens and the USD gains; and as the value falls, the USD weakens.

> USD/JPY = 107.40
> USD/CHF = 1.1035
> USD/CAD = 0.9989

Note that increasingly the slash ("/") between currency symbols is being dropped, because some computer programs don't know what to do with it and it is unnecessary.

Thus EUR/USD becomes EURUSD.

Crosses

Active markets are also made in cross currency (non-USD) pairs (e.g., the euro against the yen). Quoting rules are the same as for the U.S. dollar pairs. Thus the EUR/JPY is the JPY value of one euro.

Example: EUR/JPY = 107.35 means one euro is worth 107.35 yen.

In this relationship, as the value rises, the euro gains against the yen; and as the value falls, the euro weakens.

ELEMENTS OF A TRADE PLAN

A trade plan may be simple or complex. Its goal is to give you a basic map or guide for your trading activities. By making decisions in your trade plan, you can react quickly to changing market conditions.

Money Management

The authors of this book have a combined experience in the markets of almost 100 years. While we differ individually on a number of issues, we are unanimous on one topic: Money management is the most important aspect of successful trading.

Money management is the art and science of managing your money in the market—both in the aggregate and for individual trades.

Key elements of a good trading plan include:

- Money management parameters.
- Markets to trade.
- Trade objectives and stop-loss amounts.
- Basic trading methods.

Money management is covered in more detail in Chapter 2.

Trading Method

Chess players are familiar with the saying, "Chess is a sea in which a gnat may drink and an elephant may bathe." Ditto technical analysis. The range of technical analysis methods and systems is simply enormous. There are more than 200 books in print on the subject, and the corpus of material published since technical analysis became popular in the late twentieth century would fill a small-town library. Chapter 3 is a short tour of the technical analysis landscape. Retail traders tend to use technical analysis exclusively, whereas professionals often temper their work with fundamental analysis, discussed in Chapter 4.

As a new trader, you should aim to keep your trading method simple. There is much to learn in FOREX, and you'll need to find time also for learning the basics of money management, analyzing the markets, making calculations, and executing trades.

Attitude

Fear and greed run the markets. Controlling them is the key to long-term success. Successful FOREX traders seem to share certain attitude characteristics. See Chapter 6 for a comparison of good trader characteristics versus bad trader characteristics.

Heuristic

A heuristic, in simplest form, is a question-and-answer process to get from data to a conclusion. Every chess player worth his salt has an analysis heuristic he uses when it is his turn to make a move. Classical chess games are played with time limits, analogous to the real-time movement of the markets. A heuristic can be an invaluable asset in making sure your trades are in line with your methodology, as a diagnostic tool, and to keep you from straying because of the enormous emotional impact of real-time trading.

A heuristic should be a fairly simple process-based approach to analyzing markets, finding candidate trades, entering a trade, exiting a trade, and diagnosing the trade and/or doing a short postmortem of the trade. We like to think of a trade plan as a process loop in which we can make changes on an evolutionary rather than revolutionary basis.

Chapter 8 introduces author Mike Archer's Snowflake heuristic, including a simple trend-following trading method.

Diagnostics and Postmortem

An important component of any trade plan is a diagnostic loop—analyzing your trades on a daily, weekly, and monthly basis. The simpler your trading method, the easier it is to diagnose problem areas and make midcourse corrections. Do a short postmortem of each trade—win or lose, what went right and what went wrong—shortly after closing it and while it is still fresh in your mind. Then, move on; never dwell on it or gloat.

It is important to briefly analyze each trade you make after it is complete. You may wish to devise a short checklist and see how each trade measures up against the points on that list.

SUMMARY

Before you begin trading, you must first become familiar with the mechanics of FOREX trading. Use the Global-View Learning Center, Global-View forums, and a demo account, and focus on the order process, basic calculations, and the basic pace and rhythm of the markets.

The elements of your trade plan should work together in harmony. The plan should be simple. As Charlie Goodman would say, "After all, the markets can only go up or down." The trade plan should be designed with a heuristic that allows for all elements of the trade process, including a postmortem and incorporation of incremental changes as needed. FOREX markets move quickly, and the leverage factors of 50:1 to 400:1 require that decisions in real time be made quickly, without undue analysis. Learning the basics correctly is an important first step to achieving this goal.

Recommended Global-View Links

Learning Center: www.global-view.com/forex-education/forex-learning/

FOREX Trading Handbook: www.global-view.com/forex-education/forex-trading-handbook/

SWIFT Codes: www.global-view.com/forex-trading-tools/swfta.html

CHAPTER 2

The Importance of Money Management

M oney management includes trading wisely and husbanding your trading resources. FOREX speculation involves significant risk taking. Never risk what you cannot afford to lose. You cannot trade without trading capital, so capital preservation is critical. One key to holding on to your capital is the appropriate use of leverage. The required Commodity Futures Trading Commission (CFTC) warning statement on the Global-View web site contains a lot of wisdom for traders of any instrument. This chapter also discusses appropriate leverage strategies and provides a list of trading rules.

Coming into the trading game, it is important to realize that all traders have many losing trades. Be aware of this before starting. Stop loss orders are often not used by novice traders; use them, as they are critical to your trading survival.

It is not our intention in this chapter to be negative, but the majority of the items covered here are "don'ts" as opposed to "do's" if only because new traders seem to major in "don't." The following are some important thoughts from an experienced European trader.

Trading is not mainly about making money but more about CAPITAL PRESERVATION. Think about it. NO CAPITAL, NO TRADING!

Each time you enter a trade you should think "How much I am ready to lose!" and not "How much I am HOPING to make!"

Trading is simple, but it is not easy!

CFTC WARNING

Many of us see a warning label or disclosure statement and just gloss over it. The required CFTC warning statement about FOREX trading on margin contains useful information that is worth taking a few minutes to read and think about. Many of the topics covered in this chapter relate to the items mentioned in this required statement:

> *Trading foreign exchange on margin carries a high level of risk, and may not be suitable for all investors. The high degree of leverage can work against you as well as for you. Before deciding to invest in foreign exchange you should carefully consider your investment objectives, level of experience, and risk appetite. The possibility exists that you could sustain a loss of some or all of your initial investment and therefore you should not invest money that you cannot afford to lose. You should be aware of all the risks associated with foreign exchange trading, and seek advice from an independent financial advisor if you have any doubts.*

KEY TO SUCCESS AS A TRADER: PRESERVE YOUR CAPITAL

Capital preservation is the key to trading success at all levels, from the small individual trader to the sophisticated large hedge fund manager, and it must be goal number one. Without sufficient capital, a player cannot participate in the markets. In the warning statement, the CFTC states that "The high degree of leverage can work against you as well as for you."

A common error of new traders is overleveraging their trading capital. Later in the chapter we discuss how to calculate your leverage and recommend a commonsense approach to how much of your trading capital to put at risk on any given trade.

THE INSIDE SCOOP (JAY MEISLER)

Typically, it seems that traders don't come to us until they are about to blow their accounts. The source of the problem is usually a lack of discipline that turned a manageable loss into a crisis situation. I remember one instance where a trader who used to be in regular contact disappeared from sight. I sensed something was amiss when attempts to contact him went unanswered. He was embarrassed to tell what happened as he saw the capital in his account dwindle with each passing day. By the time he contacted me, he had already blown his account.

The problem started with a short-term trade taken following the release of some economic news. The market moved against him and he never recovered. An attempt to earn 20 pips wound up losing over 700 pips as the market trended the other way. Doubled-up trades failed. Hope replaced solid analysis. Prudent money management and discipline were tossed aside. Proper risk/reward measurement had long since passed.

In situations like this, when a trader asks for advice on a losing position (I would hope before it reaches a critical point), I ask one question: "If you were to start with a clean slate right now, would you take this position?" If the answer is no, then the trader has answered his own question and should exit the position. If asked for my advice before a trade is placed, I ask: "What is your profit target and what is your stop?" This is because a trader needs to establish a risk/reward objective on a trade before trading. Also, one *must* have a stop in place in order to live to trade another day if the trade does not work out as planned.

WHAT IS LEVERAGE?

Since outright percentage price moves in currencies often tend to be significantly smaller than those on equities or on some commodities, a 10 to 20 percent annual price swing in the value of one currency versus another is considered to be substantial. FOREX trading in the commodity markets or with an online broker is done on a leveraged basis to amplify (or leverage) potential trading gains or losses. In other words, a small margin deposit can buy control over a much larger position. A margin deposit is best described as good-faith or earnest money. *It in no way limits the potential loss on a position.* The buyer or seller of a position in the FOREX market *is liable for any losses on the full position*, and of course would benefit from any gains. For example, a USD500 margin at some firms might control a EUR100,000 position (equal to $148,000 at an exchange rate of EUR/USD 1.4800).

Leverage is often expressed as a ratio:

Leverage = Trading Position/Required Margin

Thus in our example:

EUR100,000 @ 1.4800 = USD148,000

The typical required margin is USD500:

USD148,000/USD500 = 296

The leverage is:

296:1

On the regulated commodity exchanges, the comparable FOREX leverage might be about 65:1. Some FOREX brokers advertise leverage as high as 400:1.

EXAMPLE OF A HYPOTHETICAL TRADE

With a trading margin of USD500 controlling a EUR100,000 (USD148,000 equivalent) position, a 1 percent increase in the value of the EUR/USD would generate a *gain* of $1,480 on a long position. A 1 percent decline in the value of the currency would generate a comparable *loss* of $1,480—and as an account holder, you would be liable to make good on the entire loss.

Calculation:

A EUR100,000 position is worth USD10 per one-pip movement.

A 1 percent change in the value of the EUR/USD would be:

.01 × 1.4800 = .0148
.0148 = 148 pips (smallest whole number)
+148 pips × $10 per pip = $1,480 gain

Note: Some firms now quote prices in fractions (tenths) of a pip.

Leverage is a powerful force that can work for or against the currency speculator. Because it is so powerful, we recommend that traders of all levels of experience keep their leverage well below the levels allowed by most online firms. Remember that capital preservation is the number one goal of the trader. Here is some money management advice from a successful North American dealer:

If you're long USD like I am, you need to make sure your money management is in order. That means appropriate stops, appropriate leverage, appropriate position sizing with respect to your account size.

> *Also ... if the position moves too far against you, then don't be afraid to accept the loss. It's better to live and fight another day than to draw down your account so much that you can't trade anymore.*

Keep in mind that the account holder is held financially liable for the full losses taken on any account regardless of the margin initially required. A missed margin call (demand for additional funds) will see the trading position closed swiftly by the broker to limit its exposure to losses, and the broker will pursue the account holder for any deficit in the account.

MONEY MANAGEMENT RULES

Some simple guidelines may help keep you in the game long enough to learn winning ways. Breaking even is okay, too.

- **Go slow.** If you are new to trading, start out with one of the paper-trading demo accounts offered by most brokerage firms. Get a feel for the mechanics of trading and for how the markets operate. Read the free Global-View FOREX Forum. Use the Learning/Help Forum to ask questions about *how* to trade. On the FOREX Forum you will see a lot of trading ideas posted by a wide range of traders 24 hours a day when the markets are open. You will also see a wide range of trading styles. Pick some posters you like and follow their trading ideas and how they make their decisions. Don't look for them to tell you what to do. *In the end, it's YOUR decision how to manage your money, not theirs.* Develop your own trading approach as quickly as possible.
- **Start out with a mini-account.** Trading with real money is a lot different than paper trading. Try out a mini-account and *keep your leverage low.* Forget the dollar value of your profit/loss (P/L). Trade for pips. You can always increase your leverage later. In the ideal case, you might be able to fund a full-sized account with the profits from your mini. Take your time!
- **Expect to have *many* losing trades.** They come with the territory in FOREX trading. If you talk to some of the professionals in the big institutions who have survived for many decades, the best will tell you that the markets have taught them humility. Most will say that they would be happy to be correct 51 percent of the time. They will also tell you that, given the global scope of the markets, things often happen that surprise even the most experienced participants.

- **Have the strength of your convictions, but don't be stubborn.** If you find it hard to admit when you are wrong, then you might not be suited for trading. However, flip-floppers have a hard time as well. Do your preparation for a trade. Have the strength of your convictions but don't get married to an idea that is not working for the reasons you thought it would.
- **Avoid "Jubbs."** There supposedly was a London bank trader named Nigel Jubbs who was well known for putting his stop losses at the most obvious of chart points, and he was constantly being stopped out. Consequently, those placing stops at obvious chart points are often called Jubbs. Avoid them.
- **Avoid the myth of diversification.** Some currency pairs are highly correlated to others. These correlations tend to change over time, though. Check out the correlations before diversifying your portfolio of positions, or you could find that there is more risk in your position portfolio than you thought.
- **Don't overtrade, and don't be afraid to sell currencies short.** Professional traders trade as comfortably from the short side as the long one.
- **When in doubt, stay out.**
- **Trade with the trend, not against it, especially when momentum is accelerating.** Retail traders often prefer to play extremes of ranges rather than trading breakouts. So, when trading against the trend, be quick to take your profits (or losses).
- **Use positive risk/reward objectives.** The expected gain from a trade should be two to three times the amount you figure you might lose.

The following are words of wisdom from a successful Australian speculator to a less experienced trader on a Global-View forum:

> *There's no security in FX due to the use of leverage for the retail size trader. You need a substantial amount of capital to overcome this.*
>
> *Also, as pointed out, demo accounts aren't manipulated and provide a false sense that you can beat the market. It's got to do with risking nothing vs. risking real dollars. The mental aspect of trading is difficult for people with little or no experience.*
>
> *One small businessman lost everything he had in $/cad, something like 1.2 mln dollars—this can be the reality of this business and something you must establish rules for in your trading. Also just because someone says I made a ton of money last year or last month is irrelevant—it's more in their ability to weigh their risk vs. reward over the long haul.*

THE INSIDE SCOOP (JOHN BLAND)

A good lesson is the story of Long-Term Capital Management (LTCM), which was a hedge fund founded in 1994 literally by some rocket scientists and Nobel Prize winners in economics, among other luminaries. To make a long story short, in 1998 it created a mini-financial crisis that spilled over into the FOREX market when it lost $4.6 billion in less than four months. LTCM folded in early 2000. Its losses were not in FOREX but do illustrate how the best-laid plans of the best and the brightest traders can go badly astray. This has been repeated on a much larger scale that led to the global financial crisis in the second half of 2008. Trying to forecast where the FOREX market is headed is often like trying to build a computer model to predict the weather. There are just too many unknown variables to track.

USE STOP LOSSES

From a Far East trader on the Global-View Forums:

> *Do not worry about what market will do. Just worry about what you will do when market reaches your "pain point" or "happy point." You will have an easier life as a trader that way.*

The FOREX market is not just the province of speculators. Currencies are the basic medium of exchange for countries. Governments and politicians have a vested interest in managing the values of their currencies. Thus, while an economist might be looking at relative rates of growth, interest rates, trade balances, or other macroeconomic indicators to anticipate future values, money can suddenly move in massive amounts due to financing equity investments, mergers and acquisitions (M&A) flows, infrastructure plays, central bank reserve management, and so on. It's because of these frequent and unexpected distortions to the rhythm of the markets that it is vital that a stop loss point be determined for *every* position *before* it is entered. To protect themselves against unforeseen price moves, all successful professional traders operate with stops. You never know what is going to happen out of the blue in FOREX markets.

There is a tendency for less experienced traders to be reluctant to take losses, counting on ranges holding to see their levels again. This strategy works during range markets but can prove disastrous when markets trend and momentum accelerates. This results more often than not in seeing an account wiped out as hope replaces sound analysis and money management. One thing is certain: If you start out trading without stop loss protection, you are just setting yourself up for learning the hard way that stops are required for long-term survival.

One word about stop loss orders: They do not guarantee a trade at a specific price. If your stop loss price is touched, it triggers a market order to buy or sell (depending on your position). That could be executed very close to your price or quite distant from it, depending on market conditions.

HOW MUCH TO RISK ON A TRADE

> Markets can remain illogical longer than we can remain solvent.
> —Gartman's *20 "Not-So-Simple" Rules of Trading*

How much of a loss should be at risk on a trade depends a lot on what kind of trading you are doing. A day trader is likely to risk considerably less than a long-term position trader, but as a rule of thumb it is inadvisable to risk any more than 5 percent of the total risk capital in your account on any individual trade. So if you have $10,000 in your account, risk no more than $500 on any individual trade. Remember, you are going to have a lot of losing trades!

You can calculate the appropriate position size for a trade by dividing the dollar amount you are willing to lose by the number of pips to your stop loss. Don't confuse your percent of equity loss tolerance with the margin requirement, though. They are unrelated. Assume:

$500 loss tolerance

EUR/USD 148-pip stop (1 percent) or .0148 based on 1.4800 spot price
   Calculation:

$500 ÷ .0148 = EUR33,783 position (or EUR30,000 in round numbers)

Thus, if you are willing to risk $500 on a trade with a 148-pip stop, your position should be EUR30,000.

You can adjust your stop loss requirement and increase or decrease your leverage to arrive at a proper balance. The point is that you don't want to blow your entire trading account on a handful of unfortunate trades.

THE INSIDE SCOOP (JOHN BLAND)

Take the case of my first speculative customer back in 1979. This was a sophisticated assistant treasurer of a major corporation who had previously been a consulting customer of mine in corporate currency exposure management and had been quite successful. This individual opened a personal FOREX account and lost virtually his entire balance over several weeks on his first (long Deutsche mark) trade. His leverage had been modest, but he refused to accept the fact that his trade was not working for the reasons he thought it would. This happens much too often with new traders. Manage your money. Conserve your equity. Also, risk capital must only be money that you can afford to lose.

READY TO TRADE?

> To trade successfully, think like a fundamentalist; trade like a technician.
> —Gartman's *20 "Not-So-Simple" Rules of Trading*

Here are some trading rules:

- **Get organized.** Keep records of your trades. What was the rationale for the trade, and what happened? It's a fact that you will learn more from your losers than from your winners. You can be right for all the wrong reasons, but when you are wrong, try to figure out why.
- **Be a specialist.** Don't trade a lot of currency pairs randomly. Pick out two or three and find out everything you can about them in depth.
- **Find the best broker for you.** See Chapter 7 for more on this topic.
- **Get information on the current economic situation.** Technical traders often eschew the fundamentals. Granted, it can be hard to learn how the fundamentals work, follow them, and make trading decisions based on them, but the effort is worth it. Start out with some basic knowledge of the fundamentals. A daily data calendar and forecasts for the top-tier indicators can at least improve the timing of your trading decisions (see Chapter 5, "Trading the News").
- **Remember the key market axiom that "It's not the news but the market reaction to news that matters."** So if the USD does not rally on good news, it tells you that there is something additional working against it just now.
- **Don't let a winner become a loser.** For heaven's sake, it's hard enough to be right on a trade. You can keep a winner from becoming a loser by letting gains accumulate and by running a trailing stop to protect the profits. A number of academic studies have shown that traders are often too slow to take their losses and too quick to take profits.

- **Don't pyramid your position.** Some recommend adding progressively smaller positions to a winning trade. This is called pyramiding. It might work in some markets, but we don't like it in FOREX trading.
- **Don't hedge to cover a bad position.** Some brokers now offer traders a chance to hedge an existing position with an equal and offsetting one. All a hedge does is increase the brokerage fees you pay because of the bid/ask spread. Rather than hedging to cover a bad position, just get out. Clear your head and move on.
- **Think of a trade as taking a calculated risk on which you either gain or lose.** Don't let emotions rule your decision. Don't chase your losses, and at all costs avoid doubling up to try to recoup a loss. Take your loss and move on. Losses are just a part of the business. Expect to have many.
- **Don't put on a straddle to avoid taking a loss.** Cross positions (straddles) can be just as risky as (or more risky than) outright trades. A cross position (straddle) in FOREX is an equal (size) and offsetting position in another currency. For example, a long EUR/USD position could be offset by a short GBP/USD position in the belief that the EUR and GBP will more or less equal the USD.
- **Never meet a margin call.** Liquidate. You should never reach this point on a trade if you manage your leverage and stops prudently. If you get a margin call, you are probably risking too much. Reduce your leverage and/or make your stops closer. Trading is all about capital preservation.
- **Remember that errors happen.** We know a former bank trader unused to electronic trading who too frequently hits the "Buy" instead of the "Sell" button by mistake. If this happens to you, take your loss right away. Don't let a small error get away from you.

There are many approaches to trading. The following is a post from one of the Global-View forums from a West Coast trader. He favors pyramiding his winning positions.

> *Leveraging is the hardest thing, I guess.*
> *My attitude is to start at the easiest place.*
> *Enter maximum leverage at your support or resistance point. If the market does not respect your level, don't add to the position; just either reverse or close.*
> *If the market is volatile and able to break levels in a trading day, then add to winning positions on the break.*
> *So it's the same as you read in books. Manage your losses to as low as possible, book profits if it doesn't break levels and add to winning positions to maximize return should the market be trading*

that way. It's definitely not easy to trade perfectly correctly every day but I think on the days where your levels are good and the market is moving a lot you must really trade aggressively leverage wise.

Just keep in mind I only focus short term so you need a different approach for wider trade parameters over multiple days.

SUMMARY

The CFTC warning statement for commodity and FOREX traders contains a lot of wisdom. Be aware of the message it tries to convey. Understand that everyone takes many losses in FOREX trading. Manage these losses and your trading capital and you will improve your chances for surviving in the long term. Allocate your trading capital to allow for a significant number of trading opportunities. Be sure you seek profits in a multiple of at least two or three times risk.

Money management—not trading method—is what separates the winners from the losers in currency trading.

Recommended Global-View Links

Learning Center: www.global-view.com/forex-education/
forex-learning/

Help Forum: www.global-view.com/forums/forum.html?f=4

Basics of Trading Video Course: www.global-view.com/forex-education/trading-manual/dir.html

Technical Trading

T here are two methods for analyzing markets in general and FOREX markets in particular: technical analysis and fundamental analysis. Many traders use both, but technical analysis predominates today. There are still many fundamental-based professional traders, but almost all retail and amateur traders use technical analysis exclusively. Most large FOREX funds are driven by computerized trading systems in a field referred to as quantitative analysis, which often access both technical and fundamental data. This chapter looks at some of the more popular technical trading methods—and a few lesser-known methods.

The debate over which is better—technical analysis or fundamental analysis—has raged for decades. Each side has its strengths and weaknesses.

Fundamental analysis attempts to forecast prices by reference to the economic events underlying the currency for a given country—or the two currencies in a traded pair. These events are typically offered as quantitative statistics such as balance of payments, monetary growth, and the like. There is no doubt that ultimately long-term trends are fundamentally driven. But as Lord Keynes said, "In the long run we are all dead." When you are dealing with leverage factors of 100:1 and higher, how important is the long run? Can you sit out a $5,000 loss on a small trade to eventually make $100?

Opinions from an Australian trader on the inability of markets to price in future events:

The markets are incapable of actually seeing beyond the data which is presented to them. Risks are not something to be factored or priced in but are unforeseen changes in the landscape that will be revealed at some future date.

There are two other issues the technician will proffer in the argument against fundamentals:

1. Some of the fundamental factors are not quantifiable.
2. The relationships between the factors are constantly changing, and in complex, nonlinear ways. The weights of each factor—and there are perhaps hundreds of them—fluctuate enormously and are probably unpredictable.

But even the technician will acknowledge that one should trade with the major trend—a trend certainly determined by fundamentals. "The trend is your friend" is an old and remarkably helpful market adage. Don't fight the trend; trade with it.

From a London based trader:

If a true fundamental analysis was to be applied to the current market then we would see a completely different picture.

What is a "true fundamental" analysis?

For now we have a predominance of technical over fundamental influence in the market. One could project many inferences on the market for this reason.

It sounds like you are saying that technicals dominate when no trends can be found, but technicals include trends so I'm not sure what this means at all besides the fact that there is no agreed-upon single technical analysis nor any agreed upon fundamental analysis technique. They just look at different sources of information....

Chapter 3 was written by Mike Archer. Author Bland (a fundamentalist) and Meisler wrote Chapter 4. Readers can see for themselves the point-counterpoint between the two schools of thought.

WHAT IS TECHNICAL ANALYSIS?

The technician begins with the axiom that everything is in the price, ready and waiting for analysis. The methods by which this data is manipulated—tortured if you will—are enormously varied and often quite creative and complex.

Prices are the primary data available to FOREX traders. Because there is no central clearinghouse, volume (the number of trades executed) and open interest (the number of open or outstanding trades) available to commodity futures traders are nonexistent. Efforts have been and are being made to synthesize those factors for currency pairs to give FOREX traders additional data with which to work.

A fundamentalist might argue there is nothing in past prices that would foretell future prices. The data is but a dead record of the past. A moving average tells everything about the past but nothing about the future. The technician counters that every buyer in the market must sell to exit and every seller in the market must buy to exit. That information, they hope, is somehow coded in the record of past prices. Author Archer is developing a system, the Trend Machine, that uses cellular automata in an attempt to decode past prices and reconstitute them into forecasts.

Econometric modeling is something of a hybrid approach. The statistical information of fundamentals is manipulated mathematically to create a pricing model. Since, as noted earlier, the relationships and weights of these factors are nonlinear, the only model that might work is one using nonlinear mathematics or structures such as chaos, catastrophe, or cellular automata.

Most broker-dealer trading platforms have a large palette of technical tools for the trader—charts and indicators. A number of third-party vendors offer more robust technical analysis packages. See Chapter 13 of *Getting Started in Currency Trading, Second Edition* (John Wiley & Sons, 2008) for some current offerings.

If you do use a third-party analysis suite, remember that if it does not integrate with your broker's trading platform (many do), the prices and signals off your technical tools may differ slightly from those on the trading platform.

TECHNICAL ANALYSIS LANDSCAPE

The primary division in technical analysis is between chart reading and indicators. A chart is essentially a picture, or graphic record, of prices. Some charting methods are very old; candlestick charts date to the sixteenth century.

Indicators generally fall into two classifications: trend following or trading. Indicators became popular in the 1970s and there are hundreds of them. Indicators in turn are generally of two flavors; they are designed for either sideways markets or trending markets.

A secondary division might be found between methods and systems. A method is typically a combination of technical analysis tools, used together but not fully automated. A system is a method that has been fully automated and runs without outside interpretation or judgment. Most large hedge funds now use systems, and the entire field is referred to as quantitative analysis and algorithmic trading.

Most technical traders use both charts and indicators. But try to keep your toolbox simple and be wary of overlap where two or more tools measure the same thing—for example, two indicators that both pertain to sideways markets. Systems and methods are essentially combinations of tools used by a trader. A system is generally an automated, nondiscretionary approach, whereas a method still requires the trader to make the final decision.

Charts

Bar Charts   Bar charts (Figure 3.1) are not the oldest form of charting, but they are the most commonly used. All broker-dealers offer bar charts as part of their charting packages.

A bar represents some fixed, closed-end time frame. In stocks and commodity futures, it is typically one week or one day. In FOREX, bar charts may range from one minute to one month. The most popular for trading tend to be five-minute to one-hour charts. Each bar is a vertical line representing the high and low plus short horizontal lines indicating the close (to the right of the bar) and oftentimes the open (to the left of the bar) for that time frame.

Classical bar chart formations with interesting names are still watched for by traders. A double bottom appears in Figure 3.2.

Unfortunately, the more popular a chart formation or indicator becomes, the less often it is likely to appear. The market discounts information. For example, consider the head and shoulders formation, diagrammed in Figure 3.3. As traders begin to see it form on a price chart, they often anticipate the right shoulder and begin selling. The result will be that the shoulder never actually is built and the formation fails to materialize.

Point and Figure Charts   Point and figure charts (Figure 3.4) date from the late nineteenth century. It is said insiders used them to manipulate

FIGURE 3.1 Bar Chart
Source: FXtrek IntelliChart™. Copyright 2001–2007 FXtrek.com, Inc.

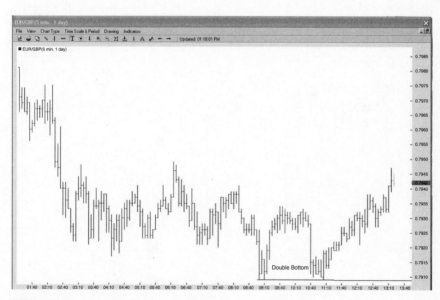

FIGURE 3.2 Classical Bar Chart Formation
Source: FXtrek IntelliChart™. Copyright 2001–2007 FXtrek.com, Inc.

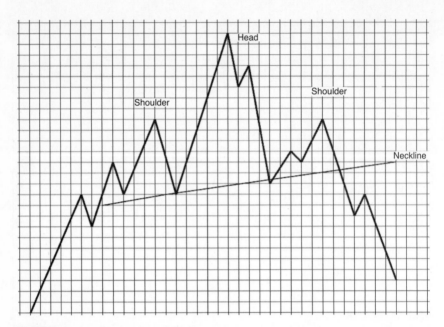

FIGURE 3.3 Head and Shoulders

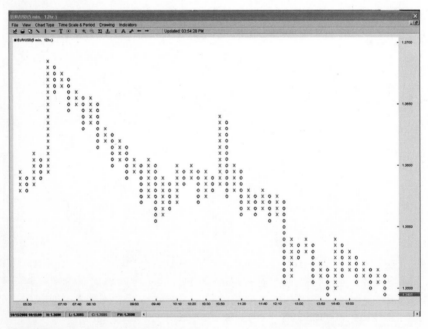

FIGURE 3.4 Point and Figure Chart
Source: FXtrek IntelliChart™. Copyright 2001–2007 FXtrek.com, Inc.

railroad stocks. Although now out of favor, they are easy to use and interpret. Unfortunately, very few broker-dealers offer point and figure charts (they are available from third-party vendors, however).

Whereas bar charts are time frame sensitive, point and figure charts are only price sensitive; you cannot tell when a price occurred on a point and figure chart. Uptrends are shown as a vertical column of *X*s and downtrends as a vertical column of *O*s. The trader must decide two parameters: the value of each *X* and *O* box and how many boxes are required to cause a reversal (i.e., begin a new column in the opposite direction). Three-box reversals are the most common, but one-box and five-box reversals are also used by traders.

Point and figure formations may be more reliable than bar chart formations, if only because point and figure charts are less in use by today's traders.

Candlestick Charts   Candlestick charts (Figure 3.5) compete with bar charts for popularity. They date from the Orient in the sixteenth century. Several books offer instruction on how to interpret them. Most

FIGURE 3.5   Candlestick Chart
Source: FXtrek IntelliChart™. Copyright 2001–2007 FXtrek.com, Inc.

broker-dealers offer candlestick charts on their trading platforms because of their popularity and the wealth of methods for their interpretation.

Swing Charts Swing charts have fallen out of favor. They are very similar to point and figure charts, but use vertical lines instead of *X*s and *O*s.

There are four primary types of swings, shown in Figure 3.6. These swings can also be seen on bar charts. They are bull, bear, inside, and outside (referenced to the previous swing). A bull swing has a higher high and a higher low. A bear swing has a lower high and a lower low. An inside swing has a lower high and a higher low. An outside swing has a higher high and a lower low.

While all broker-dealer platforms offer integrated charting tools, there are also many third-party vendors with excellent charts. We like FXtrek (www.intellicharts.com) for quality, cost-effective charts, but there are several others to consider.

Indicators

As mentioned earlier, indicators are generally of two flavors. They are either designed to spot trends or for use in sideways markets. Indicators may be scaled in accordance with price data and/or one's trading method.

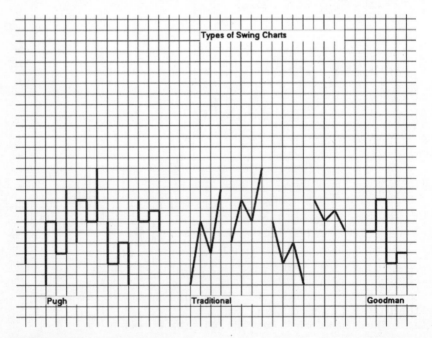

FIGURE 3.6 Four Swing Types

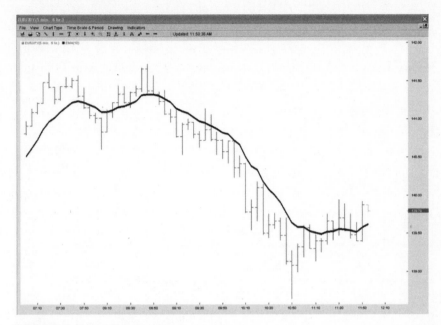

FIGURE 3.7 Moving Average
Source: FXtrek IntelliChart™. Copyright 2001–2007 FXtrek.com, Inc.

Most broker trading platforms offer dozens of different indicators. But, for the most part, they may be divided into the two types mentioned.

Moving Averages Moving averages (Figure 3.7) are used to spot and follow trends. They are an average of prices over some period of time, recalculated for each time-series data unit. A five-unit simple moving average is described by Price 1 + Price 2 + Price 3 + Price 4 + Price 5, divided by 5. The value is plotted with Price 5. The value for Price 6 would be described by Price 2 + Price 3 + Price 4 + Price 5 + Price 6, divided by 5.

Moving averages may be weighted in a variety of ways—logarithmic, exponential, or as a function of volatility.

Oscillators Oscillators (Figure 3.8) are used to spot and follow sideways markets. They may be calculated in a wide variety of formulas, but they actually differ very little. The most popular oscillator is J. Welles Wilder Jr.'s Relative Strength Index (RSI), first mentioned in his book, *New Concepts in Technical Trading Systems* (Trend Research, 1978), although there are others, such as stochastics, MACD, and so forth.

The Welles Wilder formula for relative strength is:

$$RSI = 100 - (100/1 + RS)$$

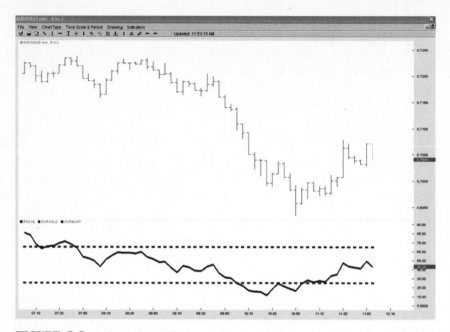

FIGURE 3.8   Relative Strength
Source: FXtrek IntelliChart™. Copyright 2001–2007 FXtrek.com, Inc.

where RS is the average of X days with closes up divided by the average of X days with closes down.

As you can see, the Relative Strength Index also has a moving average function.

Many so-called indicator batteries are composed of a mix of moving averages and oscillators. Typically, one is used to generate buy and sell signals and the other is used to filter out bad trades. See Chapter 21, "A Simple System," for an example of an indicator battery using a moving average and an oscillator.

Contrary Opinion   Contrary opinion basically boils down to: If everyone is bullish, prices will fall; if everyone is bearish, prices will rise. Why? "Everyone is bullish" indicates that everyone who thinks the market will rise has already bought (gone long). It takes buying power to push a market up. If no buying power is left it can only fall. "Everyone is bearish" indicates that everyone who thinks the market will fall has already sold. It takes selling pressure to push a market down. If no selling pressure is left, it can only rise.

From a North American trader on contrarian trading:

> *On "intuitive" trading, or contrarian traders, therein lies another wide-open field. Intuitive traders in general believe they have the pulse of the market, and the information they are relying on is director of their "intuition." Quite frankly, intuition alone is a tough sell ... in the old days we used to "read the tape," and then form an opinion, but it was never likened to a crystal ball. Real market intuition comes from decades of personal experience, and exposure to everything under the sun ... thus the adage "expect the unexpected."*
>
> *An educated contrarian trader does not merely say, "well, the market's up, therefore I'll go short, because laws of gravity state that whatever goes up must come down." However, a good contrarian often takes clues from the market, like today, when we get bad data news and the market goes up. That's a message. Successful contrarians I've communicated with have a very rigid approach and rule set for all actions to be taken in the market....*

In commodity futures, contrary opinion is quantified. Because there is no central clearinghouse in FOREX, such a quantification of opinion is more difficult. Author Mike Archer has started a FX Contrary Opinion Poll on his web site at www.fxpraxis.com in an attempt to quantify contrary opinion for major currency pairs.

Methods and Systems

As mentioned earlier, methods are combinations of trading tools used by a trader. A system is essentially an automated trading method. Systems have become very popular in the past few years and are used by many of the large FOREX hedge funds.

Crossovers Crossovers (Figure 3.9) are most common with moving averages, but may be used with other indicators. In a crossover, the indicator is calculated in two or more scales; when the indicator in one scale crosses over the indicator in the other scale a buy or sell signal is generated.

In this example an 8-unit and 34-unit moving average crossover is shown. Note two items of interest: (1) The longer 34-unit moving average filters out a lot of the whipsaw, or noise, of the 8-unit moving average, and (2) the 34-unit moving average is an excellent indicator of the longer-term trend.

Indicator Batteries As mentioned earlier, an indicator battery is two (or more) indicators used together. An ad hoc rule base is often used to

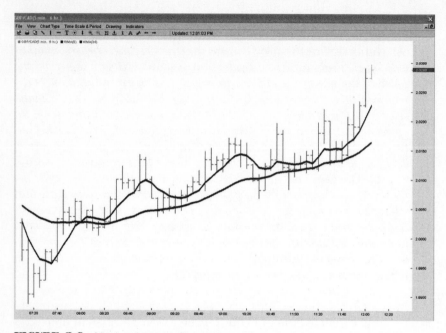

FIGURE 3.9 Moving Average Crossover
Source: FXtrek IntelliChart™. Copyright 2001–2007 FXtrek.com, Inc.

determine what coincidence of behavior between the two generates a buy or sell signal. Author Archer's program, JOSTAN FX, is an expert system that uses more than 100 indicators and over 5,000 different parameter sets. That information is driven through a rule base to determine the best indicator battery for a given market environment.

An Expert Advisor (EA) is an indicator battery that has been automated with a small rule base. Many trading platforms and third-party tools allow the trader to build and test EAs.

Goodman Swing Count System The Goodman Swing Count System (GSCS) is one of the primary components of author Archer's trading method. He has described it in detail elsewhere, including in *Getting Started in Forex Trading Strategies* (John Wiley & Sons, 2007) and the second edition of *Getting Started in Currency Trading* (John Wiley & Sons, 2008). See Chapter 27 of the present book for a tutorial in GSCS as an aid to understanding the "15 Trades and Their Stories" of Part Two. The GSCS is a swing analysis tool, similar to Elliott Wave theory.

Market Environment Charting   Market environment (ME) charting is the other major weapon in Mike Archer's trading arsenal. See Chapter 28 on ME applications in Part Three for more information. Market environments quantify the sideways and trending aspects of a market in a more precise manner than do conventional indicators.

Drummond Point and Line   Like all trading methods, this works for some traders, but not for others. Those who like it tend to love it, and the entire corpus of theory is a bit secretive. It is not mechanical (a system); it is fuzzy in some aspects and requires individual interpretation and judgment.

DiNapoli Levels   This method is based on using Fibonacci ratios and numbers in trading but offers some unique twists and ideas to mold it into a comprehensive approach to trading. Fibonacci numbers, discovered by the thirteenth-century Italian mathematician Leonardo of Pisa, called Fibonacci, are calculated by summing two numbers together to arrive at the next number in the series. It begins: 0, 1, 1, 2, 3, 5, 8, 13, 21, 34, 55, 89, 144, 233, . . . Two other market forecasting methods also rely on Fibonacci numbers and ratios: Gann angles and Elliott Wave theory. Many traders and theoreticians believe market prices—including currencies—move in accordance with the Fibonacci series.

The DiNapoli levels method is covered in detail in books like *Trading with DiNapoli Levels: The Practical Application of Fibonacci Analysis to Investment Markets,* by Joe DiNapoli (Coast Investment Software, 1998). It has also been used by Derek Ching in his learning modules on www.hawaiiforex.com.

Precomputer Technical Methods

Herein is a potpourri of different trading tools mostly from the days before computers. There are many more such tools. In the 1940s, 1950s, and 1960s it was common for researchers to self-publish their unique trading systems. Some of these were quite pricey and printed in very limited quantities, so they are quite valuable today.

Glyph Charts   Glyph charts (Figure 3.10) are a form of swing charts. First used by Charles Goodman, they are swing charts based on a specific time frame—most commonly daily. A common swing chart uses only price; it is the glyph charts' distinction to combine a swing chart with a

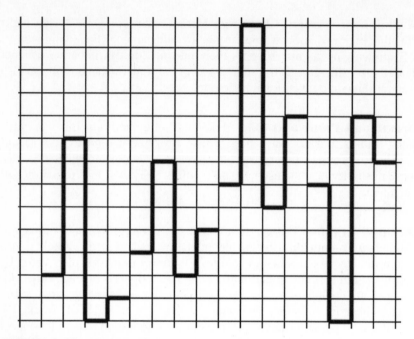

FIGURE 3.10   Glyph Chart

time frame. Analysis of glyph swing types can be very useful to the FOREX trader.

A glyph chart shows the open, high, low, and close for a specified time frame. The open always occurs first; the close, last. The high and low are charted according to which occurs first. These are very useful charts, but they take up a lot of space since each time unit requires multiple line entries. The zoom and scroll of modern trading platforms would be of great assistance in using them.

Nofri Formations   This simple but logical and elegant method was described by commodity futures floor trader Eugene Nofri in his book *Success in Commodities: The Congestion Phase System* (Success Trading, 1975). The most common of the book's 16 basic formations is shown in Figure 3.11. When two bars up (or down) are followed by two bars down (or up) with the fourth bar within the range of bars 1 and 2, the prediction is bar 5 will be in the direction of the first two bars.

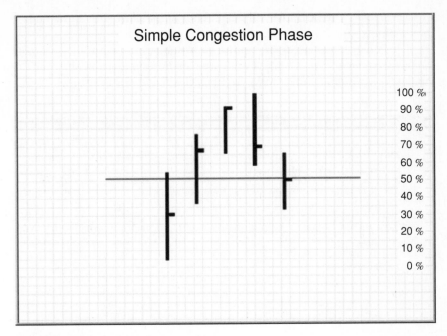

FIGURE 3.11 Basic Nofri Formation

SUMMARY

A trading method is many things to different traders. Most retail traders are technical traders, and technical analysis is the backbone of their approach.

Remember, your trading method is only one component of your trade plan. Most experienced traders will agree—despite the enormous amount of literature to the contrary—trading method is *not* as important as money management or attitude. Always aim to keep it simple; the big money is made by catching a significant trend and holding on for dear life. Even if you are a day trader—as most FOREX traders are today—it pays to trade with the trend, so focus on trend-following methods and remember that good trends take time to develop. Be willing to sit on your hands a good deal of the time you trade. If you feel you are getting lost in the woods on a five-minute chart, switch to a one-hour chart for a few minutes of perspective. You have to be prepared to have more losers than winners until you catch a trend; therefore, manage your capital carefully to be able to stay in the game. There is risk in holding, of course; this is one of the reasons most FOREX traders slip in and out of the market over the course of a major trend.

This chapter has presented only a very small sampling of the technical analysis landscape; it is huge. Part Three also offers articles on technical analysis—including author Mike Archer's GSCS and ME Charting.

Recommended Global-View Links

Daily Chart Point Calculations: www.global-view.com/forex-trading-tools/chartpts.html

FOREX Database: www.global-view.com/forex-trading-tools/gvidata.html

Live FOREX Rates: www.global-view.com/forex-trading-tools/live_fx_rates.html

CHAPTER 4

Fundamentals for FOREX Trading

T he age-old debate among traders about which is the better way to make decisions—technicals or fundamentals—misses the point. The two are not mutually exclusive; they are complementary. Activity in the interbank FOREX market is far larger than the retail trading platforms and commodity markets. The relative volume of retail trade is insignificant compared to institutional activity. Many institutional dealers rely heavily on the fundamentals, so it behooves the retail trader to have a passing knowledge of the fundamentals, if for no other reason than to understand what the big players are up to. This chapter aims to provide an insight into what factors fundamental traders consider when they make their trading decisions.

WHAT IS FUNDAMENTAL ANALYSIS?

The fundamental trader seeks to figure out the reasons behind buying or selling currencies in the FOREX markets in order to predict how those making such transactions will behave in the future. The technical trader simply accepts the fact that these transactions are taking place and looks for familiar price patterns to repeat. This chapter takes a quick look at some of the principal fundamental influences on the markets. Because knowledge of the fundamentals usually requires both academic preparation and considerable market experience, they are often used more frequently by traders who have a professional background. If you approach both analysis tools with an open mind, you might find that some of the elements of a fundamental approach might prove to be useful along with technicals. Figure out what works for you.

ALL PRICE MOVES ARE NOT CREATED EQUAL

Many assert that the fundamentals are already priced in the markets. Decades of trading experience suggest that this theory is utter nonsense. Take a look at how the direction of the markets can be abruptly reversed by a central bank decision or an economic release. As for the difference between fundamental and technical analysis, the two methods approach the markets from different directions. Technical traders look for future guidance from past and present price patterns, while fundamental analysts like to dig in and try to figure out what is behind the price patterns that the technical traders are readily accepting.

A basic flaw with pure fundamental trading is that it is often impossible before the fact to identify which fundamental factors will be dominating trade, because those factors tend to change quickly. A key flaw in pure technical trading is that it can lack the depth that comes from fundamental analysis. In other words, not all price moves are created equal. Here is how a bank dealer from the southern tier of Europe approaches the FOREX markets:

Today's data really puts into context those three basics that move fx rates: relative growth differentials, yield differentials, and other stuff. In a rising growth/low volatility environment, yield differentials matter more. In the current falling growth and risk aversion environment, yield differentials matter little. It's primarily about future relative growth expectations, and how some economies are soon to be perceived as falling more behind the curve than others.

An approach that might be considered is to use whatever technical approach works for you and supplement that strategy with an awareness of what is happening fundamentally.

THE INSIDE SCOOP (JOHN BLAND)

Recent studies of the reaction of FOREX markets to key economic releases in the hour after the data is published, over the day, and afterward suggest that the news was *not* priced in. The data also appeared to have impacted the direction of the markets in certain cases. In others, the data reinforced existing trends. It is unwise not to be aware of what releases are scheduled over the next two weeks and what is expected from them. The extreme volatility after some key releases can play havoc with your stops or give you an excellent opportunity to enter new positions. Some traders remove protective stops and/or vulnerable positions before key data is released (see Chapter 5 for a list of high-volatility data releases).

INTEREST RATES

Think of foreign exchange as just another commodity. Money tends to flow to where it earns the most and moves away from where it earns the least. An investment in a currency has "costs." The first and most volatile cost can be its exchange value against the home currency of the investor and the second is the ongoing interest rate cost of financing the position in that currency. Below we will discuss how interest rate differentials impact the cost of trading (rollover) and how rate movements have an impact on macro moves in the foreign exchange markets.

Rollover Costs

Although it is not transparent at all times to retail traders, FOREX transactions all have baked in a cost based on interest rate differentials. Sometimes this cost can be negative so that a position earns something, but there is always a daily net interest rate gain or loss cranked into the rollover or forward rates. In other words, you earn on the rollover when holding a higher-yielding currency, and the opposite is true when you hold a lower-yielding currency.

THE INSIDE SCOOP (JAY MEISLER)

Daily rollover and all forward swaps are calculated by using the differential in short-term interest rates. For example, in the case of a USD/JPY position, the bank dealer will use the cost of one-day euro/dollar (USD LIBOR) versus one-day euro/yen (JPY LIBOR) interest rates to calculate the per-day net swap cost (profit) for holding a currency position. A long position in a higher-yielding currency earns when it is funded with a lower-yielding currency. In contrast, it costs to hold a lower-yielding currency when it is financed with a higher-yielding counterpart.

It is a simple formula, and if the swaps get out of line with the deposit rates, the market will arbitrage them back into line. A simple way for you to calculate it is to look at short-term rates in various countries.

Thus a JPY purchase for USD has to be financed at some level by borrowing USD to hold on to a JPY bank deposit. If it costs 5.50 percent per annum to borrow USD for one day and a JPY deposit earns 0.50 percent for one day, the cost of running a long JPY position against the USD would be 5.00 percent per annum. A transaction in the opposite direction would earn 5.00 percent per annum. This is where the rollover costs or credits come from. In this example, the charge or credit for one day would be minimal, but for long-term capital flows, the cost over the course of a year could become considerable.

There are cases where interest rate differentials have been substantial and have remained that way for considerable periods of time. Since the early 1990s, the Bank of Japan has kept interest rates low in an effort to lift its economy out of deflation (declining prices). Thus the cost of borrowing JPY has been close to zero for years. Hedge funds and others (Japanese investors) have been borrowing cheap JPY and investing those funds in high-yielding currencies, such as the AUD. This is often referred to as a carry trade. Those with a longer-term perspective currently can borrow JPY, invest in AUD, and earn a 6.10 percent interest rate spread for a year. Of course the trade involves exchange rate risk, but that's the risk that many investors both inside and outside of Japan have been taking for a good while. In this example, those borrowing JPY (at a cheap interest rate) will buy AUD, and then place the proceeds of the transaction into an AUD bank deposit. This transaction results in JPY selling and AUD buying that fundamental traders will try to anticipate.

JPY borrowers (hedge funds and others) have also borrowed JPY to generate the cash to pay for investments in equities, oil, gold, NZD, and other vehicles. These trades have generated capital flows out of Japan, which kept the JPY weak for years as these investments were paid for by new JPY liabilities.

Note that these strategies are not a one-way street. The financial crisis in the second half of 2008 has led to massive unwinding of these "carry trade" positions, boosting both the yen and dollar versus all currencies, as global markets were forced to de-leverage. This created heightened volatility and risk aversion, which both rose to historically high levels. While technicians might say it was all in the charts, these extraordinary moves in the FOREX market were led by fundamental factors. Differentials in short- and long-term interest rates often establish the underlying flow (or currents) in the markets, as in the case of a river. For this reason a lot of time is spent in the major institutional trading rooms trying to forecast future interest rates. It is the role of a country's central bank to support its economy. Central banks, such as the U.S. Federal Reserve (the Fed), have a dual mandate to contain inflation and support economic growth, while other banks, such as the European Central Bank (ECB), have a single mandate to ensure price stability. In recent years, more and more of the central banks have started to target a specific inflation level. The theory is that if inflation is contained, economic growth will take care of itself. Global-View.com makes available in its public pages free central bank analysis accompanied by relevant charts that are updated daily.

One trading strategy that might be considered is to find whatever technical approach works best for you and to supplement those signals with an awareness of what is happening fundamentally.

Inflation Control Mechanism

One key brake and accelerator that central banks use to drive the economy is the price of short-term money (e.g., overnight rates). They impact the cost of borrowing via open market operations and control of the money supply. Central banks use monetary policy to control aggregate demand and thereby inflation. Economic theorists postulate that monetary policy is a more effective tool when a central bank wants to slow down an economy than it is when the goal is to stimulate growth. Most feel that fiscal policy (increased government spending) is a more effective tool for stimulating growth.

Almost all central banks target inflation to one extent or another. Therefore, it makes sense to keep track of the inflation measure that a central bank is targeting. In most cases this number is published monthly (quarterly in the case of Australia). If the measure the central bank is targeting is running too hot, future monetary restraint can be expected. If it is running below its target range, future monetary ease can be expected. Global-View keeps track of these data and publishes them in a chart format as they are released. A sample of the Eurozone's harmonized indexes of consumer prices (HICP) is shown in Figure 4.1.

Note that both the headline (all items) and core (headline minus food and energy) indexes are shown. Central banks often like to look at both price measures because food and energy prices are thought to be very volatile, while the core measure is an indication of how underlying prices are performing.

Another key for FOREX traders is an indication of what the markets are currently pricing in for future interest rates. A valuable tool in this endeavor is the futures market prices for three-month Euro USD LIBOR deposit rate or other currency interest rates. LIBOR is the London

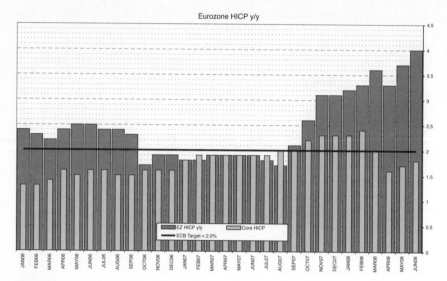

FIGURE 4.1   Monthly Eurozone HICP (All Items and Core)

Inter-Bank Offered Rate. The three-month deposit (interest rate) futures tend to be the most liquid and tell the analyst where the market says three-month-duration interest rates will be at the maturity of the contract. Thus the June three-month Eurodollar interest rate futures allow traders to lock in where three-month rates will be in the middle of June. Since three-month deposit rates are normally heavily influenced by where the central bank will be setting its overnight deposit rate target in that three-month period, the futures give the FOREX trader an explicit forecast for monetary policy at that time.

Figure 4.2 shows a chart that is updated daily on Global-View.com, and indicates (dotted line) that the outlook for Fed policy in the example below is for declining rates to about the 2.50 percent level by June and then roughly steady rates through the first quarter of the following year. Note also the comparison between the dashed line and the dotted-and-dashed line as the outlook for the economy weakened substantially in the four-week interval between market snapshots.

Last, other indexes followed actively by the markets are the various national purchasing manager indexes released monthly. Studies have found that these indexes can be closely correlated with gross domestic product (GDP) data. Traders like them because they are about as close to real-time data as can be found; they come out much sooner than GDP data, which typically arrives only after a two-to-three-month lag.

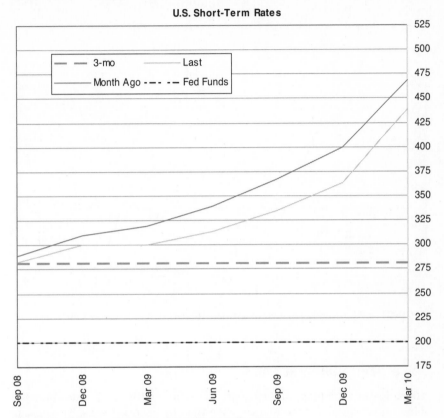

FIGURE 4.2 Implied Three-Month Eurodollar Rates

Figure 4.3 shows comparable U.S. PMI manufacturing data. The dotted "50" line is the point dividing economic expansion from contraction. As in the case of the inflation reports, the markets can be very sensitive to the various purchasing managers index (PMI) releases. Month-to-month swings can be misleading, so it is often better to stand back and look at the broader pattern of the chart, and how one economy is behaving relatively to another.

In this chart, it is clear that the U.S. economy has been slowing. At this juncture, the U.S. economic slowdown was ahead of that of the Eurozone. The U.S. economy subsequently turned sharply lower, but those looking ahead were taking the view that since the United States decline began earlier, that it would emerge from its slowdown before Europe. Keep in mind that markets are always discounting future events. Traders are always looking beyond current news to what it implies about the future.

FIGURE 4.3 Monthly PMI Manufacturing Surveys (U.S. and Eurozone)

Longer-Term Interest Rates

The price of long-term money (e.g., two-year to 10-year bonds) is determined much more by the marketplace than by central banks. The cost or yield on long-term money tends to reflect what investors and borrowers expect for economic growth and inflation over the life of the instrument. If the yield does not compensate for expected inflation or the perceived exchange rate risk, investors will shy away from the security. If borrowers feel the cost of funds is too high, they will look elsewhere. Generally, hot money tends to flow from where the perceived adjusted (for inflation and FOREX risk) money is cheapest to where yields are highest. Long-term investors tend to seek out the currencies with the highest real (inflation-adjusted) yields, rather than the currencies with the highest nominal returns.

Traders often look at the relationship of the cost of long-term money (e.g., 10-year government bonds) relative to the cost of comparable shorter-duration instruments (e.g., two-year government bonds). A normal yield curve is when longer-term interest rates are higher than short-term rates. There is a premium paid for locking up one's money for a longer time period, and higher long-term rates suggest that the economy is expected to be performing in the future at least as well as it is now. The yield curve is said to be inverted when long-term rates are below short-term rates. This configuration suggests that in the future markets expect interest rates will be lower, and this means the economy will be slowing. Traders often use the shape of the yield curve as a predictor of the strength of the economy and thus exchange rates.

A professional Far East money manager had this perspective on the shape of the yield curve:

> *The banks certainly want the yield curve as steep as possible but their money desks only serve to help flatten it in their quest for easy money—lend long-term high, borrow short-term low. The sudden steepening of yield curves has helped many banks in the past. The Fed is aware that an inverted yield curve was an ominous sign of an imminent recession so I guess their substantive moves in monetary policy were probably aided by this finding.*

Figure 4.4 is an example of how the value of the EUR/USD can be influenced by the differential in two-year interest rates between the Eurozone and the United States. Capital flows traders closely follow short- and long-term interest rates and the relative performance of equity markets.

Capital flows can also result from mergers and acquisitions (M&A) transactions. These transactions can be substantial and often take place on a timetable unrelated to market trends. The price distortions they generate tend to be short-lived, but can present a trading opportunity when they can be identified in a timely manner.

TYPICAL FUNDAMENTAL MARKET FRAMEWORKS

Fundamental traders often construct market scenarios that serve as the framework for their basic market view for positioning. Within that overall framework, many successful market participants use technical trading tools to execute their trades.

Purchasing Power Parity

Purchasing power parity (PPP) is the basic FOREX paradigm taught in universities and economics textbooks. In sum, it says that similar goods in different currency areas should be worth the same when FOREX valuations are taken into account. If the goods are too expensive in one trading partner versus another, foreign exchange values should adjust to bring them

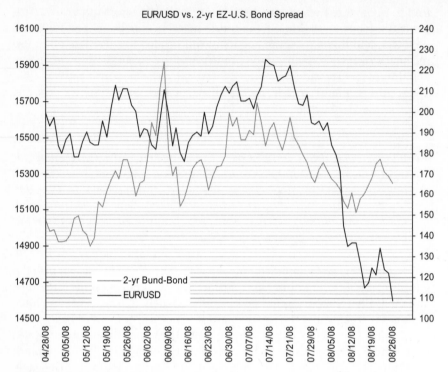

FIGURE 4.4   EUR/USD versus Two-Year Eurozone–U.S. Government Bonds

back into line. Those following the PPP approach watch the trade-weighted value of currencies to see if they are over- or undervalued. A factor that can impact the future relative valuation of currencies is differentials in inflation levels. For example, a higher relative inflation rate in an undervalued economy would tend to mitigate the undervaluation of that currency. PPP fundamental traders keep close tabs on inflation and trade data. A Canadian trader pointed out:

> *Fed's [Jeffrey M.] Lacker: "... the job of a central banker is to protect the purchasing power of currency. ..."*

Relative Growth Scenarios

Those traders who react to relative growth patterns tend to want to buy the currencies of the economies that are growing or expected to grow fastest. This approach can be related to capital flows because a fast-growing economy will tend to draw in funds from abroad to finance its growth, and global stock fund managers will want to participate in that economic growth by buying equity positions in the firms that are participating in that growth.

Traders focused on relative growth tend to keep close tabs on monthly and quarterly growth statistics.

Political Markets

Everything can be in place for an economy (low inflation, solid growth prospects, etc.), but political uncertainty can be toxic. Understandably, investors shy away from political uncertainty, because what good is a great investment if getting paid back is in question? Uncertainties can stem not only from political instability but also from credit concerns about the country concerned. Another dimension to political markets is when political instability in one country can impact activity in another. A good example might be disruptions in the international flows of energy.

Trading focused on political markets requires keeping tabs on global political as well as economic news.

Official FOREX Market Manipulation: Pegged Exchange Rates

At times, the exchange rate of one country can have a fixed value against another (often the USD). A variation on this theme is the crawling peg. In this case, one currency moves against another with a highly structured adjustment mechanism. A currency that should adjust its valuation might not because its government will not permit such a price move. An Aussie trader said:

> *Once the pegged currency un-pegs it removes a huge source of pressure and USD selling.*
>
> *I have said for a while that the knee-jerk reaction is to sell USD. I think the de-pegging and a more balanced FX income stream actually relieves a lot of USD selling pressure. These guys will be getting paid in Euros or Yen or whatever so why do they need to keep selling out of their USD? It's the same with China. As Europe becomes a bigger consumer and destination for Chinese exports the reserves will rebalance themselves. Also the US consumer slowing means less USD being spent on Chinese imports.*

Here is a typical pre–New York opening trading analysis by a bank dealer from New York City.

> *Perfect morning for a well-timed central bank "price check" or step it up towards another level of intervention. Seems something has*

to be down so that the Mid-East does not de-peg from USD. The NY interbank open should be interesting.

Managed Exchange Rates

Every currency has its value monitored by its monetary (exchange) authorities and at times manipulated against other currencies. Among the freely floating currencies, the JPY is probably the most heavily manipulated. Tokyo manages the value of its currency though the actions of government-directed investment funds that buy and sell JPY ostensibly for portfolio management reasons. In so doing, the government can intervene to manage the value of the currencies while leaving its official intervention agency (the Bank of Japan) with clean hands. There are countless cases in other situations where central banks have explicitly taken into account the value of their currency when making monetary policy decisions. In short, it is best to figure out what currency authorities want for their currency as a part of any exchange rate analysis.

The following is a comment from a professional European trader.

I remember reading something that argued China was moving away from being pegged to the dollar, favoring the euro. I'll see if I can find the material, but the underlying prospect stuck.

TRADING IN A CRISIS ECONOMY

The financial crisis that rocked global markets and boosted the dollar during the third quarter of 2008 was an extraordinary event, one that highlighted the importance of recognizing when the rules have changed and you should not treat the market as business as usual. This means that when there is extraordinary fundamental news that supersedes technicals, step back and gather as much information as possible that will allow you to assess the risks, and adjust your trading strategies accordingly. For example, the EUR/USD fell from a high of 1.6040 on July 15, 2008, to a low at 1.3882 on September 11, a 13.45 percent drop in less than two months. It then fell to a 1.2331 low less than two months later, another 9.7 percent fall from the high.

This was an unprecedented move and one driven by massive position liquidations. It also saw little in the way of a meaningful retracement as global players scrambled for dollar liquidity. We heard some disaster stories during this period about traders betting on retracements in a one-way market that was fueled by massive dollar demand for liquidity and massive liquidations of positions. A phrase used for this type of trading is trying to "catch a falling knife."

While this was an extraordinary event and one we hope is not repeated in our lifetime, it serves as a lesson to be aware of the broader picture. Don't trade in a bubble. Recognize when your normal approach is not working due to changing market conditions. Use the Global-View forums to gain a broader perspective. From a Global-View member:

Global-View's website is a gold mine, and your opinions are the gold to me. I have been copying and pasting your posts of all these forums for 6 years into my files, and I often read them too, for they are my guidance of how to survive in this forex ocean.

SUMMARY

Fundamental analysis seeks the underlying cause-and-effect relationships behind the price moves you see on a broker's trading platform. The ongoing goal of a fundamental approach is to identify which factors are currently influencing the price action. They tend to change over time. It would be wrong to try to claim that either the fundamental or the technical trading approach is superior. Figure out what works for you best and keep an open mind. Global-View.com provides support to both kinds of traders. In terms of bias, the FOREX Forum skews more heavily in the direction of the technical trader, while the GVI FOREX forum (for more experienced traders) is more oriented to the fundamental trader. Both types of traders are supported on both forums.

Recommended Global-View Links

Daily Interest Rate Forecasts: www.global-view.com/forex-trading-tools/sta.html

U.S. Federal Reserve Policy Preview: www.global-view.com/forex-trading-tools/rates/usratesa.html

Blog—Selected Daily Bank FOREX Research: www.global-view.com/forex-trading-tools/research/

CHAPTER 5

Trading
the News

T rading the news—trading into or right after a news release—can be complex and risky. Nevertheless, retail FOREX traders have a love affair with trading after economic data or other news is released. Two reasons for the love affair are there is something tangible to trade off and there is generally volatility right after the news is reported. This volatility creates opportunities for quick profits but also poses risks to those who do not understand the mechanics of the interbank market, especially during these periods of volatile price action.

The purpose of the following example is not to defend brokers but to educate the retail trader as to the realities of trading the news.

THE INSIDE SCOOP (JAY MEISLER)

Following is a typical example of the risks inherent in trading a news release:

On Friday, February 1, 2008, the U.S. employment report for January was due at 8:30 A.M. EST. The consensus forecast for nonfarm payrolls was +70,000. When the data was released, it revealed that nonfarm payrolls were −17,000. The market reacted immediately. The EUR/USD, which had been quoted around 1.4895 just prior to the data being released, gapped higher and rose to 1.4955 before retreating.

One retail trader put in a market order on his trading platform to buy EUR/USD at 1.4910. The currency spiked higher after the news, and his market order to buy was filled at 1.4955, the high for the day. While the trader may have a legitimate issue over the level at which the trade was executed, it was not realistic to have expected the buy order to be filled at the level it was placed, given the way the market gapped. Needless to say, it was a shocker and a costly fill. Those who placed buy stops may have experienced similar results.

The aim of relating this story is to emphasize the risks of trading the news and not to expect business as usual until market conditions settle down and return to normal. This is how the real market operates. Adjust your strategies accordingly.

CAVEAT EMPTOR (LET THE BUYER BEWARE)

The pros know what to expect following a major economic or other news report. They expect liquidity to thin, gaps in pricing to occur, bid/ask spreads to widen, and for the market to be volatile until the news is digested. Less experienced traders, by contrast, often expect business as usual. They expect their trades to be executed at the prices they see on their platforms and for their stops to be honored. In other words, they expect to get their orders filled at prices that may or may not exist or that are there for only a fraction of a second before moving. This often leads to complaints about orders not being executed or about so-called requotes. However, by the a time market order hits the broker's server, the price may no longer be there and in fact may have moved considerably from that level. A requote occurs when a market order is placed at a level that a broker cannot execute.

Some refer to this as slippage, but it may simply be a market issue when prices are changing at a rapid pace. Brokers do not control the market pricing mechanism and base their quotes around what is currently trading in the wholesale (interbank) market. Some brokers attempt to maintain fixed spreads, whereas others widen their bid/ask spread to reflect what is actually trading in the interbank market. This is not an attempt to defend broker practices; rather, it is an effort to educate traders, especially the less experienced ones, about the workings of the market. No firm could afford to provide gap insurance in periods of volatility when prices have disappeared in the interbank market. Some brokers tried to offer this in the early days of retail trading, but it is no longer a common practice and it is unrealistic to expect it.

MARKET ORDERS

This brings up the issue of market orders. A market order is the most common and basic type of order and is entered without a specific price limit (otherwise called a limit order). Once a market order is entered, the trader relinquishes control over the price at which it will be filled. Essentially, the trader is asking the broker or trading platform to execute the trade at the best price available at that moment in time. This also brings up a point about placing actual stops versus using mental stops, which is illustrated in a post from the Global-View forums:

> ... *nothing wrong with mental stops as long as you are very disciplined in executing them. Having said that, you run the risk of giving yourself a really bad fill if some unexpected news comes out or your computer goes down, etc. Why not just leave the orders with the broker?*

During normal times, the execution price should be close to the levels prevailing at the time the order is placed. However, during times of increased volatility, such as right after a news event, the price at which the order is executed (whether it be a buy or a sell) might be significantly different than the quoted price at the time the order was placed. Those who place market orders after a news event are leaving themselves at the mercy of the market. Sometimes they can get lucky with a good fill, but other times they may not be as lucky. The same is true for stop entry orders placed to try to catch a directional move after a news event, as the execution level could be significantly different from that specified in the order.

TRADING THE NEWS—COMPLEX AND RISKY

A full chapter could be written about the various combinations of reactions that can take place after a news event. Sometimes the market will react and sustain a move. Other times, it may react briefly in one direction and then reverse. Some traders prefer to sit out trading news events and rather use the way the market reacts as a clue to underlying strength or weakness of a specific currency. There is a saying in the market that "It is not the news but the market reaction to news that tells the tale."

Thus the ability of a currency to shrug off good news or rally despite bad news can send a signal to the astute trader. In addition, the market is ever changing, sometimes trading with the news, sometimes against it, and sometimes before it. Here is a useful observation by a trader from New Zealand:

> *Trading the release of fundamental figures is not the same as it was a few years ago. The market used to react a lot more than it does now at the release of major fundamental news. There is a way to trade major figure releases that was put forward when the market used to be more reactive.*
>
> *It appears recently that the market reacts more before the fundamental release based on consensus opinion.*

DO YOUR HOMEWORK

Now that you have an understanding of how the market operates after news, it is important to discuss doing your homework before considering trading the news. This discussion focuses on U.S. economic indicators, which are most widely watched, although the same analysis can be made for data releases from other countries.

There are different levels of indicators—first-tier and second-tier. First-tier economic indicators, such as the U.S. monthly employment report, get the most attention and often see the biggest reaction after being released.

The first step in learning how to trade the news is to find out what the market is expecting. This can be found in the consensus forecast, which is the median of expectations of economists, generally surveyed beforehand by major wire services. The significance of knowing what the consensus forecast for an economic indicator is cannot be emphasized too strongly, as it is critical in determining how the market will react to its release. Global-View.com provides an economic calendar for the coming two weeks, which includes the most recent result and consensus forecast. In addition, the Global-View forums have a countdown clock to the next key economic or news event, which counts down the time to the event and includes the most recent result and consensus estimate.

The consensus forecast is what the market expects. Knowing the consensus allows the trader to determine what is broadly expected before the actual data release. This is important because such news is usually already priced in. So, by time the news is reported, the market is often positioned for the expected event. This is why a surprise—when the actual data deviates from consensus forecast—often sees a sharp price reaction.

Besides the consensus forecast, there is also sometimes a so-called whisper number, which is usually a last-minute private or institutional forecast. This number can vary significantly from the consensus, and is sometimes thought to be a premature leak of the data. Whisper numbers are notoriously unreliable, though. The following is an approach from a northern European trader on how to trade into news releases:

> *You need to get analysts' upcoming forecasts/expectations and their take on the releases and start to picture it together for yourself.*
>
> *I'd go to every broker Global-View has listed and look on their sites for research, analysis, calendar and also utilize the links on this site.*
>
> *Then trading before and after news releases may make a little more sense.*

A revelation by a technical trader:

> *Subject: Fundamental analysis*
> *Hi friends! Can anybody recommend a good Internet source about fundamental analysis or maybe somebody has something that is possible to send by mail? Trading 95% technical now and feel very lost when numbers are released so I really want to learn more fundamentals.*

POPULAR RELEASES FOR NEWS TRADERS

FOREX trading still remains heavily oriented toward the release of U.S. economic data. FOREX, bond, and equity markets all tend to be driven by expectations for interest rates. Fed policy drives the short end, and longer-term considerations (e.g., economic growth expectations, inflation estimates, etc.) drive the long end. Thus the markets look at economic data releases in terms of their likely impact on central bank policy and on growth and inflationary expectations.

THE INSIDE SCOOP (JOHN BLAND)

Studies indicate that the most volatile market reactions over the day of release are to U.S. data. The monthly U.S. employment report prompts the most violent price swings; the Institute for Supply Management (ISM) manufacturing purchasing managers index (PMI), because it is so closely correlated to gross domestic product (GDP), is second; and inflation data—usually the consumer price index (CPI)—is always in the top five. Other key releases are monthly trade figures, existing home sales (especially recently), and Fed policy decisions. While other data releases might be more important over time, this short list includes the indicators that tend to generate the strongest market reactions.

There is a wealth of U.S. releases during the month and the relative weight given each release tends to change over time.

Monthly U.S. employment. The U.S. data report given the greatest weight by the market is the monthly employment report released on either the first or the second Friday of the month (see Figure 5.1). Traders tend to focus mainly on the change in nonfarm payrolls each month, using it as a near-contemporaneous reading on the strength of the economy. Economists drill deeply into these data and use them as the basis for many of their economic forecasts of other data.

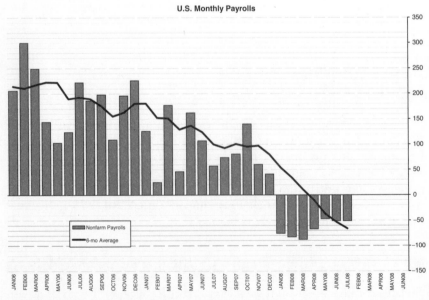

FIGURE 5.1 Change in Monthly U.S. Nonfarm Payrolls

Purchasing managers indexes. Just about every country in one form or another releases a manufacturing or service sector purchasing managers index. The manufacturing PMIs are about as close as possible to a real-time measure of the health of the manufacturing sector. As a result, dealers love these releases. Manufacturing PMIs are generally based on five major indicators: new orders, inventory levels, production, supplier deliveries, and the employment environment. Services PMIs measure manager perspectives on the status of sales, employment, and their outlook. The prices paid and employment components of these reports are closely watched as well.

The so-called boom/bust or zero line for an economy is set to 50. Any reading greater than 50 indicates the manufacturing or services sector is expanding. A reading under 50 represents a contraction. Comparative charts such as Figure 5.2 indicate the relative strength of two economies.

Consumer price indexes. The final universally followed monthly (quarterly for Australia) data is the latest inflation release for every country. This is because just about every central bank targets inflation to some extent. The Canadian data shown in Figure 5.3 is representative of what the market sees. Most central banks

FIGURE 5.2 Monthly U.S. and Eurozone Manufacturing PMI Indexes

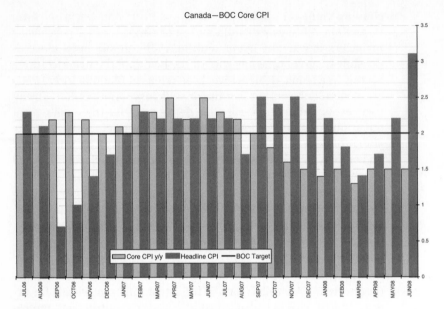

FIGURE 5.3 Bank of Canada Core Consumer Price Index

target underlying inflation (core CPI, excluding the volatile food and energy prices), but also keep an eye on the headline data release.

Balance of trade. At one time the U.S. trade release was the most followed monthly release from any country (Germany, United Kingdom, Japan, and so on). In recent years, the focus on the massive U.S. trade shortfall has been fading. Surpluses in trading partners such as Japan and Germany were once a major focus as well. Monthly U.S. trade data is shown in Figure 5.4. With the U.S. trade gap with China now involving a currency effectively with a fixed-rate regime, trading around the trade data release has not been as active as in the past. The current declining U.S. trade gap is now seen as an indication that the low value of the USD has been stimulating the export sector.

Other indexes such as the housing sector and durable goods orders come in and go out of fashion as headline releases depending on the focus of the markets at the time. The items just shown are those that seem to be of high interest no matter what the current focus of the economy and Fed watchers is.

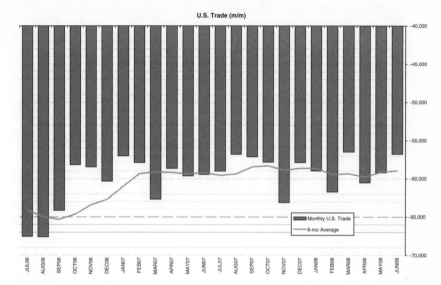

FIGURE 5.4 Monthly U.S. Balance on Goods and Services

SUMMARY

Suffice it to say that trading the news can be complex and often risky while offering opportunities to make profits due to sharp short-term market movements. Risks are present both in the lack of liquidity immediately following a news release and in the often erratic price swings that result from it. Add to that the challenge of interpreting a news event (e.g., economic data) as to whether it is bullish or bearish for a currency and whether it is already discounted in the market price. It is the opportunities that have created the retail trader's love affair with trading the news. Do your homework!

Recommended Global-View Links

Economic Calendar: www.global-view.com/forex-trading-tools/weekly. html

Primary Data Sources: www.global-view.com/forex-trading-tools/QL1. html

Central Bank Forecasts: www.global-view.com/forex-trading-tools/sta. html

CHAPTER 6

Trader Profiles

Good Traders, Bad Traders

FOREX traders have different profiles, primarily based on what time horizons they like to trade—ranging from very short-term to very long-term. Find the one that suits you best and bring all of your trade plan considerations in line with it.

Good traders share common characteristics; so do bad traders. Discovering your bad traits early is a key to not getting knocked out of the game before you have an opportunity to get a firm toehold.

WHAT IS YOUR TRADER PROFILE?

Determining your trader profile early on in your FOREX career is very important to your chances of success. Too many traders jump from one type of trade and profile to another quickly and often. The markets are enormously complex and deep; finding a trading profile is essentially finding your own niche in the market. Once you have your unique space, you can drill deeper for improvements.

The primary considerations in determining a trade profile are:

- How long—on average—do you expect to hold positions?
- How much profit—on average—do you wish to achieve for each trade you make?
- How much risk—on average—are you willing to take on each trade?

One important consideration: The longer you are in a trade, the more you can benefit from a developing trend. Conversely, the longer you are in a trade, the more you are at risk of a bone-shaking, chart-jarring news release or announcement—the equivalent of a successful bluff in poker.

The answers to these questions will lead you to one of the following profiles:

- Guerrilla
- Scalper
- Day Trader
- Position Trader

A *Guerrilla* in FOREX is typically seeking very short-term profits, perhaps 10 to 25 pips. Costs, though low in FOREX, can be a significant issue for the Guerrilla because he or she is so frequently in and out of the market.

A Guerrilla might use a 5-minute chart to follow the market, a 30-minute chart to determine the longer-term trend, and a 1-minute chart to time trade entries and exits. Guerrilla is not a good profile for the new trader; it is best left to professionals with direct access to the interbank market and very small bid/ask spreads.

A *Scalper* is also a seeker of short-term profits, on the order of 25 to 50 pips. A scalper might use a 10-minute chart to follow the market, a 1-hour chart to determine the longer-term trend, and a 5-minute chart to time trade entries and exits. Scalper is a workable profile for the small retail trader, although it is important to have a view of the overall trend to gauge whether you are trading with or against the prevailing trend.

A *Day Trader* wants longer-term profits, on the order of 50 to 100 pips. He or she might use a 15-minute chart to follow the markets, a 4-hour chart to track the major trend, and a 5-minute chart for entries and exits. Day Trader is a good profile for the new trader. Author Archer is a Day Trader. There is a rollover cost if you trade over more than a single session, but it is typically very small. If you intend to day trade, be sure you know your broker-dealer's specific rollover policy and costs.

A *Position Trader* wants to trap a large segment of a major price movement, of a magnitude of over 100 pips and usually 200 to 500 pips. He or she might use a 1-hour chart to track the markets, a 15-minute chart to time entries and exits, and a 1-day chart for trend determination. Position Trader is a good profile but a difficult and perhaps risky one for the new or part-time trader. The longer you hold a position, the more you are at risk from the price bluffs every market sees from time to time. A price bluff is a sharp change in direction and/or volatility, often occurring as the result of a news announcement. Bluffs keep traders honest—very honest!

Each trader profile requires different scales of not only charts and time frames but indicators and money management parameters. Refer to Chapter 2 for more insight into managing your money vis-à-vis your trading profile.

If you aim for a 1:3 risk/reward ratio, a Guerrilla will risk 5 to 10 pips per trade, a Scalper will risk 15 to 20 pips per trade, a Day Trader will risk 25 to 30 pips, and a Position Trader will risk 40 to 50 pips. Keep in mind that in normal FOREX trading 10 pips up or down can occur very quickly—within minutes, if not seconds.

No two traders are alike. The variance in trading methods is the most acute. Even two traders using identical indicators and scales may interpret them differently. The differences in money management techniques and attitudes are much less. Good traders tend to share money management and attitude traits—and so do bad traders.

GOOD TRADER VERSUS BAD TRADER

Once you've carved your niche, you will want to examine the characteristics of traders in the overall FOREX space. Good characteristics and bad characteristics cross all profile boundaries. Herein the authors have compiled a list from their own experiences and observations on the differences between good traders and bad traders.

The Good Trader

Good traders have firm control over their emotions.

Good traders never think of prices as too high or too low—they are interested only in the direction of a market.

Good traders make evolutionary adjustments to their trade plans, rarely revolutionary ones.

Good traders do not pyramid. Pyramiding profits is risky; pyramiding losses is suicide.

Good traders—even part-time ones—consider trading a business, not a hobby.

Good traders can tell when they are on and when they are off and never trade if and when the latter is the case.

Good traders are prepared in advance for all possible market action during a session. They may be wrong but are rarely surprised.

Good traders never trade just to trade but follow their trade plan and trading heuristic consistently.

Good traders understand the importance of good money management and attitude.

Good traders trade only with money they can afford to lose.

Good traders take small losses and let profits run.

Good traders use stops and rarely pull them or change them after a trade is entered.

Good traders do not anthropomorphize the markets. The markets are never "out to get you."

Good traders give the markets time to work. Once they take a position they sit on their hands and wait for developments with both a stop loss level and a take-profit objective established in advance.

Good traders know when to hold them, know when to fold them, know when to walk away, and know when to run.

As you will see, the bad trader is very close to the obverse of the good trader!

The Bad Trader

Bad traders trade without a plan.

Bad traders think all they need is a trading method and ignore money management.

Bad traders trade without a stop or change it frequently.

Bad traders trade too large a position for their capital.

Bad traders trade too many markets at once.

Bad traders jump from market to market and do not specialize in three, four, or five pairs and crosses.

Bad traders do not control their emotions—they get giddy and over-confident after a profitable trade and despondent after a losing trade.

Bad traders have unrealistic expectations.

Bad traders add to losing positions.

Bad traders make frequent and major changes to their trade plan and trading method.

Bad traders overtrade.

Bad traders don't keep good records of their trades and seldom review any records they do keep for learning purposes.

Bad traders anthropomorphize the markets.

Bad traders don't give the markets time to tell the tale and often make ad hoc decisions after taking a position for no substantial reason.

Bad traders hold too long, fold too soon, walk when they should run, and run when they should walk.

FOREX trading is a delicate business; little things can, and do, mean a lot. Think of the leverage in FOREX at 100:1 versus the leverage in securities at 2:1 as the difference between driving at 100 miles per hour and driving at 20 miles per hour. Everything happens faster at 100; a small error is magnified and you have much less time to react to stimuli. Ergo, be prepared for all eventualities before you even log in to your trading account.

THE INSIDE SCOOP (MIKE ARCHER)

Many traders I have mentored are absolutely astonished to find that simple postmortems of trades will lead them to one or two things they are doing wrong on a regular basis. They are even more amazed to find how much the bottom-line ratio of trading profits to losses can be changed with only slight midcourse corrections. New traders are too often prone to throw out the baby with the bathwater—making revolutionary changes to their trade plan when evolutionary adjustments are all that are needed.

Figure 6.1 shows the bare-bones record of a trade campaign of one of author Mike Archer's students. The left-hand columns show what actually happened; the right-hand columns show what would have happened if he had not pulled his stop on just one trade (in bold). It was the difference between a losing campaign and what could have been a modestly profitable campaign.

SUMMARY

Determine a trading profile and time horizon that suit your own personality, style, temperament, capital, and trading method. New traders should zero in on the Scalper and Day Trader profiles.

At the end of each trading session, review the good trader/bad trader characteristics. What did you do "good" and what did you do "bad"? You will notice bad habits quickly. Work on eliminating them; do not let them

FOREX Trade Campain 100k Lots

Pair	Position	Entry	Exit	Pips	Profit/Loss	Pair	Position	Entry	Exit	Pips	Profit/Loss
EUR/USD	Long	1.2777	1.2882	105	1050	EUR/USD	Long	1.2777	1.2882	105	1050
EUR/USD	Long	1.2809	1.2891	82	820	EUR/USD	Long	1.2809	1.2891	82	820
EUR/USD	Long	1.2801	1.2746	-55	-550	EUR/USD	Long	1.2801	1.2746	-55	-550
EUR/USD	Short	1.2929	1.2989	-60	-600	EUR/USD	Short	1.2929	1.2989	-60	-600
EUR/USD	Long	1.2855	1.2802	-53	-530	EUR/USD	Long	1.2855	1.2802	-53	-530
EUR/USD	Short	1.289	1.28	90	900	EUR/USD	Short	1.289	1.28	90	900
EUR/USD	Short	1.2974	1.3027	-53	-530	EUR/USD	Short	1.2974	1.3027	-53	-530
EUR/USD	Long	1.3001	1.2939	-62	-620	EUR/USD	Long	1.3001	1.2939	-62	-620
EUR/USD	Long	1.3067	1.2907	-160	-1600	EUR/USD	Long	1.3067	1.3017	-50	-500
EUR/USD	Short	1.2933	1.281	123	1230	EUR/USD	Short	1.2933	1.281	123	1230
				-43	-430					67	670

FIGURE 6.1 A Trading Record Analyzed

become ingrained in your trading. As we all know, bad habits are hard to break the longer we have them.

Recommended Global-View Links

Learning Center: www.global-view.com/forex-education/forex-learning/

Basics of Trading Video Course: www.global-view.com/forex-education/ trading-manual/dir.html

FOREX Trading Video Course: www.global-view.com/forex-education/ trading-manual/fxdir.html

CHAPTER 7

Selecting a FOREX Broker

The best way to assimilate the information in this book is by practicing on a free demo account. This allows you to see how the various calculations interrelate and how prices of the various pairs and crosses move over time. You can also explore different types of charts, indicators, and order types. Perhaps most important, you will get a feel for the rhythm and pace of the real-time currency markets. Watch for how much prices typically move on different chart scales (5-minute, 15-minute, 1-hour, 1-day) in both pips and dollars. Observe the interrelationships between the various chart time scales. Note that trends of significance do take time to develop and prices very seldom move either straight up or straight down without corrections and consolidations. See if you can spot specific characteristics of different currency pairs.

Be sure to download the documentation to a broker's trading platform and spend some time studying and learning all the key features. It is usually available separately from the trading platform download, but is always available under "Help" on the platform itself.

The broker-dealers listed in this chapter's "Broker-Dealer Spotlight" section also offer a wide variety of instructional materials on their web sites, including articles, how-to's, tutorials, and webinars. We encourage you to supplement the materials in this book with those offerings.

BROKER-DEALER DUE DILIGENCE

You may consider opening a demo account with perhaps two or three of the broker-dealers reviewed in our "Broker-Dealer Spotlight," one at a time. Of course, there are many others from which to choose. Consult Appendix B, "Resources for the FOREX Trader," for more. Remember, no broker is perfect; real-time trading platforms are extremely complicated software programs. Further, a broker that works well for one trader may not be another's cup of tea. You should do your own due diligence when choosing a broker.

If you have already worked with a demo account and feel comfortable with a broker's trading platform, the next step would be to open a mini-account and trade very small lots of perhaps 100 to 1,000 units.

What to Do with a Demo Account

- Practice the basic FOREX calculations.
- Make test trades to get a feel for how the markets move.
- Work with your preliminary money management parameters and make adjustments as needed.

THE FIRST DECISION: MARKET MAKER OR ELECTRONIC COMMUNICATIONS NETWORK?

Most retail FOREX brokers are still market makers. That is, they are the counterparty to your trade. They act as an intermediary to the interbank market. An electronic communications network (ECN) acts simply as a pass-through or matchmaker for your trades—although they typically reserve the right to act as counterparty in the interest of maintaining an orderly market flow.

Both types have advantages and disadvantages. Market maker platforms are easier to use for the beginner. These platforms also typically have a more robust selection of charts and indicators potentially useful to the new trader. Market makers, as counterparty to your trade, also strive to provide liquidity and an orderly market. But as counterparty they are in a sense trading against you. In our "Broker-Dealer Spotlight," all but MB Trading are market makers at the retail level.

The National Futures Association (NFA) sets requirements for broker-dealers who register with the Commodity Futures Trading Commission (CFTC). You may find more information about a registered broker, including basic financials, on the NFA web site (www.nfa.futures.org/). It has a specific page of compliance for retail FOREX dealers (www.nfa.futures.org/compliance/forex.asp). You may also type in "forex" in the NFA search box for much more information. For a discussion of the issues retail FOREX traders have on a day-to-day basis, see Chapter 28 in Part Three.

Our inclusion of a broker should not be construed as a recommendation, and the omission of a broker should not be seen as a condemnation. Each trader must do his or her own due diligence and make his or her own decisions. (See Figure 7.1.)

THE INSIDE SCOOP (MIKE ARCHER)

You will find most serious traders have accounts with at least two and sometimes several brokers. Even after you select a primary broker, keep a mini-account open with another broker. In case of an emergency—say, your primary broker's platform goes down—you have an out. In the same vein, your computer should have a battery backup in case of power failure and a secondary Internet connection in case of an outage by your primary provider. Be sure to know your broker's telephone backup number for placing orders if that becomes necessary.

BROKER-DEALER SPOTLIGHT

No one broker is right for every trader. Nor is any broker perfect. We recommend you open demo accounts with several broker-dealers and see which one works best for you.

GFT FOREX

GFT (www.gftforex.com) is one of the largest online retail brokers. As a world-leading FOREX company, GFT has received numerous awards for growth, technology, and entrepreneurship. Since starting in 1997, GFT has built a base of retail and institutional customers in more than 120 countries.

In the GFT online Resource Center you may get a copy of two booklets, *Introduction to Forex Guide* and *Guide to Currency Trading*. GFT is popular with smaller firms, which use GFT's platform and clearing services as an introducing broker (IB).

GFT's DealBook trading platform is among the most feature rich in the industry. DealBook allows for a number of third-party add-ons for the more experienced trader.

Broker-Dealer Due Diligence Checklist

Name

Web Site

Contact

Demo Account   Yes   No

Mini Account   Yes   No

Minimum

Full Account

Minimum

Type   ECN   Market Maker   No Dealing Desk   IB

Backbone   Java   Windows   Flash   Other

Recommended Browser

Charts   Bar   Line   P&F   Candlestick   Swing   Specialty

Indicators   Moving Averages   Oscillators   Others

Chart Tools   Scaling   Scrolling   Time Increments   Printing

Platform Customization

Third-Party Integration

Historical Data

Orders   Limit   Spot   Market   Combination   Sytlaicep

Order Backup Procedure

Trading Hours

(continued on next page)

FIGURE 7.1 Broker-Dealer Due Diligence Form Checklist
Reprinted with permission of John Wiley & Sons, Inc. *Getting Started in Currency Trading: Winning in Today's Hottest Marketplace, 2nd Edition* by Michael Duane Archer (Wiley, 2008).

Spreads	
Margins	
Leverage	
Currencies Traded	
Exotics	Yes No
Option	Yes No
Rollover Policy	
Financials	
Reviews	
Documentation	
Customer Service	
Likes/Dislikes	
Summary	

FIGURE 7.1 *(Continued)*

Contact:

Global Forex Trading
4760 E. Fulton, Suite 201
Ada, MI 49301
Tel: (616) 956-9273
www.gftforex.com
info@gftforex.com

FOREX.com

FOREX.com (www.forex.com) is a division of GAIN Capital Group, LLC, a market leader in the rapidly growing online foreign exchange industry. Founded in 1999 by Wall Street veterans, GAIN now services clients from more than 140 countries and supports average trade volume in excess of $200 billion per month. FOREX.com is regulated in the United States by the Commodity Futures Trading Commission (CFTC) and in the United Kingdom by the Financial Services Authority (FSA).

FOREX.com receives frequent industry and customer honors and recognition as a leading retail FOREX trading provider.

- 2008 Best Retail Platform by the readers of *Profit & Loss* magazine.
- 2008 Best Forex Brokerage finalist, *Technical Analysis of Stocks & Commodities* Reader's Choice Awards; semifinalist in 2006 and 2007.
- 2007 Best Retail Platform finalist, *FXWeek*'s e-FX Awards.

FOREX.com's proprietary trading platform combines ease of use with remarkable flexibility and a highly intuitive user interface, advanced customization features, and a full suite of professional charting and order management tools.

FOREX.com's advanced educational tools include online training courses and workshops, as well as live, interactive webinars. FOREX.com's licensed, highly experienced market strategists help customers learn how to get the most out of FOREX.com research and resources, and can also provide one-on-one trading consultations and mentoring to clients as needed.

An award-winning research team offers intraday market commentary, including the exclusive FOREXInsider and the widely read Market Updates, as well as weekly, daily, and intraday research, covering both fundamental and technical analysis.

Customer support is available by phone, e-mail, or live chat seven days a week, including 24 hours a day during market hours.

Visit www.forex.com to learn more about the company and to register for a free, 30-day practice account.

Contact:

FOREX.com

44 Wall Street

New York, NY 10005

Tel: 1-877-FOREXGO (367-3946)

www.forex.com

info@forex.com

FXCM Group

With more than 100,000 live accounts trading through FXCM's trading platforms, the FXCM Group (www.fxcm.com) has over $95,000,000 U.S. in firm capital. For live traders, FXCM offers Self-Trading Accounts, denominated in seven different currencies; Managed Trading Accounts, primarily for investors who are too busy to trade but realize the potential in this market; and Automated Trading through FXCM's Forex System Selector.

FXCM's FX Trading Station offers no dealing desk (NDD) execution, giving users access to streaming prices provided to FXCM from some of the world's largest banks and financial institutions with spreads as low as 1 pip. Contact:

Forex Capital Markets, LLC

Financial Square

32 Old Slip, 10th Floor

New York, NY 10005

Tel: +1 212 897 7660

www.fxcm.com

info@fxcm.com

FXDD

FXDD (www.fxdd.com) is a leader in the global FOREX arena, providing real liquidity and a 24-hour market for foreign exchange trading. Dedicated customer support is available 24 hours a day, and access to client accounts is available by phone, fax, or Internet.

Services include the award-winning MetaTrader software and FXDD Auto (an automated signal-based trading platform). Along with great trading tools, FXDD offers in-depth training and trading education, as well as daily market commentary by Greg Michalowski. There are numerous additional resources to increase a trader's scope and knowledge of the markets.

FXDD is a fast-moving, large company that puts emphasis on delivering the best pricing and access to the global markets for its customers. Live trading accounts are offered at no charge and there are no monthly maintenance fees. The FXDD Learning Center offers training, webinars, tutorials, and a useful FAQ section.

FXDD offers a variety of trading platforms, including the very popular MetaTrader as FXDDMetaTrader and also FXDDTrader, FXDDPower-Trader, and FXDD*Auto*.

Contact:

FXDD

75 Park Place, 4th Floor

New York, NY 10007

Tel: (212) 791-3488

Fax: (212) 937-3845

www.fxdd.com

info@fxdd.com

GCI Financial Ltd

GCI (www.gcitrading.com) is a worldwide regulated FOREX broker-dealer with over 10,000 customers across a wide spectrum. The GCI Resource Center offers a variety of chart services, quotes, and learning aids for the trader.

GCI is a regulated securities and commodities trading firm, specializing in online foreign exchange brokerage. GCI executes billions of dollars per month in foreign exchange transactions alone. In addition to FOREX, GCI is a primary market maker in contracts for difference (CFDs) on shares, indexes, and futures, and offers one of the fastest-growing online CFD trading services. GCI's more than 10,000 clients worldwide include individual traders, institutions, and money managers. GCI provides an advanced, secure, and comprehensive online trading system. Client funds are insured and held in a separate customer account. In addition, GCI Financial Ltd maintains net capital in excess of minimum regulatory requirements.

GCI offers a full range of retail and institutional FOREX services as well as instructional material for the new trader.

GCI's leading online software allows trading from the dealing rates table or directly from the integrated real-time charts. You can set alerts, place conditional orders, and take advantage of GCI's Thomson Reuters news feed, live quotes, comprehensive real-time position and account tracking, and mobile trading. Both Java (currency option trading capability) and Windows (trade-from-charts functionality) are provided to every GCI client.

Contact:

GCI Financial Ltd
831 Coney Drive
Belize City, Belize
Tel: +1 284 494 7738
www.gcitrading.com
info@gcitrading.com

dbFX

dbFX (www.dbfx.com) is Deutsche Bank's online margin FX trading platform for individual investors and small institutions. dbFX enables retail clients to trade FX directly with the world's leading FX liquidity provider on a professional platform tailored to their needs. Deutsche Bank has been voted the No.1 Foreign Exchange House for the past four consecutive years by the Euromoney FX poll and now brings this expertise to the retail market.

The dbFX trading platform provides clients with comprehensive market information and a high level of execution as well as customizable risk management and easy online account maintenance. Clients have 24-hour online access to live streaming prices, live web based charts, from which they can trade, plus access to a breadth of Deutsche Bank's Foreign Exchange services, such as award winning market research and analysis as well as quality pricing and execution.

dbFX also offers a variety of customized solutions for Money Managers, Introducing Brokers and high frequency traders who trade via APIs and provides 24 hour client support in 9 languages.

Contact:

dbFX

Registered Address: Winchester House

1 Great Winchester Street

London EC2N 2DB

Tel: 1-877-343-3239

www.dbfx.com, www.dbfxarabic.com and www.dbfx.com.hk

info@dbfx.com

Email: info@dbfx.com

MB Trading

MB Trading (www.mbtrading.com) is the only ECN in our Spotlight. It offers online webinars for learning how to use its trading platform effectively. A free application program interface (API) is also offered for advanced traders with their own trading systems. Reviews and customer service are very good. MB Trading recently acquired its IB, EFX Group, which will be integrated into MB Trading. MB Trading offers direct access to stocks, FOREX, futures, and options.

MB Trading was founded in 1999 to provide active online traders with a high-end technology solution for fast executions with low commissions. The primary objective was to enable customers to use a variety of third-party tools and applications while receiving direct access to the global markets. MB Trading's proprietary smart order engine, known as MBTX, intelligently scans market makers, ECNs, exchanges, and pools of liquidity for the best available execution price in all of the asset classes that they cover.

MB Trading has received numerous awards, including #1 On-Line Broker in *Barron's* Annual Online Broker Rankings multiple years in a row as well as Top Trade Technology in the same reviews.

Through Manhattan Beach Trading, Inc., the financial services holding company, MB Trading offers online stock, FOREX, futures, and options trading using its proprietary platform, the MBT Navigator.

The MBT Navigator is the only order management system (OMS) that integrates seamlessly into a variety of third-party end-user applications, such as eSignal, QCharts, Quotetracker, Neoticker, OmniTrader Pro, and TopGun. Clients can simultaneously place orders, view account information, and watch quotes and charts, all on one screen.

For developers, MB Trading hosts a wide variety of options, offering third-party developers full support to connect to their applications via FIX or SDK.

Contact:

MB Trading Futures, Inc.:

Corporate Address 1926

E. Maple Ave El Segundo, CA 90245

Tel: 480.212.1112

Direct: 480.304.5409

Toll Free: 877.212.1112

Fax: 480.304.5071

www.mbtrading.com/fx

support@mbtrading.com

Saxo Bank

Saxo Bank A/S (www.saxobank.com) is a modern investment bank specializing in online investments in the international capital markets. The company was founded in 1992 and became a licensed bank in 2001. Saxo Bank is headquartered in Copenhagen, with operating offices in London, Singapore, Marbella (Spain), Geneva, and Zurich.

Saxo Bank acts as a facilitator and enables clients to trade currencies, shares, CFDs, futures, options, and other derivatives as well as manage their portfolios via its online trading platform, SaxoTrader.

SaxoTrader 2 offers all the trading capabilities of the original award-winning SaxoTrader platform, plus many important features and improvements to help you trade more effectively: Advanced Charts, Flexible Workspaces, Instrument Explorer, and New Price Board. Contact:

Saxo Bank A/S
Tuborg Havnevej 18, 2nd Floor
DK-2900 Hellerup
Copenhagen, Denmark
Tel: +45 39 77 40 00
www.saxobank.com
info@saxobank.com

FX Solutions

FX Solutions (www.fxsolutions.com) is a leading online foreign exchange broker. The Company provides IB's and White Label Partners FX trading and risk management in over 40 countries through its Global Trading Systems (GTS) platform. Compliant with CFTC and NFA regulations, FX Solutions' custom-engineered suite of applications includes one-click trading, automated execution on more than 99% of trades (period of April 1, 2008 – June 30, 2008), a proprietary price feed and competitive fixed-spread pricing—resulting in low effective spreads. FX Solutions has web sites and complete customer support in multiple languages.

FX Solutions, LLC
1 Route 17 South
Saddle River, NJ 07458
201-345-2210 ph
201-345-2211 fax
www.fxsolutions.com
info@fxsolutions.com

THIRD-PARTY SERVICES

The popularity of FOREX has given rise to a very robust third-party vendor marketplace. The range of services is extraordinary. For a more complete list, refer to Michael Archer's *Getting Started in Currency Trading, Second Edition* (John Wiley & Sons, 2008).

Trade The News (www.tradethenews.com). An excellent service if you trade the news or are interested—as you should be—in how news impacts a specific market. Trade The News' Credit/FX audio package covers worldwide breaking news and instant analysis 24 hours daily for bond, Treasury, fixed income, currency, and FOREX traders. The Credit/FOREX squawk, similar to a police radio in your ear, covers economic numbers; interest rate, bond, and commodity futures markets; central banker speak, energy news; terrorism and geopolitical developments; and natural disasters in real time. The Credit/FOREX audio broadcasts are coupled with the NewsStation text platform, where written analysis appears a few moments thereafter. Trade The News also offers an audio packages for Global Equities and Futures Markets.

IntelliCharts—FXtrek (www.fxtrek.com). An excellent charting package. The platform is offered as a third-party hookup by many FOREX broker-dealers. You can trade using a broker's order execution and the FXtrek charts. (See Figure 7.2.)

NinjaTrader (www.ninjatrader.com). A very dynamic and robust package for trading, charts, indicators, system development, and testing. Extraordinary documentation. (See Figure 7.3.)

ForexTester (www.forextester.com). In a similar space with Ninja-Trader. Not as robust, and focused on the system development and testing side of things. Easy to get up and running. If you have advanced applications, ForexTester supports C++ code. (See Figure 7.4.)

AFTER THE DEMO ACCOUNT

Most brokers offer a micro- or mini-account as the next step after a demo. A micro-account can typically be funded with between $300 and $500, and a mini-account with $1,000 to $2,500. These are useful next steps after a demo account—and before flying solo with a full account. You can trade as few as 100 units with a micro-account; 10,000 units is the standard mini-account base. A full account typically requires $7,500 to $25,000 to trade 100,000 units of a currency pair.

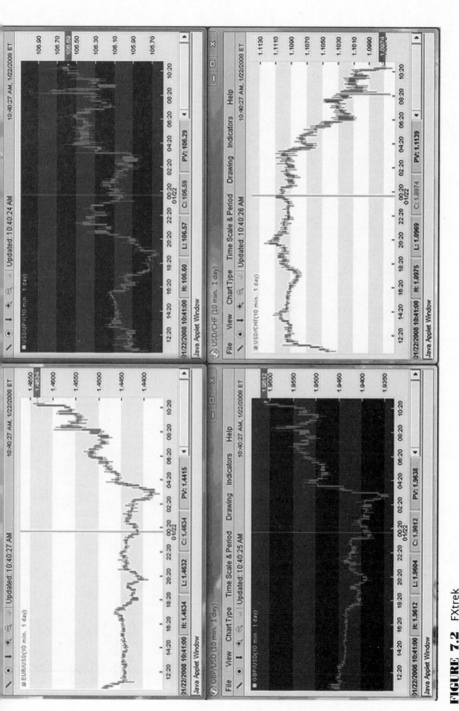

FIGURE 7.2 FXtrek

Source: FXtrek IntelliChart™. Copyright 2001–2008 FXtrek.com, Inc.

FIGURE 7.3 NinjaTrader

FIGURE 7.4 ForexTester
Courtesy of ForexTester, www.forextester.com.

SUMMARY

The logical progression for the new trader is:

Demo Account → Mini-Account → Full (Standard) Account

Do your due diligence on two or three brokers. Determine which one suits your own needs and style the best. Sometimes it is only a matter of personal taste that is the deciding factor—a useful indicator, a chart type or time frame, or simply the look and feel of the platform.

We've provided you with the basics in Part One. Part Two is a discussion of 15 of author Archer's trades. Like all traders, he is far from perfect and makes more bad trades than good trades! But the 15 trades in Part Two will give you food for thought in how to apply the basics of FOREX trading. Archer uses the Goodman Swing Count System (GSCS) extensively for trading. A systematic overview of GSCS is provided in Part Three. You may wish to refer to that overview as you study the 15 trades.

Recommended Global-View Links

Global-View Web Site: www.global-view.com

FOREX Broker-Dealers: www.global-view.com/forex-brokers/

PART TWO

15 Trades and Their Stories

P art Two of *Forex Essentials in 15 Trades* is a compilation of 15 trades—some winners, some losers—from author Archer's recent trading praxis. They represent a variety of common situations FOREX traders encounter. You may learn more from the losers than from the winners, but we hope you can learn something from all of them. Avoiding losing trades or at least limiting your risk at the beginning is more important than finding winning trades. During the learning process, breaking even is the name of the game.

Each trade comprises a discussion and one or more snapshots of charts I used when making these trades. Included is a discussion of the primary theme of each trade. Along the way are some stories that are pertinent—if not to the specific trade, at least to the factors that underlie them. I have met some very interesting people in 35 years of trading. In one way or another they all taught me something: David Van Treuren, Sherry Lemon, Jack Zales, Frank Semone, Howard G. Hunt, John Kauhini—to name, and thank, just a few of them. The most important to my development as a trader were Eugene Hartnagle, James Bickford, and—of course—my mentor, Charles B. Goodman.

CHAPTER 8

Heuristic-Based Trading

A lthough I am engaged in developing two algorithmic trading systems, the Trend Machine (a cellular automata–based system) and JOSTAN FX (an artificial intelligence expert system), I don't use automated algorithmic systems to trade currently.

I remain an old-fashioned discretionary, seat-of-my-pants chart trader. I use nothing but charts to trade, no indicators. I do troll the Global-View forum two or three times a week to get a sense of what other traders are thinking on specific markets, to see if I am missing something big, to learn about the fundamental underpinnings, and to scout for the possible contrary opinion opportunity. My trading is not mechanical. I have traded for 35 years and studied tens of thousands of charts. I firmly believe in keeping it simple (KIS). While I seldom go against my trade plan, I am not hesitant to trust my instincts from time to time. Nonmechanical methods are less prone to the occasional price bluff than are algorithmic systems. The idea of 25-year-old quants with functionally no market experience running tens of billions of dollars in FOREX quite simply makes me shudder. A debacle is coming—when, I do not know.

I don't trade the news, but note all announcements pending for the currencies I trade. I watch to see how the market reacts to these as an indication of the major trend. For an excellent analysis of the quantitative aspects of news announcements, see *Forex Shockwave Analysis*, by James L. Bickford (McGraw-Hill, 2007).

THE SNOWFLAKE TRADING HEURISTIC

Critical to my trading is the heuristic I have developed over the years. I call it the Snowflake heuristic and consider any trading heuristic that is process based in this manner to be a Snowflake approach. The idea of a Snowflake heuristic is for the trader to gradually zero in on a trade, working from the most general considerations to the most specific. For more on my thinking in this regard, see *Getting Started in Forex Trading Strategies* (John Wiley & Sons, 2007), where much of this methodology is described as the Codex process.

"Boxing a trade" was Mr. Goodman's phrase for the process of finding a trade—going from a general observation of a market to a more specific analysis and finally to actually entering an order. I think "Snowflake" describes it and my additions to it more accurately.

1. Analyze the market.
2. Identify candidate trades.
3. Determine money management parameters.
4. Enter the trade.
5. Monitor the trade.
6. Exit the trade.
7. Postmortem the trade.
8. Analyze the market.

The postmortem is an important step. I have found that small, incremental changes to my trade process can mean a large difference on the bottom line. But once my postmortem is finished, I do move on and do not think about the trade itself again.

Much of my trading method is based on two methods I learned from my mentor, Charles B. Goodman, and further developed on my own over the years since his passing in 1984. (The first two chapters in Part Three—"Currency Futures Trading Basics" and "FOREX Lessons from Shanghai BC"—explain this in greater detail.) I have refined Charlie's approach and customized it to my own trading style and personality.

The Snowflake trading heuristic is quite simple. As an eclectic, I am not a slave to any methods or ideas. I want to spend the majority of my time watching, questioning, and analyzing markets. I do try to follow the Snowflake heuristic to some degree for every trade. I am not by nature an organized person, so it requires real effort for me. You begin with a general shape for a trade and continuously overlay it with heuristic steps until the shape is clearly defined and you have a trade. This idea was first introduced to me by Randy Ingermanson as an approach to writing. His Snowflake Principle obviously has applications to many domains. Play this short Java applet to get a visual sense of Snowflake: http://math.rice.edu/~lanius/frac/koch/koch.html.

I am generally a day trader, although I have been known to be a scalper and to use scalping as a method of testing the waters and building a position in a pair. I monitor 10 to 15 markets at any given time. They are said to be "in the hopper." The pairs and crosses in the hopper are not fixed; I sometimes rotate currencies in or out as I see things on charts or as the spirit moves me. I review charts of 25 markets—5-minute, 15-minute, 30-minute, 1-hour, 3-hour, 1-day, 1-week—on a weekly basis. If a chart catches my eye or I read something interesting in the Global-View forum, I might make hopper changes.

Of those 10 to 15 markets, typically seven or eight will be on a watch list for which I keep basic notes. Three or four will be candidates that I observe and analyze more closely for Goodman Swing Count System (GSCS) trading formations, and one or two will actually be trades in progress. I rarely have more than three open positions at one time. Even with a relatively simple heuristic and trading method I have used for decades, it is still a lot to keep track of for me. Certainly one advantage of the algorithmic trading system method is that a computer can follow more markets than any one person can follow.

There are four steps to the primary trade (Snowflake) heuristic: Watch, Hopper, Candidate, and Trade. Prospective trades move from the former to the latter. Of course, many potential trades are eliminated during the process. The heuristic approach can also be useful for money management and attitude, although the trade heuristic is most critical. All of these are covered in the sections that follow.

Before examining the heuristic in more detail, here are a few tips to consider along the way.

- Unless you use an automated trading system, you are constantly juggling and judging a variety of inputs from the market. Being on for trading is essentially having all these elements working together smoothly. I take 10 minutes before each session to try to get those elements working smoothly in my mind and catch up on the market action that I have missed. I take 10 minutes after each session to take a mental snapshot of at least my current candidate trades and open trades. I never leave a session without stop-loss and a take-profit prices sitting in the market.
- Give a trade time to work. Most new traders are in a rush and spend too much of their time watching the shorter time frame charts. Remember, even in such active markets as FOREX it takes time for a trend

to develop. If you don't believe me, look at a few daily and weekly charts. You'll see some enormous trends—but they took days, weeks, and months to develop.

- Do not let a profitable trade turn into a loser, ever! You can always reenter a market. "If in doubt, stay out!" Assuming you are a day trader, once a trade has gone 20 to 25 pips in your favor, consider taking partial profits and moving your initial stop on the balance up to close to breakeven. For an idea of how much to move a stop, look at the average price rhythm for the secondary trend (the trend opposite your position).

Hopper Heuristic

At the hopper level—where prospective trades begin their journey—I am watching the major trend (directional movement):

- Price rhythm
- Time rhythm
- Volatility
- Thickness
- GSCS formations—Return, Double Intersection, Goodman Wave

These provide me a basic feel for the market in question. Should it become a candidate, I already have a good understanding of what is happening. At the hopper level, whatever your particular methods, you are only wanting to have a general understanding or feel for a particular market.

Candidate Heuristic

Once a prospective pair is cleared to be in the hopper, I watch for more specific signs to move it to candidate status.

A currency pair or cross cannot become a candidate on the basis of trend, price rhythm, time rhythm, volatility, and/or thickness. It is the appearance of a potential GSCS formation that moves it from hopper to candidate status.

At the candidate level I am mostly interested in ordinal GSCS formations.

If one of these occurs, or looks like it may occur, I am then watching for an entry point and calculating cardinal GSCS values. I am sometimes happy to trade without making extensive cardinal calculations. I have seen so many charts that I usually have a sense of what is fish and what is fowl.

"Ordinal" refers to direction only, with no specific values of price attached. "Cardinal" refers to measurements with specific price values.

Trade Heuristic

I keep both a daily and a weekly trade plan. This is much like a doctor's log for a patient. I can pick it up anytime I "see the patient" and know the situation, ready to absorb new information. This was an idea I picked up from Frank Semone, and it is an excellent tool—clean, simple, and effective.

I get a buy or sell signal from a GSCS formation. Since I have been monitoring things from hopper to candidate, I am already prepared to move.

Money Management Heuristic

I set stop losses and price objectives based on the cardinal GSCS measurements and market environment (ME) elements of time rhythm and price rhythm. I may trade with no stop loss entered in the market—although I strongly recommend against the new trader doing this—but I *never* leave a session without both stop-loss and take-profit prices in the market.

I recommend the new trader use fixed dollar stops and objectives, placing them in as soon as a trade is executed—and leave them alone. If it is a long-term trade, you may wish to *gradually* move up your stops to protect a portion of your profit.

Attitude Heuristic

I do not open a trading session if I am not 100 percent emotionally ready to trade or if I have less than three hours of time. I prefer in-depth trading sessions of 8 to 10 hours, and you will often find me trading from 2:00 P.M. EST to midnight. If I have other things of importance to do, I complete those tasks so my mind is clear to trade. I close the door to my home office. My wife and son know that means to stay away. Sometimes I play classical music in the background. I keep a notebook ready to jot down important notes, reminders, things of interest, and memory joggers. I punch in and out of a trading session on a sheet—using an old time clock from my Hawaii futures office. I know how much time a week I have devoted to trading and how long the trading sessions were. Each month I like to calculate my profit/loss in pips per hour of trading.

I keep very brief notes at the beginning of the session and end of the session noting my overall attitude.

Postmortem Heuristic

I keep accurate records of each trade—date, pair, time in, price in, time out, price out, lot size. I also note the formation that triggered entry and the basic ending values—win/loss, amount. All trading platforms keep this information and many of them allow you to pull it off into a spreadsheet. I prefer doing it by hand.

At the end of every 10 trades I review all my notes, looking for sources of both strength and weakness. I am especially interested in finding ME Profiles (see Chapter 28) in which I have done exceptionally well (or poorly). I know from experience that small changes to my method can make big changes to the bottom line. Eliminating one bad trade can move a campaign from the minus column to the plus column. I try to make small, evolutionary changes rather than large, revolutionary changes. I treat trading as a process and think carefully before I tinker or otherwise interrupt the process. I then move the data to a set of spreadsheets where, if necessary, the numbers can be more intensively crunched.

Chart Scales

I use three scaled bar charts for each market I follow. This may vary from time to time—and I may use a fourth or fifth chart scale for a confirming look at some specific in the heuristic. If I see a chart with a potential GSCS formation I will use it.

Primary Scales

- 5-minute chart—timing
- 1-hour chart—watch
- 1-day chart—trend

Secondary Scales

- 15-minute chart—watch
- 30-minute chart—watch
- 3-hour chart—trend
- 1-week chart—trend

Which ones I use vary to some degree, but I am always thinking in terms of a watch chart (15-minute, 30-minute), a major trend chart (3-hour, 1-day), and a timing chart (5-minute). I avoid watching the 5-minute chart, because it moves too much and makes small price jiggles look overly important. Few traders use the 1-day or weekly chart, but they are worth a look—not just for the major trend but to see how truly long-term many FOREX prices moves are. We can get excited about a 100-pip move but fail to remember the major trends can be several hundred pips in length and months in duration.

A KIS (KEEP IT SIMPLE) SYSTEM

Before moving on to my trades, let me show you a very simple system for trading. It is, I think, ideal for the new trader. You can use it later as a candidate heuristic when you have developed a more sophisticated trade heuristic.

"The trend is your friend" is an old saying in the market. It is perhaps the best of many market proverbs. It is very difficult to get badly hurt if you simply trade with the major trend. The rub—how do you determine the major trend?

Trend is relative. A trend on a 1-day chart may be composed of numerous smaller trends and trading or congestion areas. But it can generally be accepted that the bigger the chart scale on which a trend shows, the more reliable it is. Currencies do tend to run in very long-term trends (a tidbit of information well worth considering). If you do not believe me, take 10 minutes to examine some daily and weekly currency charts. The major trend is also a function of your trader profile. A 15-minute chart might be major to a Guerrilla, while it is probably a timing chart for a Position Trader.

A trend, of course, may at any time stop, go into a congestion or sideways mode, or reverse completely. Again, the longer-term the trend, the more reliable it is. Nonetheless, one wants to get on a trend earlier rather than later. Predicting prices requires some degree of anticipation.

The simple system uses only two chart scales from those listed earlier, but without reference to the GSCS formations. There are six steps:

1. Look for a long-term trend on either the 1-day or 1-hour chart. Ideally, look for a long-term trend on the 1-day chart and a current subtrend in the same direction on the 1-hour chart.

2. Look for the price rhythm on the long-term trend for both the primary trend direction and the secondary or correction trend direction. If these rhythms have a close average, you have a candidate.

3. Wait for a price rhythm average move in the secondary trend opposite the primary trend.

4. Move to the 5-minute or 15-minute chart. Average the primary and secondary trends.

5. Enter the market on the first move in the direction of the primary trend after an average move of the secondary trend. I call this the Dagger entry principle.

6. Place your stop at approximately 50 percent of the value of the secondary trend above or below your entry price. Place your take-profit price at approximately 75 percent of the value of the primary trend above or below your entry price.

If you wish to try for a larger piece of the price pie: For every 10 or 20 pips the market moves in your direction, move your stop half that distance closer. You may also use the Dagger to raise or lower stops: Wait for the market to pull back toward your stop and then move back up or down. When it does this, raise or lower your stop to just below or above the pullback price. Figures 8.1, 8.2, and 8.3 are examples of the Dagger formation. While the structure remains the same, the specifics of each market may make them look somewhat different. Every market is unique!

FIGURE 8.1 Dagger A
Source: FXtrek IntelliChart™. Copyright 2007 FXtrek.com, Inc.

FIGURE 8.2 Dagger B
Source: FXtrek IntelliChart™. Copyright 2007 FXtrek.com, Inc.

You may gradually add tools to the simple system such as time rhythm, volatility, thickness, and GSCS formations until you have a fairly sophisticated but logical and understandable trading method. You may find other trading tools of value; the field is very large. But limit your set of tools so you spend time watching and analyzing the markets and not trying to keep up with your toolbox. The tendency is to use too many tools—and tools that overlap and do not complement one another.

FIGURE 8.3 Dagger C
Source: FXtrek IntelliChart™. Copyright 2007 FXtrek.com, Inc.

SUMMARY

As you go forward, remember to:

- Think in terms of going from a general understanding of a market to gradually "boxing a trade." Work from Watch to Hopper to Candidate to Trade. At the end, your Snowflake should look like a trade!

- Start trading with a very simple trend-following method. You may use a variety of the simple system or a combination of a moving average and an oscillator indicator. Use the moving average to determine the trend. Use the oscillator to time entries based on secondary reactions to the trend.
- Develop and follow a heuristic or set of heuristics, but keep it simple (KIS). As your trading becomes more sophisticated, improve and add to your heuristic.
- Keep records and use them to analyze your trading campaigns. Make evolutionary, not revolutionary, changes to your trading method.
- Spend 10 minutes after each session to update your records and 10 minutes at the beginning of each session to get in sync with the markets.

The 15 trades in the following chapters attempt to give my heuristic process and general thinking when researching and making a trade. I've included relevant anecdotal stories along the way. A reminder: Unless you use an automated trading system, discretionary trading is always part art, part science. With 35 years of trading experience, intuition is also part and parcel of my trading. I have seen tens of thousands of charts, and sometimes—despite the heuristics—something will seem right or wrong that cannot be easily explained.

CHAPTER 9

Trade #1: A Symphony of Numbers

Money Management

*M*oney management is the most important factor in your trading program.

I have yet to speak to a trader successful in the long term who did not agree with this statement. Money management is much more important than your trading method. If you find yourself devoting too much time to a trading method, you may already be off track.

THE SIX COMPONENTS OF MONEY MANAGEMENT

There are six interrelated components to building a coherent money management system. It is difficult to discuss them individually, because they are so closely intertwined. Pip values, for example, depend on the lot size; lot size in turn depends on one's trader profile.

Trader Profile

As we discussed in Chapter 6, you should be either a Guerrilla, a Scalper, a Day Trader, or a Position Trader. I am a Day Trader with dreams of being a Position Trader. The best profiles for the new trader are Scalper and Day Trader. Guerrilla trading is too fast and you need a high percentage of winners to succeed. Being a Position Trader leaves you open to earth-shattering news announcements. You may call profiles by other names, whatever you like; the reality behind the monikers is how many pips you aim for, at minimum, before you pull the trigger and enter an order. I know a trader who calls himself a zebra because he uses one set of tools for trading the long side, and another set to trade the short side.

As a Day Trader, I want 100 pips before entering. Of course I will take less if that is all the market will give me. A Scalper will want 50 pips. A Guerrilla may aim for only 20 pips, whereas a Position Trader may want 200 pips.

Risk/Reward Ratio and Profit/Loss Ratio Aggregate

Your risk/reward ratio is the amount you might lose versus the amount you hope to gain. The profit/loss ratio aggregate is the number of winners over losers, given a series of campaign of trades. The higher your profit/loss ratio aggregate is (see below), the lower your risk/reward ratio needs to be. The new trader should assume he or she will lose 70 percent of the time, or 7 out of 10 times. Let's take a look:

If your risk/reward is 3:1, meaning you risk $100 to make $300, then an aggregate profit-to-loss of 1:2 will allow you to make consistent profits over a period of time. Thus, one winner at $300 against two losers at $100 yields a net profit of $100. Scalpers and Guerrillas have the lowest risk/reward ratio, so they require a higher profit-to-loss to remain profitable over a period of time.

Trade or Lot Size

Your trade or lot size is determined primarily by the amount of money you deposit in your account. The Campaign Trading Method (CTM), described later in this chapter, recommends you allocate your trading capital and lot size for at least three campaigns of 10 trades each.

Leverage

Leverage is a little fuzzy in FOREX. The broker-dealer will set a maximum leverage you can use, but on a per-trade basis you determine it by your trade size and/or account size.

I recommend the new trader begin with a leverage of 10:1 and no more than 20:1. Go up every time you have a profitable campaign or campaign series of 10 trades; down when you have a losing campaign or series. In this manner you will not be trading at higher leverage levels until after you have shown some market success.

Aggregate Equity in Play

This is the percentage of your account that is used for margin at a specific time. It is determined by the number of trades open concurrently, your leverage, and your trade size.

I recommend the new trader never have more than two trades open concurrently and never have more than 50 percent of account equity in play. New traders may wish to begin with a lower threshold—perhaps 10 percent—and work up as they progress and gain confidence.

The key to success is to have all of these money management components working together. If one is out of line, problems will result. Since these factors are all interdependent, you need to do some experimenting with a FOREX calculator to see how changing one of them will affect the others. I recommend the new trader spend several hours with a good FOREX calculator. This exercise will also help a great deal in learning how to quickly make basic FOREX calculations. Most broker-dealers have a calculator either on their web site or attached to the trading platform. An excellent one can be found at www.forexcalc.com. Start with a sample trade, then successively alter the value of each variable three or four times and see how it impacts the other variables.

THE CAMPAIGN TRADING METHOD

I strongly recommend that the new FOREX trader use a dollar profit objective and stop loss based on a fixed risk/reward ratio. Coupling this with a KIS (keep it simple) trading method and realistic expectations is your best chance to get traction in the markets. Staying power is the key. The longer you are in the markets, the more you will learn, the better trader you will become, and the more likely you will be to find the big winner. As a new trader, breaking even over the period of your first campaign will put you ahead of 90 percent of your peers.

I learned the Campaign Trading Method (CTM) from futures trader extraordinaire Bruce Gould. Even though they are written for the futures participant, his newsletters from the 1970s are loaded with valuable nuggets of wisdom and advice applicable to FOREX. The entire series of newsletters, bound, may be ordered from www.brucegould.com.

Begin with your grubstake amount. Let us say it is $3,000. Next, divide it into three portions of $1,000 each. Now, divide each of those into 10 segments of $100 each. You now have 30 opportunities to succeed, each risking $100.

If you set a 1:3 risk/reward ratio, you need to aim for $300 profit per trade. If you do this and have seven losers, you are out $700. But the three winners made you $900.

From these calculations you can determine the lot size you can comfortably trade. You will also want to consider market volatility. The more volatile a market, the more quickly it will move $100 in either direction. Try to get time on your side.

Directional movement is the net price change over a specified period of time. Volatility is how much prices gyrate along the way.

ANALYZING THE TRADE

In this trade I bit off more than I could chew. Holding a position larger than your comfort level can often affect your decision making. The result—as here—is a substantial loss instead of a small loss or even a break-even trade.

The trade seemed to line up so well vis-à-vis my heuristic that I decided to enter an order twice my normal amount. Unfortunately, the market does not care about what you think or your heuristic or trading methods. We traders have a tendency to anthropomorphize about the market and assume it will respond to our wishes. It will not. We affect the market just twice, and then only slightly: A buy adds pressure to the upside for the split second the order is executed, and the subsequent sell has the same modest result.

After a losing trade you should sit back for a short time to clear your mind. It is very natural for a bad trade to affect one's emotions. After you have cleared your mind and you feel settled, analyze the trade and make a few notes. Try to define what went wrong in a single sentence. Once you have made 20 or 30 trades, you can review these and see if a single problem or set of problems is dominating. If so, take corrective action. A small adjustment can make a large difference to the bottom line.

For each trade I am providing the basic statistical information so the trader may find and review the appropriate charts with his or her own charting service. Here are the statistics for the trade shown in Figure 9.1:

Pair: EUR/USD

Entry Date: May 15, 2008

Exit Date: May 16, 2008

Long/Short: Long

Entry Price: 1.5474

Exit Price: 1.5399

Profit/Loss: Loss of 75 pips

Theme: Money management

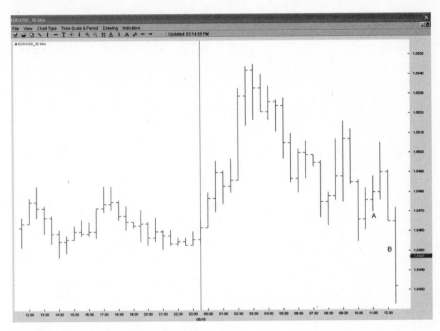

FIGURE 9.1 A Symphony of Numbers
Source: FXtrek IntelliChart™. Copyright 2001–2007 FXtrek.com, Inc.

I went long at A and should have exited when the lows on the 30-minute chart were broken (B). I overstayed my welcome and lost 75 pips in what should have been close to a break-even trade. *Always* use stops, no matter how experienced or certain you are of a trade!

SUMMARY

Be sure you not only understand the six money management components in and of themselves, but also know how they work together and impact each other. Use a FOREX calculator such as the one at www.forexcalc.com to make up example trades, manipulate the variables, and learn how they interact.

Often it is an aid to see these concepts in use. Do a search for such keywords as *pip, risk, ratio, leverage,* and the like on the Global-View forums.

At the outset, devise a KIS trading method and use the Campaign Trading Method with fixed (dollar) values for stop-loss and profit objectives.

CHAPTER 10

Trade #2: Know When to Hold Them . . .

Money Management

Y ou may remember the song "The Gambler" by Kenny Rogers. It offers advice for a poker game, but it's also very pertinent to FOREX trading.

There is an old adage in the markets, not as well known as it should be: "Run fast or not at all!" This means if you miss the opportunity to exit with a small loss, your best approach is to sit it out and wait for the market to bounce and—you hope—save you.

THE BOUNCE

In my early years of trading commodities I was almost ruined by a position in orange juice futures. Success had gone to my head early on (see Chapter 16, "The King Kong Syndrome") and I assumed—incorrectly—the market did my bidding. I initially purchased five contracts of O.J. at around 75 cents. One cent in O.J. was then $150. The market trended down, and I added more contracts at 72 cents, 69 cents, and 66 cents over a period of perhaps two or three weeks. I simply could not believe I was wrong!

As the markets closed on a Friday I realized that if prices opened lower Monday I would need to begin selling to meet margin calls. If prices went as far as 62 cents I would be essentially wiped out. It was not a pleasant weekend. Holding for the bounce may have enormous psychological impact on the trader.

One weekend during this trade I went pheasant hunting with my broker Kenny Malo of Peavey & Company and several of his hunting buddies. They seemed to very much enjoy sitting in the dark, damp, swampy field in the bitter cold of morning waiting for a target to appear. Kenny remarked to me at one point, referring to my orange juice futures, "If it was this cold in Florida you'd be in good shape!"

The telephone ringing woke me up at 6:30 A.M. Monday morning. It was the prophetic Kenny Malo. "Hey, guess what, Michael! There was a freeze this weekend in Florida—a big one. The orange juice crop is gone! Futures are locked limit up."

I of course thought he was joking but soon knew otherwise. I had been saved big time by the bounce—and cold weather! On the third day, futures came off limit up and I sold all but five contracts—I was just so happy to have avoided a debacle I still was not thinking clearly. O.J. futures ultimately ran to $1.30 over several weeks. I would have made a small fortune, but my equilibrium had been disturbed too much by waiting for the bounce.

Nine out of 10 times the bounce will save you; one out of 10 times it will not and the subsequent loss will be devastating. Consider the trade shown in Figure 10.1. The conclusion is clear: Don't risk the big loser that might take you completely out of the market. Swallow hard and take the small loss; run fast!

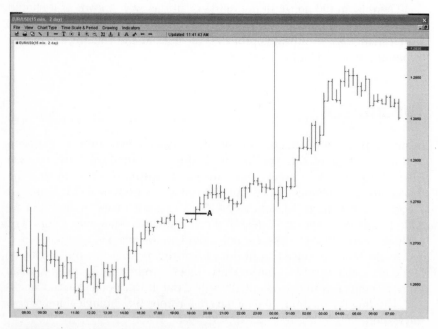

FIGURE 10.1   When It Doesn't Come Back
Source: FXtrek IntelliChart™. Copyright 2001–2007 FXtrek.com, Inc.

A stop on a short position should have been placed at "A" in Figure 10.1.

Stops—An Eternal Debate

What follows is a discussion of an eternal problem for traders: whether to use stop loss orders—and, if so, whether to place them in the market or use mental stops.

Do you place stops in the market, or do you use mental stops? Ask 10 traders their views on placing stop loss orders and you will receive at least 11 answers. Each has its advantage, but every new trader should definitely have stops *in the market* for every trade.

To understand why the debate over real or mental stops rages—and has raged in all markets for a long time—it is necessary to see the two primary reasons traders either do not place in-the-market stops, or pull or cancel stops already entered.

1. They can't accept a loss.
2. They hope the market will come back to them.

There is also suspicion that some market makers in FOREX hunt or harvest stops.

Whipsawing

This has happened to every trader—both the good ones and the bad ones. Your stop is hit, only to have the market immediately turn around and move back in the direction one had originally hoped. Figure 10.2 is an example of a market where a trader who seeks to follow the trend is easily whipsawed.

Traders in every market—especially new ones—end up getting whipsawed as they continually enter and get stopped out of the market. Whipsaw happens for a variety of reasons. Stops may be too close for the volatility of a market, the market may be in a sideways-trading rather than a trending mode, and stops may be at obvious chart points where professionals work to hit them.

After this happens a few times, traders typically start using unrealistic stops to avoid whipsawing or—more often—simply let a trade ride sans stops. But Figure 10.3 shows once again what too often happens when stops are pulled or never entered. In this example, the trader on the short side had multiple opportunities to liquidate as the market trended upward. Often the market is not so accommodating, but such price action also tends to put traders to sleep thinking they will have yet another chance

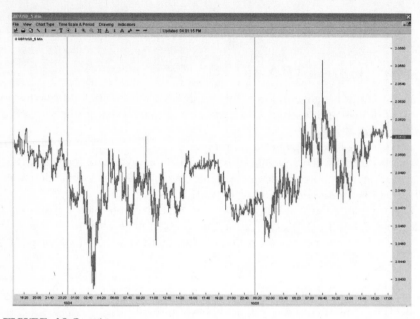

FIGURE 10.2 Whipsaw
Source: FXtrek IntelliChart™. Copyright 2001–2007 FXtrek.com, Inc.

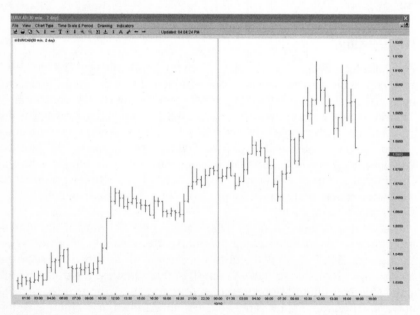

FIGURE 10.3 The Killer Loss
Source: FXtrek IntelliChart™. Copyright 2001–2007 FXtrek.com, Inc.

to bail—only to wake up to the realization that the market has gotten away from them.

This is how most new traders are shown the door: a single large loss because of the inability to place stop loss orders and live with them.

It is simply too easy for most of us to let a loss become large instead of admitting error, accepting a small loss, and moving on to another opportunity.

Stopaphobia

In FOREX, traders fear that market makers will artificially move prices up or down to hit or harvest their stop loss orders. The FOREX blogs are full of such complaints. How many are true and how many are sour grapes is impossible to determine. But as the chess master Aron Nimzowitsch once said, "The threat is stronger than the execution"; and traders use such a supposed threat as an excuse to trade without in-the-market stops. The best one can do is be selective about the broker-dealer one chooses. It is important to remember that legitimate whipsawing is almost certainly many times more common than stop harvesting.

The only way to really check for stop harvesting is to run multiple trading platforms at the same time and see if, when your stop is hit, that price also has occurred on the other trading platforms. Remember, there is no centralized clearing exchange in FOREX. While prices between brokers are normally extremely close, they all feed from different sources and groups of sources that eventually lead to the true interbank market.

Unfortunately, even this technique of comparing platforms is not foolproof. Broker-dealers do use different networks to execute trades. It may be fully legitimate that a price on one platform is not hit on another platform. If the difference between platforms is substantial—perhaps 10 pips or more—it does increase the odds that your stop being hit was a purposeful harvesting—but still does not guarantee it. Should this happen frequently when the chart does not indicate a whipsaw area, perhaps your broker simply does not have the liquidity to execute all trades in an orderly fashion.

Use In-the-Market Stops

The bottom line for the new trader: Use in-the-market stops at all times. A few small nicks are far less costly than letting a trade go extremely bad and become a killer loss. The emotional consequences of such a loss can also be extreme.

Determining Stop-Loss Prices

Another debate concerns how one determines stop prices. The two most common approaches are fixed or dollar stop and system stop. A fixed (dollar) stop is highly recommended for the new trader. One simply picks a reasonable dollar amount and calculates a stop-loss point based on that amount. A system stop is more complex. System stops are derived from one's specific trading method—either internally generated or ad hoc in some instances.

I normally use a system stop, since my methods provide me with entry, take-profit, and stop price areas. But I make sure that those would fit into parameters that match my trading profile. If they do not, I will pass the trade or use fixed stops. The recommendation for a new or an inexperienced trader is to simply use a dollar stop as recommended in Chapter 9 with the Campaign Trading Method. There is a lot going on in FOREX trading, and until you build a comprehensive trading method, adding the time and effort to factor in stops can be a lot of work and distracting.

Fixed stops should be realistic and take into account the type of trader you are and the potential profit of a trade. In Figure 10.4, the trader who

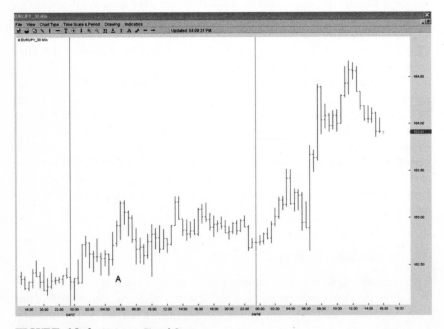

FIGURE 10.4 Using a Fixed Stop
Source: FXtrek IntelliChart™. Copyright 2001–2007 FXtrek.com, Inc.

entered the market at A and used even a small fixed-dollar stop of 25 to 50 pips could have ridden this entire move.

ANALYZING THE TRADE

The chess master José Raúl Capablanca once said, "The good players are always lucky." In the following trade I missed the gracious exit and waited for the bounce (see Figure 10.5). Fortunately for me, it came in time to keep me from a devastating loss. Some lessons are harder to learn than others.

Pair: USDCAD

Entry Date: December 2, 2008

Exit Date: December 2, 2008

Long/Short: Short

Entry Price: 1.2435

Exit Price: 1.2458

Profit/Loss: Loss of 23 pips

Theme: Hoping for a bounce

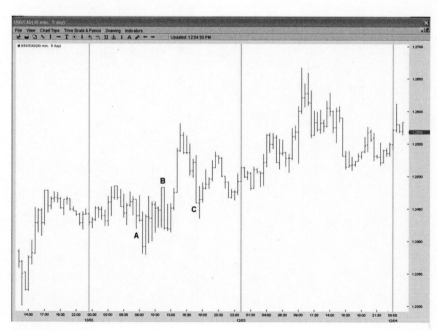

FIGURE 10.5 Hold or Fold?

SUMMARY

The best way to guarantee you will run fast from a losing position is to place a reasonable fixed (dollar) stop in the market. Yes, you will get whipsawed on occasion. But a few whipsaws will be much cheaper—financially and emotionally—than the killer loss. If you get whipsawed often, review the "Whipsawing" section and see if you can find one or two reasons that predominate. Then, work to eliminate them.

CHAPTER 11

Trade #3:
Scaling the Wall

Money Management

S caling into and out of a trade is a common and very useful money management tool. I mostly use it for entry but, again, it can be used for exiting also. Suppose you intend to take a position of 500,000 in a currency pair. To scale into the position you might take first a 200,000 position, see how it works, then add 100,000, 100,000, and 100,000 successively as the position goes in your favor. To scale into or out of a trade, simply divide your trade lot size into three parts and enter as the market goes in your direction (or exit if it goes against your direction).

Some traders refer to scaling as "taking a position." I knew two brothers, very competent silver futures traders, who built positions of 200 to 300 contracts by carefully scaling into the position as their market judgment proved itself.

THE DAGGER

I use the Dagger entry principle to enter a market most of the time; you may also use it as a scaling tool. The Dagger uses three trends to position an entry: a major trend in the primary direction of the market; an intermediate trend, the reaction to the primary direction; finally, a minor trend that moves back in the direction of the major trend. You are attempting to trade with the major trend, wait for a price reaction to it, then catch the momentum as the major trend (you hope) restarts. See Figure 11.1 and Chapter 8 for more information.

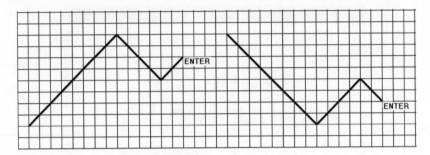

FIGURE 11.1 Example of a Dagger

You might also use the Dagger to scale into a trade, as trends often form in a sequence of small 1-2-3 Daggers. (See Figure 11.2.)

Scaling of course reduces your total profit potential—as opposed to entering all of the position at your first entry point. It may have the same effect for exiting. That is counterbalanced by being able to see more of a trade before taking a full position.

I recommend you consider using scaling only after you have completed at least one successful campaign. Have some trading experience before adding it to your money management arsenal. If your trading capital is limited, scaling may not be possible. At the very least you will need to find a broker that will accept very small lot sizes, typically a micro-account.

ANALYZING THE TRADE

In this trade I was using a formation on an hourly chart and was looking for well over 100 pips of profit. I could afford to give up some of that profit,

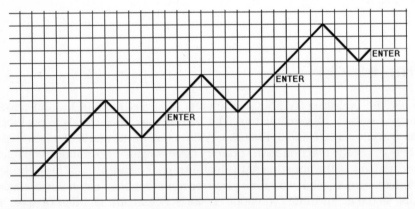

FIGURE 11.2 Using the Dagger to Scale into a Trade

should I be correct, since it was larger than my usual trade objective. (See Figure 11.3.)

> Pair: AUD/USD
> Entry Date: November 21, 2007
> Exit Date: November 21, 2007
> Long/Short: Short
> Entry Price: 0.8871
> Exit Price: 0.8740
> Profit/Loss: Profit of 131 pips
> Theme: Entering with the Dagger

The AUD/USD is one of my favorite pairs. It seems to work very well for me during the time frame I usually trade—3:00 ~PM EST to 9:00 ~PM EST. The AUD/USD is usually very thick, and in reviewing my trades I find I tend to do best in thick markets.

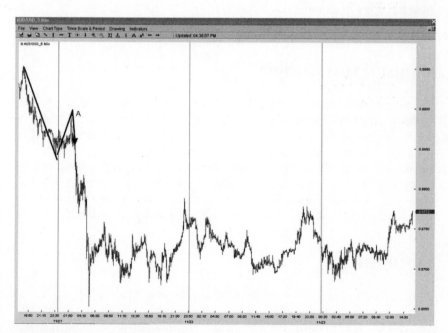

FIGURE 11.3 Scaling the Wall
Source: FXtrek IntelliChart™. Copyright 2001–2007 FXtrek.com, Inc.

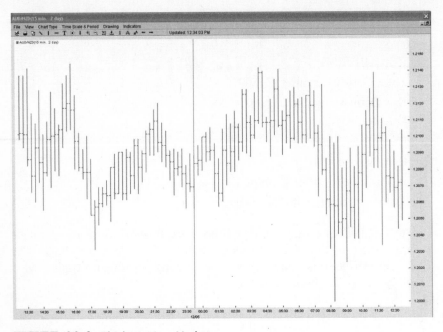

FIGURE 11.4 Thickness in a Market
Source: FXtrek IntelliChart™. Copyright 2001–2007 FXtrek.com, Inc.

MARKET THICKNESS

Thickness is an element of my market environment (ME) methodology (see Chapter 3 on technical analysis and Chapter 28 on trading with ME). It measures the overlap between two consecutive units on a bar chart. Generally, if the overlap over some period of time averages over 50 percent, I rate the market thick. If it averages under 50 percent, I rate that market as thin. Thick markets tend to move more slowly and thin markets more quickly. This is intuitively obvious: The more thickness between two bars, the less price change (ΔP) there has been for that time period. (See Figure 11.4.)

SUMMARY

Scaling into a position can be wise for a number of reasons. If you intend to take a large position, scaling can limit losses if the market moves against you quickly. Knowing you are able to at least break even can make it easier to place a larger position. But do not work with scaling in or out until you have completed at least one successful trading campaign.

CHAPTER 12

Trade #4:
The Trend Is
Your Friend

Money Management

"The trend is your friend" is an old market adage and about as good a one as you will ever hear. Trading with the trend, instead of against it, can increase your long-term odds of success enormously. The trend in this context means the major trend—the primary current direction of the market you are following. The major trend is also contextual. If you are a Guerrilla, the major trend may be the 30-minute chart. If you are a Scalper, it may be the 1-hour chart. For a Day Trader it may be the 3-hour or 1-day chart, and for a Position Trader the 1-day or weekly chart.

The trend is your friend because that is the direction the market is currently going—and that will be the direction, ceteris paribus, you want to trade. If the major trend is *up* you want to be long a pair; if the major trend is *down* you want to be short a pair.

It is really a game of percentages. You have a better chance of the market going your way if you trade with the major trend if only because most of the price ticks are in the direction of the major trend and most of the market's time is spent building the major trend. Figure 12.1 shows how the major trend consumes most of a market's price history. The more pronounced the trend, the more pronounced the percentage of ticks or price bars in the trend direction.

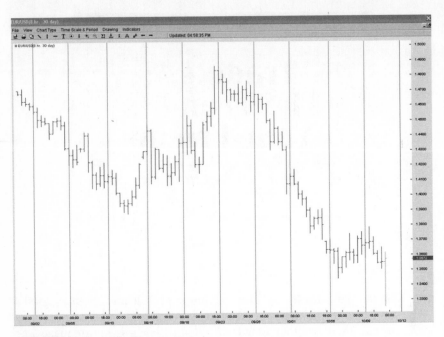

FIGURE 12.1 Eyeballing the Trend
Source: FXtrek IntelliChart™. Copyright 2001–2007 FXtrek.com, Inc.

TREND COMPONENTS

All trends at all price levels and in all time units have two components:

- The primary trend is the direction of the market.
- The secondary trend is the direction opposite the market.

No market goes straight up or straight down. (This is the philosophy behind the bounce in Chapter 10.) Every market has corrections or secondary trends. Figure 12.2 shows a typical degree of up-and-down market action within a trend. No market is ever one-way—as least not for very long.

THE MATRIX

In Goodman Swing Count System (GSCS) theory, my primary trading tool, a matrix is defined as a series of primary trend, secondary trend, primary

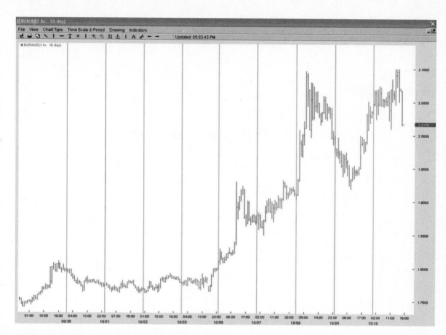

FIGURE 12.2 A Typical Trend
Source: FXtrek IntelliChart™. Copyright 2001–2007 FXtrek.com, Inc.

trend. In Goodman, a matrix is really the basic bare-bones component of market movements.

Trends may also be defined as major, minor, and intermediate (see Chapter 13, "Don't Be a Flatlander"). Trends can even be defined as a function of time (5-minute, 15-minute, hourly, daily).

HOW DO YOU DETERMINE THE MAJOR TREND?

The major trend is simply the direction or directional movement from Price A to Price B. So, how do you determine the major trend?

Traders use an enormous number of tools for that purpose, from the simple to the ridiculously complicated. KIS (keep it simple) is my watchword. You might use a moving average to determine the major trend. A moving average smooths out the flow of price data and creates a relatively stable single directional line.

To calculate a moving average: Take a number of price units, for example, 110.5, 111.0, 111.5. Sum them. The divisor you use (3 in this example)

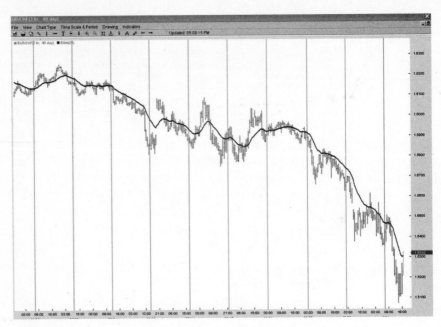

FIGURE 12.3   Using a Moving Average to Spot the Trend
Source: FXtrek IntelliChart™. Copyright 2001–2007 FXtrek.com, Inc.

needs to be in harmony with the time frame for which the moving average is calculated. Don't use a 100-unit moving average to determine the major trend if you are a Guerrilla—it is too long a period to be useful to you.

Figure 12.3 shows a moving average that indicates the major trend for a Position Trader on a 3-hour chart.

Traders also used very complicated and closely guarded secret indicators to determine the major trend. But is that really necessary?

MARKET ENVIRONMENTS

My methodology of market environments (ME) (see Chapter 28) uses directional movement and ΔP—change in price/time—to determine all trends at all time unit and price levels.

Save your effort for other activities related to your trading. To find the major trend, draw a line from the first closing price on a chart to the last closing price on that chart. (You can, of course, simply visualize the line without actually drawing it.) Is it up or down? That is the major trend. By *how much* is it up or down? is the only other question you need to ask. This tells you how strong the major trend is at the moment. Redraw the trend line periodically for an updated major trend.

Now, that was not difficult, was it? Does the moving average, which required calculation, really give you any more information? Not really. I can assure you the same is true for those complicated indicators I mentioned—they are truly much ado about nothing.

When I was in this chapter's trade I could not help but think of the Feldman brothers at Peavey & Company, who carefully, patiently milked silver futures for every penny they could get. On occasion they would go into a small side room and close the door. You could hear them arguing—shouting and yelling at each other. But when the door opened and they came out, all was peace and harmony. Partnerships are hard work; I am happy I trade alone!

ANALYZING THE TRADE

In Figure 12.4 I caught the major trend quickly from the 3-hour chart (A) and followed it by buying on the secondary trend breaks using the Dagger entry principle. I stayed a bit too long, as you can see (B). That is an occupational hazard of trend following: You do not know it is over—until it is over. But one good major trend ride can cover a great many small losses. It should be noted that a position trade of weeks is very unusual in the FOREX arena, especially for retail traders, who usually stay only for hours, if not minutes.

For each trade I am providing the basic statistical information so the trader may find and review the appropriate charts with his or her own charting service:

Pair: EUR/CAD

Entry Date: May 4, 2006

Exit Date: May 24, 2006

Long/Short: Long

Entry Price: 1.3970

Exit Price: 1.4285

Profit/Loss: Profit of 315 pips

Theme: The trend is your friend!

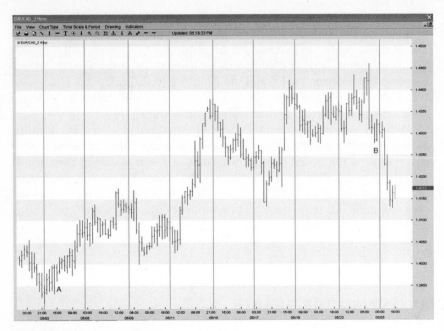

FIGURE 12.4 The Trend Is Your Friend
Source: FXtrek IntelliChart™. Copyright 2001–2007 FXtrek.com, Inc.

SUMMARY

Trading with the major trend increases your chances of success—you are playing with the odds, not against them. Do not use complicated methods to determine the major trend. Eyeballing will do most of the time. For more sophisticated methods, use moving averages or a calculation of directional movement.

Chapter 20, "I've Got Rhythm," offers another major trend perspective.

CHAPTER 13

Trade #5: Don't Be a Flatlander

Money Management

*F*latland: A Romance of Many Dimensions, by Edwin A. Abbott (1884; repr., Dover Publications, 1992), is a famous mathematics-for-the-layman book. It is about a square that is living in two-dimensional space and discovers a third dimension. It is worth reading for many reasons, but the point here is that too many new traders are flatlanders—they use only one chart to follow the markets. But there are traders at many different levels intersecting to make prices happen, and using two or preferably three charts per pair will allow you to see that third dimension the square found.

THE THREE CHART SYSTEM

Chapter 12 ("The Trend Is Your Friend") discussed using multiple charts to trade. The Three Chart System is one of the most common—and useful—money management tools in FOREX. The only downside is it takes up a lot of real estate on your computer screen(s). If you are watching three markets, that is nine charts. If you have only one screen, the nine charts will be very small, although typically you can zoom in on them for detail. Remember, you also must have your trading platform order tools up all the time.

The other approach is to simply keep one chart up for each market—so you can watch more markets—and toggle back and forth to the other scales of charts for each pair.

You can see now why most serious traders have more than a single computer monitor. Two or three is very common; I have seen up to a dozen!

I use two and have resisted the idea of adding a third. How much information can you watch at one time? is the question.

As to computer monitors, go with the biggest and best you can afford. I like wide-screen monitors, but some traders do not. Do not skimp on quality, especially resolution parameters—maximum resolution, image contrast ratio, and response time. At the time of this writing the best monitors offered 1,920 × 1,200 resolution, 1,000:1 contrast ratio, and 5 millisecond response time. Your eyes will thank you later.

My solution is a charting tool that my mentor Charles B. Goodman taught me in the 1970s. I call them box charts. Box charts allow me to see multiple scales on a single (big) chart. This tool requires software, and you can inquire about that at my web site at www.fxpraxis.com. Figure 13.1 suggests Three Chart System parameters for all trader profiles. Please note: These are only suggested parameters; they can and do differ from trader to trader and even author to author! Use your demo account to find ones that work best for your trading methods and temperament.

I typically use the middle scale chart to watch the market on an ongoing basis. The smallest scale is for timing an entry, typically using the Dagger entry principle. The chart with the largest scale is for a long-term perspective, to keep track of the major trend—and to switch to for a few minutes if you feel you are getting too caught up in the short-term price movements.

Using multiple time frame charts is a big advantage for currency traders. But there is no such thing as a free lunch. You need to decide in advance how you are going to use them in your trading program. Simply bouncing from chart to chart without a plan will not work and is apt to only confuse and befuddle.

The Three Chart System has some disadvantages. It takes time, you are constantly switching focus, and it does limit the number of markets you can follow with full attention. But I think the advantages of a 3-D perspective outweigh those difficulties.

The Three Chart System—Parameters			
	Timing Chart	**Watch Chart**	**Perspective**
Guerrilla	1-minute	5-minute	30-minute
Scalper	5-minute	30-minute	1-hour
Day Trader	30-minute	3-hour	1-day
Position Trader	3-hour	1-day	1-week

FIGURE 13.1 The Three Chart System for Traders

THE IMPORTANCE OF PERSPECTIVE

It is important to recognize—and track—the different levels of traders who collectively make the market. As mentioned earlier, switching perspectives requires refocusing. But gaining perspective is worth the effort.

I find that many traders seem to watch the 5-minute chart most of the time. That will drive you batty, quickly! Small moves will loom large, and your emotions will dance all over the place just like the prices on the chart. You will have a difficult time staying in for a long-term trend because of the constant jiggles you see on the 5-minute chart. Real trends take time to form; you need perspective to keep them in focus. For more on that see Chapter 14, "Sit on Your Hands."

ANALYZING THE TRADE

Here is a trade where the Three Chart System worked very well for me.

I used Day Trader chart parameters and show the 30-minute timing chart as a reference in Figure 13.2. Long positions were initiated at A1 and A2 and liquidated on stops at B.

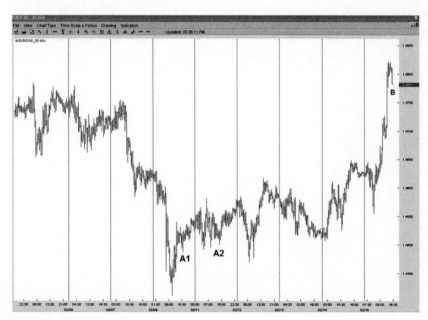

FIGURE 13.2 Don't Be a Flatlander
Source: FXtrek IntelliChart™. Copyright 2001–2007 FXtrek.com, Inc.

For each trade I am providing the basic statistical information so the trader may find and review the appropriate charts with his or her own charting service:

Pair: EUR/CAD

Entry Dates: February 10 and 11, 2008

Exit Date: February 15, 2008

Long/Short: Long

Entry Price: 1.4522 (average)

Exit Price: 1.4785

Profit/Loss: Profit of 263 pips

Theme: Perspective with three charts

SUMMARY

Do not become mesmerized by the short-term chart. Use it only for timing your entry; then bounce back to the middle-term chart to follow the markets. View the long-term chart at least once an hour to keep a perspective on the major trend. Hold a perspective on all the traders in the markets—Guerrillas, Scalpers, Day Traders, and Position Traders; don't be a flatlander.

CHAPTER 14

Trade #6: Sit On Your Hands

Psychology

This was my mentor's most common advice: "Sit on your hands, dad, sit on your hands." If he said it to me once, he said it a thousand times. It took a long time for the advice to truly sink in, but I have gained more from it than anything else he preached to me.

Ten years ago you could count on one hand the number of books on trading psychology. Today there are over a dozen such tomes. Clearly, the importance of this trading aspect is becoming more apparent to all traders. Although not written specifically for the trader, the book *Biology of Belief*, by Bruce Lipton (Elite Books, 2005), is a worthy read. The author's web site also is interesting (www.brucelipton.com).

Sitting on your hands applies to two distinct aspects of your trading. First, it means waiting for the right trade. Almost everyone gets bored and trades simply to be doing something. I find myself doing it more than I want to acknowledge, and I have been trading for 35 years. Nine out of 10 of those trades will be losers. Be patient and wait for the right opportunity. You want everything to be in line with your heuristic—money management, trading method, and psychology. If not, do not pull that trigger; just sit on your hands. It is better to miss a good trading opportunity than to make a bad trade. Breaking even trumps losing. The markets are not going away; there is opportunity every trading session.

The other reason to sit on your hands concerns the time after you have initiated a trade and are waiting for it to work. Yes, FOREX is very volatile; the markets can and do move extremely fast. I have seen the EUR/USD move 50 to 100 pips in minutes on many occasions. But normally they do not move that fast. When they do, they tend to back and fill; no market goes directly to the moon. Real trends—major trends—still take time to form. I mean days and weeks, not minutes and hours. If you want to catch a big piece of a major trend, you have to be there for it. Your broker won't add equity to your account if you are not in the trade!

TRADING VERSUS HOLDING

Along with stops, knowing when to hold them, and knowing when to fold them, perhaps the most eternal debate among traders is between the buy-and-hold and trade strategies. There are advantages and disadvantages to both views. Let us look.

- **Buy and hold.** You will catch the major trend, and if it's a big one you will profit handsomely. Trends take time to unfold; patience can be a great virtue, indeed. The longer you are in the market, the more likely you are to be impacted by a news announcement that can either make you or break you. You have to be in the market to make money, but being in the market is risky. The longer you are in, the riskier it is.
- **Trade.** You may make more than 100 percent of the major trend. If you sell at peaks and buy on dips throughout the major trend, your profits will be greater than if you use the buy-and-hold strategy. The more often you trade, the more often you can be wrong, though. Each trade is a decision of its own, and you are greatly fighting the odds if you think your decisions throughout the course of a major trend—when to sell, when to rebuy—will always, or even usually, be correct.

The less you are in the market, the less exposure risk you have to the impact of news announcements. This is essentially the Guerrilla's Creed. But the less you are in the market, the less profitable a good trade can be for you.

Figure 14.1 shows both sides of the coin—buy and hold, or trade. Whereas the minor trend moves do not look too extreme on a 3-hour chart, I can assure you they can be death-defying to live through on a 30-minute chart! These charts show the pluses and minuses of both a holding strategy and a trading strategy.

A trader can also exercise reversal trading. Instead of simply exiting the major trend and waiting to rebuy later, the trader can reverse positions and short the secondary trends. This is almost impossible to pull off for very long and is not recommended for the new trader. If you use a reversal strategy and it works consistently, you will be rich. Good luck trying!

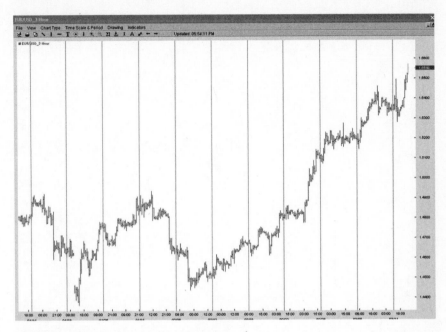

FIGURE 14.1   Buy and Hold—or Trade?
Source: FXtrek IntelliChart™. Copyright 2001–2007 FXtrek.com, Inc.

ANALYZING THE TRADE

In this trade I spotted a double intersection formation on the 3-hour chart. Considering other factors such as volatility, rhythm, and thickness, I decided to stick it out as long as I could. I did a lot of sitting on my hands during the secondary moves—and during the plethora of news items during the meltdown of 2008. (See Figure 14.2.)

For each trade I am providing the basic statistical information so the trader may find and review the appropriate charts with his or her own charting service.

Pair: USD/JPY

Entry Date: September 22, 2008

Exit Date: October 9, 2008

Long/Short: Short

Entry Price: 106.65

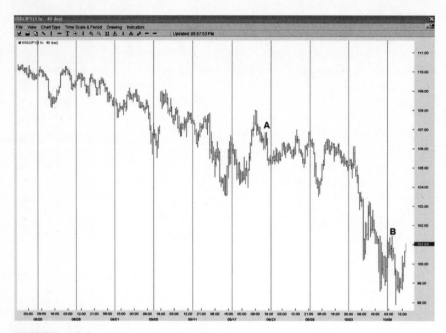

FIGURE 14.2 Sitting on Your Hands
Source: FXtrek IntelliChart™. Copyright 2001–2007 FXtrek.com, Inc.

Exit Price: 101.30

Profit/Loss: Profit of 535 pips

Theme: Holding on for dear life.

SUMMARY

A new trader should be happy to break even over a series of 10, 20, or 30 trades. Most traders are gone by that time. The longer you can stay in the game, the more you will learn and the greater the likelihood that you will be around long enough to catch at least a few big winners.

In Europe, a "Belgian dentist" refers to a very conservative trader. It may seem impossible—or crazy—to be conservative in a market as fast and volatile as FOREX; but not only is it possible, it is a good idea. Take your time picking trades; do not shoot at everything that moves. Trade small lots, and increase them with success. Use modest leverage to begin (I recommend 10:1) and increase it, again as you succeed.

Try to have at least a 1:3 risk/reward ratio on every trade. That means for every $100 you risk, you are hoping to make $300. Few traders can hope to make even 50 percent correct trades; the winners need to outdo the losers by a dollar amount to keep you in the game. This does not mean you will always have a 3:1 profit/loss ratio; we all take what the market will give us. But it is better to aim high than to shoot yourself in the foot.

As in life, the truth is often between the two extremes. In FOREX, on the one hand it is difficult to follow the buy-and-hold strategy. On the other hand, excess trading will get you in trouble, also. Try to find a happy medium between the two. The best advice: Trade the major trend. Sit on your hands but do not let them grow numb. Once you set stops and objectives for a trade, try not to change them. There is a news announcement out there just waiting to spoil your trade and your day.

CHAPTER 15

Trade #7: The Search for a Winning Personality

Psychology

A winning personality can refer to two things: A FOREX trader must have a winning personality to be effective, and markets (or in this case, FOREX pairs) seem to have their own personalities. If you can learn those, it will help you make more good trades.

TRADING TO WIN

Stable is the best word to describe what is needed to trade to win in FOREX. You do not want to be overconfident, nor do you want to be too timid. Be ready to pull the trigger when everything lines up correctly, but do not make trades just because it is something to do and exciting.

At the old Peavey & Company where I traded commodities in the 1970s, it was not difficult to spot the winning and losing traders. You didn't need to see their account statements: Winning traders tended to be quiet or even secretive, and losers were noisy, jumping around and getting excited every time new highs or new lows were made. The latter listened to every word that came over the squawk box as if it were life or death.

Good traders realize the market just *is*, and they try to adjust to it. Bad traders anthropomorphize and begin to think the market cares what they might or might not do. The good traders are very cool and objective; the bad traders are emotional and subjective. It is impossible to keep your emotions in neutral; we are all human. But it is a good idea to monitor them and try to check the extremes.

145

USING DEMO ACCOUNTS TO ACHIEVE STABILITY

I have yet to see anyone fail to make money with a demo FOREX account. When there is no money on the line, there are no emotional interferences; everyone is a winner. A demo account should not really be used for trading. It should simply serve to familiarize oneself with FOREX basics, the broker's trading platform, and the basic ways the markets move over time.

When you are ready to start trading, use a micro- or mini-account with at least a little real money on the line. A micro-account can be opened for as little as $100, and you can trade lots as small as 100—or perhaps less. A mini-account typically requires 10,000-unit lots. Consult your own money management parameters to see how much capital you need to trade those lots. I would recommend at least $2,500 to trade a mini-account.

A standard FOREX lot is 100,000 units; a bank lot is 250,000 units.

As you become successful, you can raise the size of your trading lots as well as your leverage. As you fall back (it happens to everyone), decrease lot size and leverage. I still modulate my trade size according to circumstances—how I feel, how I have been trading, my sense of how strong an opportunity a particular trade is, the specific pair, and so on.

Leverage cuts both ways; it will magnify both wins and losses. Keep your leverage factor consistent and only raise it—gradually—as you progress and profit.

Sadly, many of us are simply not cut out to trade. Know when to throw in the towel. Never risk money you cannot afford to lose. Some personalities are just not meant to trade. If I knew what those were, I would tell you. You'll need to pay your money to find out for sure.

MARKET PERSONALITIES

Markets also have personalities that can persist over long periods of time. The more you know about a market's characteristics, the easier—and better—they are to trade. I use my market environment (ME) methodology (see Chapter 28) to attempt to learn those personalities. Three factors (or elements, in ME-speak) seem to determine a market's personality:

1. **Directional movement.** Directional movement is the net change (ΔP) between two prices.
2. **Volatility.** Volatility is the aggregate amount of movement between two prices, given a minimum fluctuation value.

3. **Thickness.** Thickness is the amount of overlap (or lack thereof) between the high-low range of one price unit and the high-low range of the next price unit.

There are others (including rhythm, discussed in Chapter 20), but these are the primary elements.

The very first thing I do when I open a trading session is look at my charts for these basic personality elements. What are they? Have they changed since the close of my last trading session? You do not need complicated mathematics to track and record these characteristics.

ANALYZING THE TRADE

Here is a trade using just directional movement and volatility in scalping a market. (See Figure 15.1.)

Pair: GBP/USD

Entry Dates: August 13–20, 2007

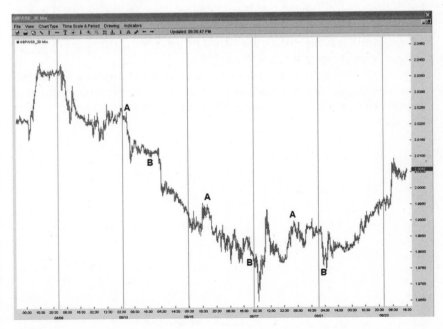

FIGURE 15.1 A Personality Trade
Source: FXtrek IntelliChart™. Copyright 2001–2007 FXtrek.com, Inc.

Exit Dates: August 13–21, 2007

Long/Short: Short

Entry Prices: 2.0240/1.9935/1.9910

Exit Prices: 2.0133/1.9812/1.9778

Profit/Loss: Profit of 362 pips

Theme: Scalping with directional movement and volatility

The reader can decide whether the author did better by trading in and out, or if simply selling and holding would have been preferable.

SUMMARY

A number of books are out now about the psychology of trading. Reading at least one or two of them is a good idea. Learn what you can about the characteristics and personalities of successful traders. Can you emulate them?

See Chapter 6 for characteristics of successful traders. Two excellent reads to get you thinking about this aspect of trading are *Trade with Passion and Purpose: Spiritual, Psychological and Philosophical Keys to Becoming a Top Trader* by Mark Whistler (John Wiley & Sons, 2007) and *Warrior Trading: Inside the Mind of an Elite Currency Trader* by Clifford Bennett (John Wiley & Sons, 2006).

The quickest way to get a bead on a market is to examine its directional movement, volatility, and thickness. By adding rhythm (discussed in Chapter 20) you will have a very good idea of the beast you are preparing to battle.

CHAPTER 16

Trade #8: The King Kong Syndrome

Psychology

I first heard of the "King Kong Syndrome" when the phrase was used by the late Pete Rednor, office manager of Peavey & Company in the 1970s and early 1980s. He used the term for anyone who made a few good trades and got big-headed about it. Pete was wise; he knew such a trader was ready for a fall. He would often wait to see what their next trade would be—and go in just the opposite direction!

This chapter's trade illustrates how even an experienced trader can lose control of his emotions and let greed take over the driver's seat.

FEAR AND GREED

Fear and greed have always driven the market. No matter how sophisticated the markets become, those two factors still tell the tale. Fear keeps traders from entering a market when they should—failing to pull the trigger—or from exiting a bad trade quickly. It can also make a trader get out of a good trade too soon. Greed is the flip side: entering a market too soon, taking on too large a position, or overstaying a trade. (See Figure 16.1.) Fear drives people out of a market; greed drives them into a market. These two emotions represent the psychological trend lines of markets.

If you've had a long winning streak, greed can easily morph into the King Kong Syndrome—a feeling that overtakes traders and makes them think they can do no wrong. Anyone who has made 5, 10, or 15 good trades in a row knows about the King Kong Syndrome. It's a wonderful feeling,

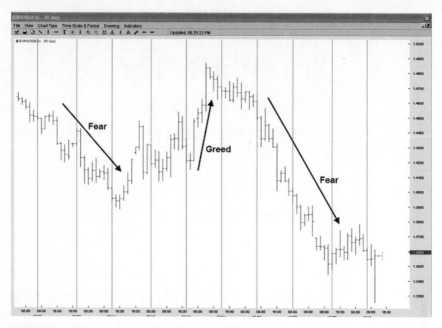

FIGURE 16.1   Fear and Greed Drive the Market
Source: FXtrek IntelliChart™. Copyright 2001–2007 FXtrek.com, Inc.

a natural high that can disappear in a trice and suddenly become the infamous reality check.

There are methods for dealing with the King Kong Syndrome. First, know that it is a natural phenomenon; be on the lookout for it anytime things go exceptionally well.

Second, monitor your emotions before and during every trading session. I keep a graph numbered from zero in the middle, down to minus five and up to plus five. I take my emotional temperature before each session, at least once during a session, and at the session's end. If I am minus four or below or plus four or above, I either don't trade, stop trading, or at least wait a few minutes and work to get closer to zero. Figure 16.2 is a visual representation of trading emotions. You do not need to keep a graph, but keep a mental note of your approximate mental state at key times—such as when entering or exiting a trade.

Third, don't be afraid to walk away from trading for a short period of time. Most traders know to do that after a string of bad trades, but it may be just as useful after a string of good trades. Missing a good trade is better by far than hitting a bad one because your emotions are tangled. You can't trade all the time, anyway. The FOREX markets are more or less

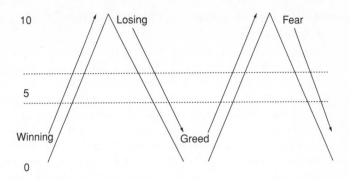

FIGURE 16.2 Chart Your Emotions
Reprinted with permission of John Wiley & Sons, Inc. *Getting Started in Currency Trading: Winning in Today's Hottest Marketplace, 2nd Edition* by Michael Duane Archer (Wiley, 2008).

continuous, unlike the discrete sessions of the futures or stock markets. You need to make notes after each of your sessions of trading so that you can review what you missed when next you trade, and ease into the market traffic without incident.

DISCRETE VERSUS CONTINUOUS MARKETS

FOREX trading can be emotionally unsettling because it runs continuously, around the clock. The stock and futures markets open and close at set times each day, but FOREX runs from 1:00 P.M. NY time on Sunday to 5:00 P.M. NY time on Friday. Beware the opening and closing sessions—especially Sunday afternoon. They can be treacherous. Markets are very illiquid and pip spreads can be outrageous until after 5:00 P.M. on Sunday.

Unless you are trading with an automated "bot," you are limited not only to the number of markets you can successfully follow but to the amount of time you can trade them. Some traders trade as and when they are able—for short two- or three-hour sessions, across all trading sessions—North American, London ("London rules"), and Tokyo. I like to trade longer sessions, five to seven hours, and can comfortably do that only in the evenings, after the North American session closes. What type of trader profile you have will determine how long a trading session needs to be to offer real opportunity. A Guerrilla can catch a two-hour session and have many opportunities. A Position Trader needs longer sessions and also needs to be comfortable leaving stops in the market on open positions when he or she is away.

These traders' sessions, whether two hours or seven hours, are discrete and do not reflect the reality of the almost continuous nature of the FOREX markets. Adjustments have to be made to be successful. Much can happen when you are away—if only for a few hours or even a few minutes.

The best method for adjusting is to make notes on the markets you are following when you quit a session. They need not be copious—just enough so when you return you can catch up quickly. Make printed charts of your markets before you sign off. When you next sign on, review what the markets did while you were away. A good method is to print a longer-term chart that goes back to where you last traded. Look at your notes and now make some opening session notes. Compare the basic motifs—directional movement, rhythm, volatility, thickness. Have they changed since you last traded? If so, how? Now you are caught up and ready to make some money.

ANALYZING THE TRADE

This trade most likely occurred because I had a case of King Kong Syndrome. I had had a particularly good streak of winners extending almost six weeks. My log shows 18 winners and only four (small) losers. I had a hunch to sit on my hands, but greed and giddiness kept me going. I did walk away after this trade, but it had cost me the equivalent of four of the winners. I had also probably been trading too much; three of my trading sessions within two weeks were over 10 hours. The King Kong Syndrome finds those who are tired and unsuspecting. I also had a bad head cold (I know, excuses, excuses). I would also like to claim it was an unfamiliar pair—but as Charles Goodman used to say, "A chart is a chart." This one is also very thick, one of my favorite trading environments. The rhythmic directional movement of major trend and minor trend simply put me to sleep. See Figure 16.3.

Do not trade unless you are physically fit. To that end the trader should keep at least a modest physical exercise program. If you do not believe this, I recommend you purchase a blood pressure monitor and take your reading both when trading is going very well for you and when it is going very poorly for you.

Pair: AUD/NZD

Entry Date: December 14, 2006

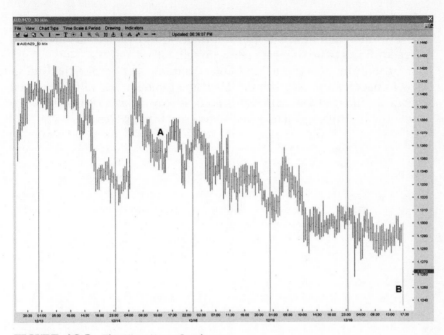

FIGURE 16.3 The King Kong Syndrome
Source: FXtrek IntelliChart™. Copyright 2001–2007 FXtrek.com, Inc.

Exit Date: December 19, 2006

Long/Short: Long

Entry Price: 1.1368

Exit Price: 1.1250

Profit/Loss: Loss of 118 pips

Theme: The road to hell is paved with them!

Mentally one can do the same thing to stay sharp: Crossword puzzles, word or number games, and chess problems all assist in keeping those little neurons firing!

SUMMARY

Most traders know to walk away for a while after a series of losing trades. It may be just as wise to do so after a series of winning trades if you are starting to feel invincible. Yes, it is difficult to walk away from a hot hand. But how often and how long can you trade with the full focus needed to succeed? It has to be your call; know thyself.

A good way to curb the King Kong Syndrome is to cruise the Global-View forums for an hour. Just the diversity of opinion and obviously keen knowledge many of the participants possess may act as a reality check for you. Into the bargain, you may find some great trading ideas.

CHAPTER 17

Trade #9: The Return of the Return

Technical Analysis

I find more Return trades than any other type or formation I study. It is based on a core idea of the Goodman Swing Count System (GSCS). The GSCS ideas are discussed in Chapter 3 on technical analysis, and a deeper look is available in Chapter 27 on Goodman basics. Along with market environment (ME), it is one of two methodologies that define my trading method. The key to using the Return successfully is separating the wheat from the chaff and selecting only the very best ones based on my experience with them.

I fondly remember traders at the Peavey & Company office literally begging Charlie to tell them what he meant by a Return. About all he would do was put his finger on the landing area (a "box" with the price objectives defined as the vertical lines and the time objectives defined as the horizontal lines) and say, "The Return is about here . . . I think."

For complete details on the Return, see Chapter 27, "A New Introduction to the Goodman Swing Count System."

ORIGINS OF THE RETURN TRADE

My mentor, Charles B. Goodman, felt the core market formation of prices was a matrix made up of three price waves: a primary trend, followed by a secondary trend, and finally a second primary trend. (See also Chapter 27 on GSCS basics.)

Charlie said that the next secondary trend (wave 4) would, ceteris paribus, retrace approximately one-half of the three-wave matrix. The distance can vary; there are a number of other Goodman factors involved. He called this fourth wave the Return wave. What is critical is that the end of the Return wave would oscillate about the end point of the matrix's secondary wave.

I use this both as a trading formation and as a timing tool. It has some similarity to the Dagger entry principle. It may be used as a stand-alone trade tool or in combination with other devices such as moving averages and oscillators.

The Return demonstrates a key difference between Elliott Wave theory and the Goodman Swing Count System. Elliott believed that the fourth wave had the same value as the first secondary wave. Charlie's discovery was that the fourth wave behaved against the entire 1-2-3 matrix, not just as a secondary to wave 3. You will note in many Elliott studies it is often the fourth wave measurement that is off.

This trading method involves buying or selling into the landing area (perhaps scaling in if it is large), entering a stop below the landing area—and waiting to see what happens. Exits can be a function of many different factors. The idea here is to see how effective trading the Return can be in FOREX. Charlie used GSCS only in stocks and especially futures. As a technician, I long ago concluded that "markets are markets," and it works as well in FOREX. Trading the Return can be used at all price levels, by all trader profiles. If other tools confirm the trade—rhythm, for example—so much the better. The Return is my go-to trading formation, and it is a good one for the beginning trader to watch for in the markets as it occurs frequently.

ANALYZING THE TRADES

In Figure 17.1, I have used a 5-minute chart to show the fine matrix detail even at Guerrilla time frames. The Return occurs frequently at all time frames and can be used successfully by the Guerrilla, Scalper, Day Trader, and Position Trader.

There is a great deal to be observed and learned from this one chart:

Matrices propagate into bigger and bigger waves. This is called nesting. The major wave here is 1-5-6-8. Note that both primary components of 1-5-6-8 are themselves composed of smaller matrices. 1-5-6 is said to be complex, while 6-7-8 is said to be flat. Flat waves tend to be followed by complex waves in a Goodman matrix propagation, and complex waves tend to be followed by flat waves.

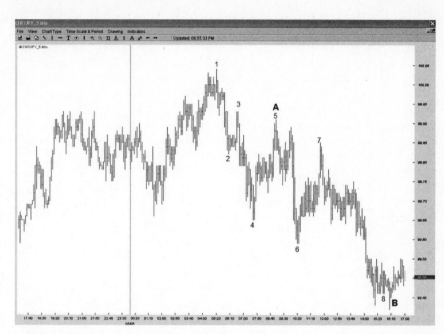

FIGURE 17.1　Trading the Return, Example 1
Source: FXtrek IntelliChart™. Copyright 2001–2007 FXtrek.com, Inc.

The Return is the selling point A. The fourth wave, 4-5, propagates from 1-2-3-4 and is *not* (per Elliott) simply another 2-3.

Pair: CHF/JPY
Entry Date: May 5, 2008
Exit Date: May 5, 2008
Long/Short: Short
Entry Price: 99.90
Exit Price: 99.45
Profit/Loss: Profit of 45 pips
Theme: Return trade, first example

Another example of the Return is shown in Figure 17.2.

Pair: AUD/USD
Entry Date: July 25, 2008
Exit Date: July 28, 2008

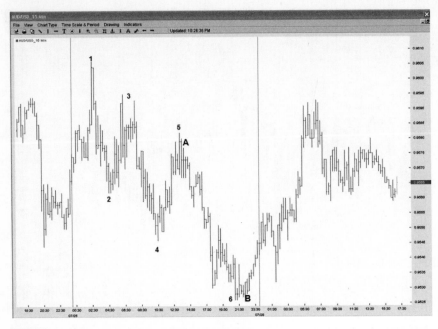

FIGURE 17.2   Trading the Return, Example 2
Source: FXtrek IntelliChart™. Copyright 2001–2007 FXtrek.com, Inc.

Long/Short: Short
Entry Price: 0.9574
Exit Price: 0.9530
Profit/Loss: Profit of 44 pips
Theme: Return trade, second example

For a final example of a Return trade, see Figure 17.3.

Pair: USD/CHF
Entry Date: September 19, 2008
Exit Date: September 23, 2008
Long/Short: Short
Entry Price: 1.1290
Exit Price: 1.0805
Profit/Loss: Profit of 485 pips
Theme: Return trade, third example

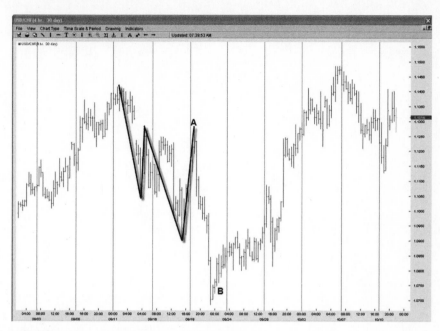

FIGURE 17.3 Trading the Return, Example 3
Source: FXtrek IntelliChart™. Copyright 2001–2007 FXtrek.com, Inc.

As you can see, the Return formation occurs at all chart levels and time frames.

SUMMARY

The Return is a solid, simple, easy-to-understand tool for the new trader to use to at least get his or her feet wet. The formation is relatively easy to spot and plentiful on all time frame charts.

Look for a clean, crisp 1-2-3 matrix and a Return wave that digs fairly deeply into the end point of wave 2. Watch for prices moving quickly into a landing area and equally quickly bouncing back—a sign the market has found good support or resistance. Enter using a flavor of the Dagger.

CHAPTER 18

Trade #10: Double Your Pleasure with Double Intersections

Technical Analysis

T he Double Intersection in the Goodman Swing Count System (GSCS) is the most reliable trading formation I have found in 35 years of trading. It is not as plentiful as the Return, but it is not uncommon, either. You will need to use the Three Chart System to accurately find Double Intersections. For more detail, see Chapter 27 on GSCS basics.

A Double Intersection is the meeting of two separate 1-2-3 waves in a single point or price area. As with the Return, the Double Intersection may be used as a stand-alone trading tool or in conjunction with other tools—GSCS or other methods and ideas.

CLASSIC CHART FORMATIONS

There are many classical chart formations, long cataloged by traders and researchers.

I do not believe these chart formations to be particularly reliable anymore, simply because too many traders are aware of them. This tends to mean the really good classical formations are aborted before they completely form because traders anticipate them and buy or sell accordingly. Nonetheless, all FOREX traders should be familiar with these formations. Several good books cover them in much depth. A good place to begin is with *How Charts Can Help You in the Stock Market*, by William L. Jiler (Trendline, 1968). The formations all carry over to other price markets such as futures and FOREX. Two others are *Technical Analysis of Stock Trends, Eighth Edition*, by Robert D. Edwards and John Magee (CRC Press LLC,

2001), and *Encyclopedia of Chart Patterns, Second Edition,* by Thomas N. Bulkowski (John Wiley & Sons, 2005).

The Global-View web site has material on chart patterns, and on occasion they are heated discussions in the forums between those who use them and find them reliable and those who consider them to be on the same level as reading tea leaves.

DOUBLE INTERSECTION COMPONENTS

Charlie Goodman was a very conservative trader. He believed in playing the percentages and waiting for only the crème de la crème of trading opportunities. Because the Double Intersection is essentially the intersection of two trading formations at a single price or area, it was his favorite trade. It is mine, also.

Several ideas combined to create the Double Intersection: 50 Percent Rule, Measured Move Rule, and matrix. These are covered in Chapter 27 on GSCS basics.

The Double Intersection is defined as two matrices intersecting at a price point or area. There are several forms of the Double Intersection. See Figure 18.1 for the most common. This is an intersection between the 50 percent retracement of the primary up matrix and the end point of the secondary down matrix.

ANALYZING THE TRADE

A Double Intersection can of course occur on any time frame chart and is potentially useful to all trader profiles. I found this one almost

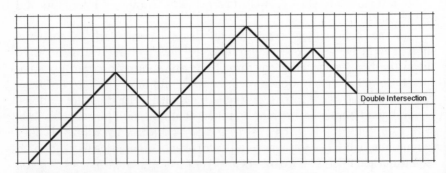

FIGURE 18.1   Double Intersection Formation

accidentally by cruising the charts looking for an opportunity. Once you have some familiarity with the pattern, you can bookmark charts that seem to be forming a Double Intersection and keep regular tabs on that market.

Pair: USD/JPY
Entry Date: June 19, 2008
Exit Date: June 19, 2008
Long/Short: Short
Entry Price: 107.66
Exit Price: 107.08
Profit/Loss: Profit of 58 pips
Theme: Double Intersection

In Figure 18.2, the point 7 represents a Double Intersection. It is the 50 percent retracement of the wave 1-2-3-4 *and* the end point of the secondary wave 4-5-6-7. The trader normally has to act quickly, selling into strength and buying into weakness—especially on shorter time frame

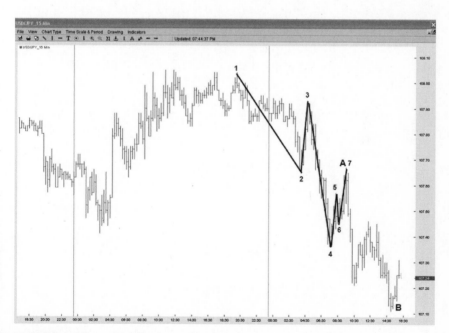

FIGURE 18.2   A Double Intersection Trade
Source: FXtrek IntelliChart™. Copyright 2001–2007 FXtrek.com, Inc.

charts. The Double Intersection is not quite as plentiful as the Return, and it requires more skill to find—but it is still fairly common.

SUMMARY

The Double Intersection is a reliable formation for trading, although you have to look to find them. Use the Three Chart System to make them easier to spot at different price levels. On short-term time frame charts you need to anticipate and act quickly.

CHAPTER 19

Trade #11: Riding the (Goodman) Wave

Technical Analysis

R iding the Wave means to trade a Goodman Wave, the propagation of the basic three-swing matrix as it builds to bigger and bigger matrices in a market. Typically one can ride a strong wave for four or more trades until it gives out and you roll snake eyes. Needless to say, making four or five profitable trades in a row can be very rewarding both financially and emotionally. But strong Goodman Waves are not easy to spot, nor particularly easy to follow. This is an advanced trading method.

It is advisable for the new trader to start small and simple. Make bigger trades and use more tools as you achieve success. You are bound to have secondary reactions to your primary trend of success. When you do, I recommend that you scale back. Go to smaller lots, lower leverage, and fewer tools. Work your way up based on success, not failure.

DEFINING THE GOODMAN WAVE

The difference between Elliott Wave theory and the Goodman Swing Count System (GSCS) is small but critical, and the reason it is repeated from Chapter 17. For Goodman, once a 1-2-3 matrix forms, the next (fourth) wave is related to the entire 1-2-3 wave, not just to wave 3 as in Elliott. According to GSCS theory, this is how markets propagate. Chapter 27 on GSCS basics explains the Goodman Wave in greater detail.

You will need to access charts at multiple price levels to accurately analyze and look for a Goodman Wave. Different price levels tend to show the different matrices better than others do. On a 5-minute chart you would need a 200-inch monitor to see the largest matrix, and on a 1-day chart you cannot make out the smaller matrices. The zoom and scroll features on most trading platforms can be helpful. Figure 19.1 is a sample screen setup. All trading platforms allow you to zoom an individual chart when you need a closer look. Many traders use multiple monitors. I use 2 30″ monitors but have seen setups with six or even eight monitors!

Out of the Goodman Wave idea grows another trading feature: the Flat/Complex Principle. It states that if wave 1 of a matrix is flat (no secondary wave or correction), then wave 3 will be complex (with a secondary wave correction). Conversely, if the first wave is complex, the second should be flat. See Chapter 27 on GSCS for more detail.

BATHTUB ANALYSIS

None of the formations in Chapters 17 through 19—the Return, a Double Intersection, or a Goodman Wave—will jump out and tell you it is there. You need to actively look for them.

Actively and critically following a market is essential. When you are watching, don't be passive. Ask questions, form hypotheses, and see how the market reacts to them. It is important to interact and engage the market even if you are not trading. Not only will it help you get in sync with a market, but you will also learn a great deal as you pass the time waiting for a good trading opportunity.

Charlie Goodman liked to take a batch of charts into the bath with him. He would formulate some hypotheses—typically simple ones—and check the charts to see if any of them were worth pursuing. He discovered GSCS in this way, in the 1940s.

You might ask about a 1-hour bar chart, "What happens on the fifth hour after two up hours followed by two down hours?" If it looks promising, you can narrow your hypothesis: "What happens when the low of the fourth hour is higher than the low of the first hour? Will the next hour be lower?"

Charlie did not have access to computers—he loathed them—but programs can be written to do extensive and quantifiable bathtub testing of hypotheses. One example is my Bar Chart Stat Pro software. Originally written in 2002, it is being extensively rewritten in 2008.

ANALYZING THE TRADE

This trade was fun; winning always is, of course. I traded a Goodman Wave until it stopped propagating. (See Figure 19.2.) Because it was going so well

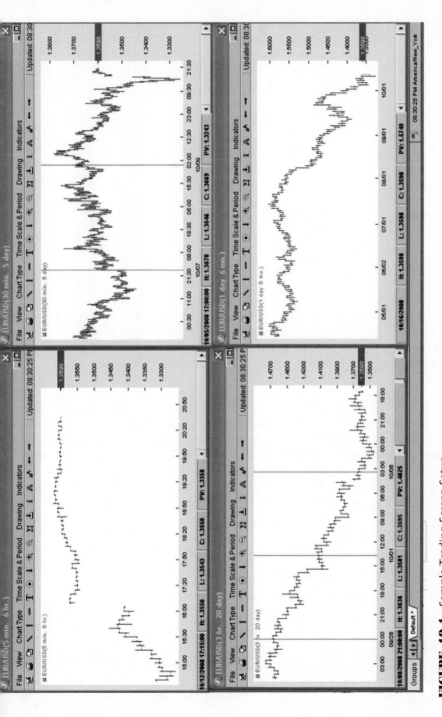

FIGURE 19.1 Sample Trading Screen Setup

Source: FXtrek IntelliChart™. Copyright 2001—2007 FXtrek.com, Inc.

167

FIGURE 19.2   Riding a Goodman Wave
Source: FXtrek IntelliChart™. Copyright 2001–2007 FXtrek.com, Inc.

I also began reversal trading, something I rarely try. When I exited a long position I simultaneously went short; when I exited a short position I simultaneously went long—a reversing tactic that I seldom use, as the long-term odds are against the trader for consistent success. Please note that other factors were involved in timing these trades, in particular measurements utilizing the 3C Rule, which are beyond the scope of this chapter.

For this trade I give only the basic statistics:

Pair: EUR/USD

Dates: May 8–12, 2008

Profit/Loss: Profit of 318 pips

Theme: Riding a Goodman Wave

SUMMARY

Riding a wave in FOREX is much the same as for a surfer: the longer and bigger, the better. But of course eventually the wave runs out and we are, at least for a time, washed ashore to dry out and look for the next wave. When riding a Goodman Wave, don't overstay your welcome. If you begin to get whipsawed, something has gone awry; do not fight it—run to dry land.

Riding the Goodman Wave is an advanced technique. At its best, you can reversal trade with each wave and do very well. *Do not try reversal trading until you have a great deal of experience and have successfully completed several trading campaigns.* Begin with trading the Return, move on to the Double Intersection, and then, finally, you can try riding a Goodman Wave.

CHAPTER 20

Trade #12: I've Got Rhythm

Technical Analysis

B ehind the apparent chaos and randomness there is often rhythm in FOREX pairs. I seldom use rhythm strictly as a trading idea, but I always use it to become more familiar with a market. When I come to a new trading session, rhythm is one of the market environment (ME) elements allowing me to get in sync quickly with how a market is behaving. It can also be a useful timing tool or last-minute check before initiating a position.

The other important ME elements are directional movement, volatility, and thickness. Shape and pretzels are also ME elements. Rhythm is a primary market environment concept. See Chapter 28 for more information about market environments.

TWO KINDS OF MARKET RHYTHM

Rhythm means a relatively uniform value between prices (price rhythm) and time (time rhythm). Prices move over time. In a market there can be rhythm to prices and/or to time.

Time Rhythm

Time rhythm is the measurement between peaks and valleys of prices. You would measure time rhythm distance along the horizontal axis of a chart.

As with everything else in a game of numbers, there is a great deal of manipulation and quantification you can do. But, with "Keep it simple" as my mantra, I like to measure the peaks and valleys in some fixed unit value.

I make an average of them over a minimum of three measurements each. If the average does not deviate much from the individual measurements, the market has time rhythm. I find that at least 75 percent of markets exhibit time rhythm in at least one time frame chart.

Apart from using time rhythm to simply get a good feel for a market—a most valuable asset—it can be used for timing and other trading aspects. For timing, just consider this example. If time rhythm seems to be near an average of five units between valleys, you may not wish to enter a buy order at three units.

Reliable time rhythm seems to be more common than equally reliable price rhythm. I am not sure why that is the case.

Price Rhythm

Price rhythm is the measurement of primary trends and secondary trends over at least three of each type of trend. As with time rhythm peaks and valleys, keep separate measures for the lengths of both primary price moves and secondary price moves. Remember that primary price moves are the moves in the general direction of a market; secondary price moves, reactions against that direction. Again, make an average of each and see how much it deviates from the individual measurements. If not much, the market has some price rhythm.

Price rhythm is also useful to get a feel for a market. Indeed, just measuring primary and secondary moves will be a constant reminder to you of the major trend. As a timing tool, price rhythm can be helpful. You obviously want to place buy orders somewhere around the average length of a secondary wave; this at least allows you to play the percentages and keep a close stop loss order should your judgment be incorrect.

Simple tools can be enormously effective. Avoiding large losses is the first step to long-term success trading FOREX.

See Chapter 28 on market environments for more detail. Time and price rhythm can both be very useful. While there are methods for quantifying them, simple eyeballing works fine. Look for rhythm in each of the pairs in your hopper each time you begin a trading session.

ANALYZING THE TRADE

In this trade I found both price and time rhythm and traded happily along, both long and short (reversing my position each time) until the rhythm broke and my luck ran out. Nothing lasts forever! (See Figure 20.1.)

Pair: GBP/JPY

Entry Date: October 24, 2007

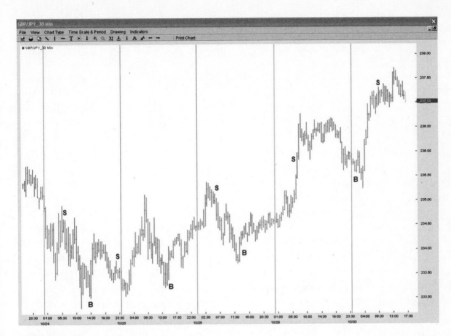

FIGURE 20.1 A Rhythm Trade
Source: FXtrek IntelliChart™. Copyright 2001–2007 FXtrek.com, Inc.

Exit Date: October 30, 2007
Profit/Loss: Profit of 636 pips
Theme: Rhythm trading

SUMMARY

Use time and price rhythm to help time trades and get a feel for a market. You can also use them to trade occasionally if both are very strong. You need to get aboard fairly early; rhythm tends to change more quickly than the other ME elements; three or four complete cycles is about the most you can reasonably expect.

As you can see from the last four chapters, I use a variety of tools, formations, and methods to trade. I am an eclectic and a pragmatist; whatever works is what I want to do! But as a new trader you should limit your repertoire. Use a simple system as shown in Chapter 8 (the Snowflake heuristic) and add tools as you feel comfortable and achieve success. The Return would be a good first tool.

CHAPTER 21

Trade #13: A Simple System

Technical Analysis

I always recommend that traders occasionally try something new: a different market, a different indicator or chart—something to get outside the box and achieve perhaps a new perspective. At the very least, stepping back from a fixed routine may help a trader get a clear view of the bigger picture; in trading the forest is often lost for the trees. Also, it is easy to get in a trading rut, and trying something new may have an effect similar to taking time off from the markets altogether.

Simpler is almost always better. The simple system in this chapter was developed by a commodity broker I once used, Eugene Hartnagle. He was a fine technical analyst and had many unique ideas. Such indicator batteries are commonplace today but were revolutionary in the early 1970s. Computer analysis was almost unheard-of in those days. I used a Data General Nova at the university for my early research. A $70,000 system then, it would be no match for a $500 barebones PC today!

HISTORY OF SIMPLE SYSTEMS

In the late 1970s after I finished a day of trading commodities at Peavey & Company, Charlie and I would often drive downtown to commiserate with brokers at Bache & Company. Among those with whom we gathered was Eugene Hartnagle. Gene brokered both stocks and commodities, but commodities were his first love. He was also quite sharp and creative with technical analysis.

I once traveled with Gene on a sales tour—to North Dakota in January! The ranchers had little to do most of the winter, and his seminars were extremely well attended.

He was perhaps the finest salesperson I ever met. Visualize a one-room schoolhouse in a very close-knit rural community. There are 15 or 20 ranchers and farmers crowded inside who have just heard Eugene give his lively talk about the money to be made in futures. He speaks as he passes out account forms to each table, like a schoolmarm passing out a spelling test.

"Now, if any of you cannot afford an account of just $5,000, please pass the forms back to me. I have quite a few stops left and do not want to waste them."

That, boys and girls, is called asking for the order!

I should mention that Gene's 1975 Cadillac Eldorado was no match for the rural roads of North Dakota in January. We became stuck quite a few times.

One afternoon Charlie and I met with Gene and several other Bache brokers at the coffee shop next to the Bache offices. The talk, as it often did, turned to charting and technical analysis of the markets. After Charlie showed us his latest market environment (shape), Eugene pulled out several charts demonstrating a simple method he had begun using. Remember that there are two basic kinds of market price action: trending markets that are moving up or down, and trading markets that are moving mostly sideways. Of course, as we have noted, trending and trading can be relative to the chart scale and time frame. See Figure 21.1 for a trending market paradigm and Figure 21.2 for a sideways trading market paradigm.

Moving averages tend to work best in trending markets, and to fail in sideways markets. Oscillators and relative strength indicators work well in sideways markets but not so well in trending markets.

Eugene's idea was to use moving averages to determine the trend, but to buy or sell only when an oscillator was oversold (buy) or overbought (sell). In technicians' lingo this combination is called an indicator battery. Eugene also used contrary opinion in his system, but such figures are currently not available for FOREX. My web site, www.fxpraxis.com, now offers a FX Contrary Opinion tool to fill this gap.

WHEN A SIMPLE SYSTEM BECOMES COMPLEX

Even a simple system can become complex. Moving averages, oscillators, and other indicators can utilize filters to compensate for gradually changing markets moving from sideways trading to trending or vice versa. They

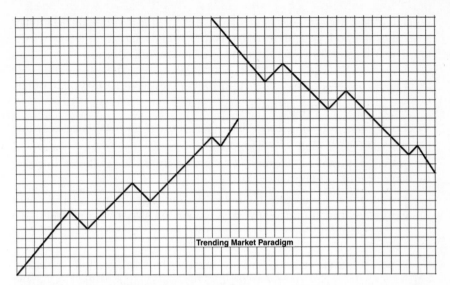

FIGURE 21.1   Trending Market Template

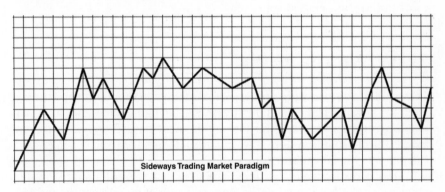

FIGURE 21.2   Sideways Trading Market Template

can also be designed to adjust for market volatility and other behavioral patterns. In addition, the specific rules used to generate trades, stops, and objectives need to be defined for such methods—usually ad hoc.

In 2004 my chief programmer, the late James Bickford, and I wrote a small program to test the simple system over a wide range of filters, parameters, and rule sets. No matter how complex the setup, results seldom varied by more than 5 percent. The simplest setups worked, on balance, as well as the most complex.

Charlie Goodman's caveat on indicators is also worth keeping in mind: Most of the time you can eyeball a chart and see the same behavior easily enough ("Is it trending or trading sideways?"). But if you want to build a system or method, you do need to quantify your tools.

The five rules for using Eugene's system are indeed simple:

1. Use the moving average as your primary entry and exit indicator.
2. Filter the entry signals using an oscillator.
3. Enter on a moving average buy signal only if the oscillator is falling sharply and/or at or below the 0 point.
4. Enter on a moving average sell signal only if the oscillator is rising sharply and/or at or above the 0 point.
5. Because you have more flexibility with entering a market than with exiting, exit on a moving average buy or sell signal without reference to the oscillator value.

If you think about this, you are actually trading with the trend but only entering on price retracements or when the primary trend has slowed down. You can do the same thing by using charts, but indicators give you a more precise, automated approach.

ANALYZING THE TRADE

In the fall of 2007 we were preparing for our annual month-long pilgrimage back to Hawaii. I had closed out my trades and had decided not to initiate anything new as we would be leaving the next day. I happened to come across the old simple system software manual, reread it, and began cruising the markets on a 30-minute time frame.

The following trade certainly indicates that Eugene's simple system shows promise but would necessitate substantial quantification and testing. For traders who feel uncomfortable with charts, there are much worse ideas than beginning with a simple system. An indicator battery, to be successful over the long term, needs to be tested over a wide range of market environments. (See Figure 21.3.)

Pair: EUR/GBP

Entry Date: October 12, 2007

Exit Date: October 12, 2007

Long/Short: Short

Entry Price: 0.8015

Exit Price: 0.7871

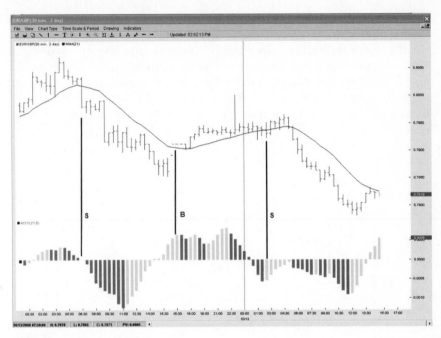

FIGURE 21.3 A Simple System
Source: FXtrek IntelliChart™. Copyright 2001–2007 FXtrek.com, Inc.

Profit/Loss: Profit of 144 pips

Theme: A simple indicator battery

Note that the oscillator filter rules kept me from a buy and a sell that would not have been profitable and allowed me to stay with the primary downtrend. This is the primary rationale behind filters—avoiding bad trades and whipsaw market action. As Charlie always reminded me, the first step to profits is not losing your grubstake; risk avoidance is the key to long-term success in FOREX.

SUMMARY

This chapter is as much about simple systems and indicator batteries as it is about breaking away once in a while and going outside the box. It is a big world out there and you never know what you might find! If you use charts, try an indicator or two or three; if you use indicators, try a chart. Even trading a new pair can be consciousness-expanding. I have seen traders pull out of a rut by simply changing the color scheme of their charts on a trading platform!

If you use indicators, remember that they are not magic. Be sure you know what they actually measure before using them. Know whether they are designed for trending markets or for sideways trading markets. A good indicator battery will have an even mix of trending indicators and sideways trading indicators. Last, ask yourself, "Can this be done more simply with charts?"

CHAPTER 22

Trade #14: A News Trade

Fundamental Analysis

R ight now trading the news is the in topic for small FOREX traders. News trading offers large, quick profits to FOREX traders. Who would not be interested in easy money? As we all know, however, easy money is seldom easy. There are a number of challenges that confront the prospective news trader.

Although I am a technical trader, I do pay attention to the fundamentals. I am especially interested in the news announcements that hit the market on almost a daily basis. Such reports as nonfarm payrolls (NFP) can give the USD pairs trader a good idea of the technical underpinnings, strength, and weakness of the USD.

Refer to Chapters 4 and 5 for the perspective on fundamentals and news trading of John Bland and Jay Meisler.

WHAT IS TECHNICAL NEWS TRADING?

News trading is attempting to profit from one of the many news announcements that hit the market almost every day. For the USD, the nonfarm payrolls report is a very popular announcement to trade. The news announcement time (NAT) is anticipated by traders. Global-View recently introduced a "countdown clock" to the next key economic event on its web site. The clock also lists the consensus forecast and most recent result for the upcoming economic indicator. In addition, Global-View provides an extensive economic calendar with consensus forecasts and most recent results.

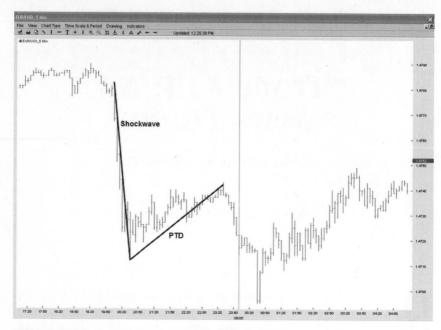

FIGURE 22.1   Price-Trace-Dispersement Chart
Source: FXtrek IntelliChart™. Copyright 2001–2007 FXtrek.com, Inc.

These announcements tend to generate large and very fast price moves; if you can catch even part of the move, you will have done extremely well for yourself. The attraction of news trading is substantial.

There are two defined components to a news trade. The shock wave of the initial news announcement is what most traders follow. But after the shockwave, very often a slower, more orderly move sets in, erasing much if not all of the shockwave value. I call this a price-trace-dispersement (PTD). See Figure 22.1.

The aftershock or PTD is often easier to trade than the shockwave because of its lower volatility and the longer time period over which it occurs.

CHALLENGES OF NEWS TRADING

News trading, per se, is very popular but not easy to do effectively. Here's why:

- It is impossible to predict with certainty which way prices will go after a news announcement.

- Most brokers do not like news traders.
- There is enormous volatility after a news announcement.
- The pattern of prices after a news announcement may vary enormously.
- There are a great number of fundamental factors that ultimately drive FOREX prices. It is impossible to quantify these factors accurately, and even if they could be quantified, the interrelationships between them are constantly in flux (the relationships themselves and the importance of the relationships). How they are related is almost certainly nonlinear. It is not unusual for prices to go in the opposite direction from the general expectation of traders.
- Market makers are the counterparties to your trades. At some level that means your profit is their loss. A quick, big win for you may well be a quick, big loss for them.
- Volatility and directional movement may spike enormously for a short period after a news announcement. Spreads will widen enormously for some market makers and on electronic communications network (ECN) platforms. Market makers are protecting themselves with large spreads (and the consequent poor order fills), while ECNs require a counterparty to execute your order. If the NAT is very bullish, no one will want to sell and prices will rise dramatically before you can find a seller to match and fill your order.
- Along with the late James L. Bickford, I have done an enormous amount of quantitative and statistical research to identify the patterns of price behavior after a NAT. One very common pattern is the price-trace-dispersement (PTD). Prices spike sharply immediately after the NAT (a shockwave), then drift in the other direction for a longer period of time. There may in fact be better trading opportunities in the longer dispersement (aftershock) period than in the initial shockwave after the NAT.

A NEWS TRADING STRATEGY

The most common news trading strategy is a hedge trade. As the time of an impending announcement grows near, the trader puts in an order to simultaneously buy and sell slightly above and below the current market price. Ideally this is entered as a one cancels the other (OCO) order so whichever way the market bolts you are in and the opposite order is canceled.

Neat! But not so fast. Brokers now rarely accept hedge orders. And pip spreads balloon enormously for both market maker and ECN brokers—although for different reasons. If you get filled 50 pips away and the move is 75 pips, you don't have much. You have 25 pips, you say? Maybe, maybe not. You still have to get out of the trade. Volatility and pip spreads can remain high for several very long minutes. Then a PTD may set in, quickly retracing the initial shockwave—and your supposed 25-pip profit.

Software is available to news trade. Traders have also devised schemes to hide their intentions—similar to how players count cards at blackjack. They might place the buy order with one broker, the sell order with another. Because of the lure of quick and big profits, a good deal of research attention has been given to news trading; unfortunately, it is well beyond the scope of this tome. The only current book addressing this topic is James Bickford's very fine *Forex Shockwave Analysis* (McGraw-Hill, 2007).

I certainly recommend that the new trader keep a calendar of news events for each trading week. I further recommend that you should be out of the market during those times. If you have an open trade going into news, be sure you have a stop entered in the market; but be prepared for a risk that it could be triggered at a less advantageous price should the market gap after the announcement.

Watch from the sidelines how a market reacts to the news. This can be very useful information going forward. Do not just watch the shockwave. The PTD aftershock can often tell you more about market underpinnings than the shockwave.

The Global-View web site offers a FOREX News Calendar, and it is enough for most of us. If you need to dig deeper, try www.tradethenews .com. On the forums you will always find traders discussing both pending and just-released reports.

ANALYZING THE TRADE

Here is an example of a successful news trade in the EUR/USD. The tactics of making such trades can be complex—and nerve-racking—so they are not recommended for the new trader. As you can see in Figure 22.2, the first reaction to the news was negative—prices quickly reversed and soared higher. It is a tough way to make 50 pips!

- Pair: EUR/USD
- Entry Date: June 26, 2008
- Exit Date: June 26, 2008
- Long/Short: Short, then long
- Entry Prices: 1.5571/1.5590
- Exit Prices: 1.5590/1.5668

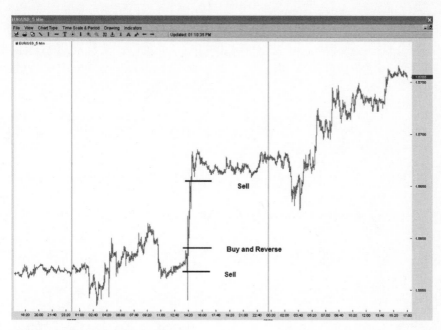

FIGURE 22.2 A News Trade
Source: FXtrek IntelliChart™. Copyright 2001–2007 FXtrek.com, Inc.

- Profit/Loss: Profit of 59 pips
- Theme: Trading the news

SUMMARY

New FOREX participants should avoid attempting to trade the news. Yes, it is all the rage, and, yes, it can be most profitable. But it is a very specialized and complex activity, not unlike arbitrage—only more dangerous. Your chances of consistent success without substantial experience, money, research, and proper tools are microscopic.

Be sure you know when news announcements in currencies you follow occur. Note them when you open a trading session. Definitely have stops in on any open positions. Then sit back and watch how the market reacts to the news. Do not just watch for the news shockwave, but pay attention to the sometimes more durable and stable PTD aftershock.

CHAPTER 23

Trade #15: I Read about It on Global-View

Fundamental Analysis

I am not a fundamental trader. I have been strictly a technician since the get-go, 1973. But I do not doubt the importance of fundamentals to especially long-term trends. In using the Global-View forums for the past year I have also learned that fundamentals can sway the short term—sometimes surprisingly quickly. It is a little like reading tea leaves to me, but I sometimes find a trend in the Global-View forum that points me to a possible trade. From there I use my own technical tools.

FOREX FOR FUNDAMENTAL TRADERS

Despite the fact that most large hedge funds now trade using automated trading systems, or bots, there are still many professional traders who are strictly fundamentalists or at least use fundamentals along with their technical work.

There is very little literature on trading FOREX with fundamentals. Perhaps it works so well it is something of a secret society. I think rather the reason is that fundamentals are hard to get a grip on for new traders. You can use indicators straight out of the box, but fundamentals take a great deal of real-time experience. Most traders do not have the patience.

In addition, fundamentals are difficult to convert to prices, whereas technical methods almost always are derived from prices. The interrelationships between fundamental factors are enormous in number. The interrelationships are always changing, and so are the weights, at any given time, of many of them.

What is important to the market for a period of time can suddenly be of little interest. I remember in the late 1970s and early 1980s that every trader held his breath pending the release of the money supply figures. This went on for years when the Federal Reserve, led by Paul Volcker, was running policy based on money supply growth. Then, suddenly, Fed policy changed and the interest was gone; the figures were released to a very tepid market response.

There is a sense that the relationships between fundamental factors are nonlinear and the conventional tools now used to monitor and analyze them are not sufficient. But, again, the importance of fundamentals to FOREX prices cannot and should not be underestimated. If you can find a way to fold them into your trading, do so.

The best way to learn fundamentals is from fundamental traders. The largest group of them I know congregate on the Global-View forums. Most traders are technically oriented, though, and this is reflected on the Global-View forums as well. Most of the fundamental traders come from an institutional trading background, and reside on the GVI Forex experienced traders forum. These traders mostly work on a blend of the technicals and fundamentals.

ECONOMETRICS

There is a hybrid research realm called econometrics. It aims to quantify fundamental information so that models of economies can be manipulated mathematically. The potential for FOREX econometric models is substantial. Up to the present, to my knowledge, all of these have used linear mathematical tools. Since the interrelation between fundamental factors is almost certainly nonlinear, it may require the use of nonlinear modeling methods such as cellular automata to make a breakthrough. Some trades may use econometric tools or methods to bridge the gap between technical and fundamental analysis, but the topic is mathematically complex and not for the new FOREX participant.

THE MUNDO

In the *Forex Trader's Companion* volumes (CommTools, 2001–2002), you will find information on the Mundo—a FOREX index similar to the Dow Jones or Standard & Poor's indexes. It has many applications and may help bridge the gap between technical and fundamental analysis.

To begin and for the sake of simplicity, we define the Mundo as the unweighted average of the four most heavily traded currency pairs:

EUR/USD
GBP/USD
USD/CHF
USD/JPY

The steps to calculate the present value of the Mundo are quite simple:

1. First, the USD must be the quote or second currency in the currency pair. Therefore, the reciprocals of both the USD/JPY and the USD/CHF must be calculated (divide the exchange rate into 1).

$$\text{If USD/CHF} = 1.2393, \ \ \text{CHF/USD} = 0.8069$$
$$\text{If USD/JPY} = 117.23, \ \ \text{JPY/USD} = 0.008530$$

2. Next, all pairs must be converted to their pip values. Multiply the EUR/USD, the GBP/USD, and the CHF/USD by 10,000:

$$\text{EUR/USD pips} = 12{,}753$$
$$\text{GBP/USD pips} = 18{,}872$$
$$\text{CHF/USD pips} = 8{,}069$$

3. The JPY/USD currency pair is special because of its wide parity rate. Multiply it by 1,000,000:

$$\text{JPY/USD pips} = 8{,}530$$

4. Now add the total number of pips:

$$12{,}753 + 18{,}872 + 8{,}069 + 8{,}530 = 48{,}224$$

5. Divide the sum of the pips by 4:

$$48{,}224 \div 4 = 12{,}056$$

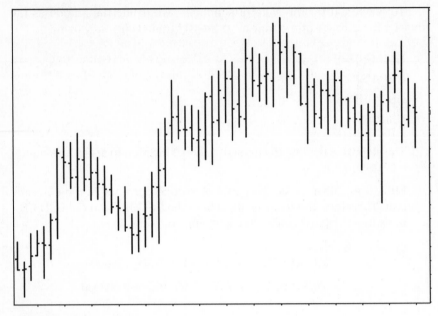

FIGURE 23.1   A Mundo Chart

6. To convert from the number of pips to the Mundo exchange rate, divide
   by 10,000:

$$12{,}056 \div 10{,}000 = 1.2056$$

See Figure 23.1 for a Mundo chart.

A recorded webinar on the Mundo is available on www.fxpraxis.com.
See Chapter 26 for more on the Mundo and possible applications.

ANALYZING THE TRADE

I was reading the Global-View Professional Forum for a few days and no-
ticed a lot of chatter about the lack of any more impending U.S. Federal Reserve interest rate cuts. In the current environment (and this can change),
lowering interest rates lowers the attractiveness of holding the U.S. dollar.
Conversely, no more interest rate cuts would seem to imply an eventual
strengthening of the U.S. dollar. The EUR/USD is the most widely traded
currency pair but very often comes with extreme volatility and sensitivity

to news events, which of course cuts both ways. At the time I did not have the EUR/USD in my Hopper, but I decided to take a look at all EUR/USD time frame charts. Figure 23.2 shows the relevant 30-minute chart.

I took a bit of a flier, selling the EUR/USD mostly on rhythm, and used a 75-pip stop loss because of the volatility of this popular pair. But it worked out very well. Once you are in a trade where you can bring a stop loss to breakeven or better, the pressure is off and you can, more or less, let it ride.

I would never have considered the trade without catching the interesting chatter on the Global-View forum.

Pair: EUR/USD

Entry Date: March 19, 2008

Exit Date: March 20, 2008

Long/Short: Short

Entry Price: 1.5695

Exit Price: 1.5611

Profit/Loss: Profit of 84 pips

Theme: The Global-View forum

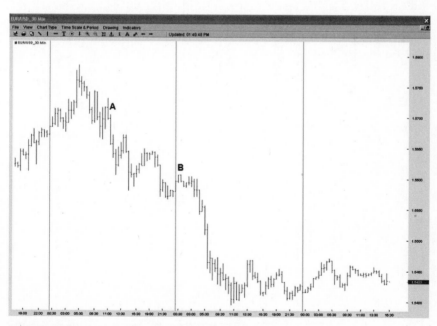

FIGURE 23.2   A News Trade in the EUR/USD

Source: FXtrek IntelliChart™. Copyright 2001–2007 FXtrek.com, Inc.

SUMMARY

Ultimately fundamentals decide market prices, especially over the longer term—the major trend. Do not ignore them. Once you have a basic technical trading method in place, attempt to find a way to use fundamentals to your advantage. The field is certainly wide open to new research and ideas.

I recommend spending at least one or two hours a week (or every day, as many do) cruising the Global-View forums to get a good feel for how fundamentals work and how fundamental traders think about FOREX. Log in at different times to familiarize yourself with the participants during different trading sessions. Cut and paste recommendations from some of the regulars and review how they did on a weekly or monthly basis. You can use the search tool to find threads on specific fundamental ideas or currency pairs. If you are contemplating a trade in any pair, you can look to the forums for how fundamental traders are viewing that market.

The most astute technical traders will use fundamentals to support and confirm their technical work.

PART THREE

Selected Readings

P art Three is primarily intended to provide the reader yet another perspective on the information provided in Part One and Part Two. FOREX is a very large and complex space; our belief is the new trader will learn the most by approaching the same information from different angles.

Chapter 27, on Goodman Swing Count System (GSCS) basics, and Chapter 28, on market environment (ME) applications, are meant to be used in concert with Part Two.

CHAPTER 24

Currency
Futures Trading
Basics

HOW DO FOREX FUTURES TRADING PRICES RELATE TO THOSE IN THE CASH FOREX MARKET?

The most active currency futures trading contracts trade for four fixed dates in the year. They settle on the third Wednesday of March, June, September, and December. In contrast to the futures market, the cash FOREX adjusts its maturity dates daily, trading primarily for monthly maturities of one, two, three, six, and twelve months ahead, with the flexibility to quote for any individual date in between. The interbank market thus trades for spot and forward delivery. The cash or interbank market is a delivery market. That means that all transactions between institutions must be settled for the full face value of each transaction. In contrast to the cash market, FOREX futures trading markets allow traders to buy and sell contracts and thus avoid the need for the cash settlement of trades. Such is always available at the quarterly settlement of maturing contracts, allowing professional arbitrageurs to keep the two markets tightly in line with one another. Currency futures are spot prices adjusted by the forwards to arrive at a future delivery price. Professional arbitrageurs job the two markets to keep them in line.

This chapter is taken from the Global-View Learning Center (www.global-view.com).

WHERE, THEN, DO THE FORWARDS COME FROM?

Many traders mistakenly believe that forwards are the market's prediction of where spot prices will be at some point in time in the future. They are not. They are generated solely by interest rate differentials. For example, suppose a USD/JPY conversion rate is needed for one year away and the price must be fixed immediately. This can be accomplished by borrowing dollars for a year, immediately converting them into yen, and placing them in a one-year time deposit. The yen deposit matures in 12 months and its proceeds at that time are used to meet the future yen commitment. The cost of the hedge is the loss on the interest rate differential. That interest rate differential can be applied to spot FOREX rates by converting them into point values. These point values are called forward swaps. Global-View provides forward swap values daily for converting spot rates to futures and vice versa as part of its FOREX resources section.

Example of USD/JPY Conversion

U.S. dollar 12-month deposit/lending rate: 6.25 percent

Yen 12-month deposit/lending rate: 0.50 percent

Interest rate differential: 5.75 percent

Dollar/yen exchange rate: 105.00; $105.00 \times -0.0575 = -6.038$ points

Of course the transaction can be reversed to lock in a dollar value against the yen. In that case, yen would be borrowed and deposited into dollars. On that trade the transaction would earn 5.75 percent. If ever the forward market gets out of line with interest differentials, traders quickly force them back into line by use of the deposit market. The market actively trades the forward point values. The International Monetary Market (IMM) maturities (value dates) are now actively quoted in the interbank market, and are often determined by a straight-line interpolation between the nearest actively traded value dates.

Quoting conventions in the interbank market and currency futures trading market (IMM):

Due mainly to historical precedent, dollar forex rates are quoted in one of two formats:

1) Dollar value of foreign fx currency unit (e.g., one British pound is worth US$1.6050).

2) Number of foreign forex currency units per dollar (e.g., 105.00 yen purchase US$1).

The IMM quotes all currencies using convention #1. This convention allows point values to have a fixed dollar value. Using convention #2, point values would have a fixed foreign currency value. This would create a logistical nightmare for a dollar-based exchange, as daily settlements would have to be converted to dollars using an arbitrary exchange rate. Convention #1 quotes are simply the reciprocal of #2, and vice versa.

For example, USD/JPY 105.00 can be converted from #2 to #1 as follows:

$$1 \div 105.00 = .009524$$

Global-View posts indicative IMM swaps each trading day. That FOREX resources link (www.global-view.com/forex-trading-tools/ spotfutcalc.html) also illustrates how the conversion of each major FOREX futures currency contract is done.

CHAPTER 25

FOREX Lessons from Shanghai BC

TRADING: A MIND GAME

You must change your mental attitude first from a normal person to that of a speculator. Almost all traders I have met, except a few successful ones who really made millions and billions trading in the market, simply waste all their time trying to learn the easiest part, like how to read data and charts, and trying to perfect entry and exit skills and the like. Trading is a mind game, and without having a right frame of mind, it is a losing game even before it starts. Training a trader's mind is the first step for any successful trader—but almost all new traders neglect that part, and that explains why more than 95 percent of traders are failures in the long run.

Acquiring the knowledge of the market is not difficult for anyone with average intelligence after a few years of hard study in the market. But it is neither the level of intelligence nor the knowledge that decides the outcome of the market operations of a trader. It is the decision-making process that is so hard for most traders to overcome, and that is the main reason for a success or a failure for all the traders. Some find it easy to make decisions and stick to them, but most find it so hard to make decisions and stick to them. Unfortunately, any decision-making process in trading is a painstaking process, and humans tend to avoid pains and go for pleasures, even if temporary ones.

This chapter consists of selected Shanghai BC posts from the archives of the Global-View.com FOREX Forum. Shanghai BC is a highly respected member of the Global-View.com community.

Assuming one has acquired enough market knowledge and acquired one's proven trading system (this is the second most important element of success in trading, in fact; an edge in any system is based on the quality of information one has, charts being only information of secondary quality, not the best one) through studies and research, a trader faces the task of making decisions to put this knowledge and system into practice. Then, how many traders can honestly say they can commit their ranch when the trade is suggested by their own system (given that trading is just a chance game) and let the profit run for weeks and months when their system tells them to? And how many can manage to cut the loss as a routine process when the situation arises? It all sounds so easy when saying it but is so difficult when doing it and affecting real money in the market.

I still do not sleep well when I am running a position, because even if the profits are running into a few hundred dollars and the system is telling you to carry on, there is no guarantee that the profit will turn into a yard or two in a month's time, and it may even turn into a loss in a day or two when something unexpected happens. It is a painstaking process in a real sense. The pain is in not knowing what will happen in the future and in the fear of losing.

So at the end of the day, assuming one has a decent trading system and market knowledge and decent information, it is ultimately how disciplined the trader is and how well that trader can take the pain of making the right decision at the right time that decides the outcome of the trade. Hence I call trading a mind game.

When I interview prospective young traders, I always look for a disciplined and strong-willed person as my first priority as long as one has decent education. But strangely, in many cases, it is some kind of genius or half-genius with lots of brains but no discipline who turns up for an interview thinking only bright people can make good traders.

In fact, I always try to pyramid while position trading medium-term once I am convinced of a new medium-term trend emerging, like in USD/JPY position trading 135–132 as an initial position, adding in 132 and 129 areas; same for AUD/USD and EUR/USD with similar strategies. But sitting on positions and watching the counter-rallies costing truckloads of money is not an easy job to do and causes lots of pain all the time. Most traders, even experienced ones, cannot bear that pain and give up too early. *But there is no other way to make big money, and we have to bite the bullet and "sit and accumulate" as long as the medium-term trend is intact.* That is why I always believe psychological aspects of trading are far more important than anything else in successful trading. It is a mind game like the bluffing game of poker.

Entries and exits can never be irrelevant for any trader for any purpose. It is just that psychological aspects of trading are much more important than entries and exits, and decisive for the success or failure of a trader in the long run. Perhaps exits are more important than entries, because any perfect or near-perfect entries are possible only in hindsight.

BC'S WORDS OF WISDOM

Any market, be it the real estate market or the FOREX market, is all about transferring money from the masses to a few lucky ones in the long run. In most real property speculation cases, the masses make money, a lot of money, but the money stays as paper profit and evaporates before they realize their paper profit into real hard cash. In most FOREX speculation cases, the masses barely survive a few years, thanks to lack of knowledge of the market and the deadly leverage. But both types of speculators serve their useful purposes in the investment food chain, contributing their hard-earned money to the market in exchange for a dream.

For any prospective traders, I hope this is not in any way a discouragement. Trading is a hard mind game and not everyone is suitable to be engaged in such a hard game. Most have neither frame of mind nor mental fortitude to survive in this hard game. Mastering technical analysis or numbers or the options business is at best a first tentative step in the right direction with no guarantee of any success. Training a right frame of mind is the most difficult but absolutely necessary part for success, and most are simply not ready to go through that hard stage of the learning process, because it is a very painful process. Trading is essentially about a painstaking process in the end, although most do not realize it—the process of overcoming fear and greed and mastering tranquility of mind in this hard school of speculation.

Every trader should find his/her method/system that suits his/her own situation and personality. And that system/method must be the one that has proven to be able to make some money through trials. So, if Tom, the medium-term trader, revealed his money-making method of the last three decades, it may not have the same effect for Dick and Harry, the day traders, and vice versa. Most traders fail for lack of a system/method and/or lack of discipline to follow through.

Trading success is all about making as much as one can when one is right and losing as little as possible when one is wrong. That is the essence of this business. So, any theory or system that looks after the above is a good one.

A system is a weapon of a soldier in this market. You must have one as soon as possible. Otherwise, it will be like fighting well-armed FOREX robbers with a handbag. The best one is a self-made one because you can never feel comfy in borrowed shoes, although borrowing good ideas from others is a good idea. Good luck.

* * *

One cannot make a dime unless one follows the herd or trend most of the time. It is just that one has to be cautious when an overbought/oversold region is approaching and know how to turn at the inflection point for the opposite trend. Following the herd needs average intelligence and courage, but identifying inflection points and taking a necessary action need not only intelligence but also a lot of courage. *Again, fortune favors the brave.*

Money management is where most traders go wrong in almost all cases, leaving only a few as the winners at the end of the day. Money management and discipline of mind are what make or break a trader at the end of the day, not the elementary entry and exit method.

FOREX/Currency Trading: It is a sentiment game with a crowd mentality where even the best players with the best forecasts are tricked out of good positions by the magic of price action.

TREND TRADING: ACCUMULATION AND DISTRIBUTION

The FOREX market, like any other market, works in a very simple way. It accumulates in a certain area for a while, and once the accumulation is over, it advances a certain distance until distribution starts, and accumulation happens again and advances a certain distance again, and repeat and repeat. Day trading may not yield the best results while the accumulation and distribution work themselves out; being double-murdered by zigzag moves while the market starts advancing out of the accumulation area, day trading is a sure way of cutting profits short. In general, day trading is not the best form of yielding the most profits in my experience, contrary to what some writers who never made real money in this game try to say.

The safe and better way in making some money must be to wait for accumulation to be over and ride the whole length of the advance until distribution starts, and then reverse as the market dictates as a short-term trade for 2 to 10 days, as the case may be.

Please study 8-hour or 4-hour line charts or candle charts, especially the patterns and 20 MA [20-day moving average] inside the charts for a few months every day, and you will discover what I mean by accumulation and distribution for short-term trades in the FOREX market. The FOREX market always needs this process, so you can decide what tactics you will use at a given stage. IMHO. Good luck.

TECHNICALS AND CHARTING

Why day trade once you get a good seat and the market is going your way? It is always more profitable to ride even the short wave for 2 to 10 days by adding up. In general, you must day trade only when you are losing. To find a buy entry seat for short-term trades, you can study the accumulation and distribution patterns and 20 MA in 8, 4 hourlies or 30-min line charts (or candle charts), together with MACD [moving average convergence/divergence] overbought and oversold indicators with their patterns. If you study them for a while, you will understand when it is the best entry point. The remainder is for money management and discipline and, of course, experience. Good trades.

* * *

On the technical side of the trading, the first thing to do is to find out the trend in one's trading time frame and the proper trading strategy for that trend. Some traders ride positions for months, while some ride positions for less than an hour or a day, and their views of the trend obviously differ. For a trader who is running a position for months, a daily fluctuation may be just meaningless noise, while for a day trader or an hour trader, a daily fluctuation could be a monstrous tsunami. Having a precise definition and a technique of identifying a trend and the turn of a trend in a trader's time frame, and adopting the right strategies for that trend, is the first elementary step in a hard school of trading. IMHO.

I keep my technical side on any pair as simple as possible, largely relying on others' moves to see how I can take advantage of the situation. So for me the strategy is to range trade. Please always give a stop order per your risk profile when you open any new position. Medium-term reversals can be confirmed only in monthly, weekly, and daily charts. *Chart reading is not to predict the tops or bottoms of any move, but to confirm the change of trend as soon as it is made and adopt the right strategies in that new trend.*

Each cycle is different from the last one, and that is the beauty of the market. It is extremely important to look at the big picture from the distance rather than studying the minute and hourly charts with a microscope. And repeat the whole show again and again till it shows a sign of turning in the daily or weekly chart. And flip. Good trades to you.

* * *

I use very primitive charting methods. Please read 8-hour charts of EUR/GBP with 20 and 40 MA, and read round figures and breakouts (from consolidations); then you will realize the method cannot be more primitive than that, but it is still deadly effective. Buy on dips toward the support and add up on a breakout of that consolidation, treating the two as one trade with the same stop loss, and keep them as long as the market moves in your way. Good trades.

As a rule of thumb, 20 MAs in 8-hour, daily, weekly, and monthly charts are useful for their directional tendency and as a resistance and support point. Not sure how much they are useful in day trading, though.

Please have a look at EUR/USD and USD/JPY weekly 10 RSI [Relative Strength Index] and AUD/USD monthly 10 RSI patterns, not levels. Then you will find out that primitive things work better when coupled with even simpler MAs. And RSI is useful only in these weekly and monthly time scales as far as I can see. You can ignore RSI in short-term scales, as the inventor of RSI, [J. Welles] Wilder, told us long ago.

* * *

Good afternoon. Agree with your observation. [George] Soros of Quantum Fund hit the nail on the head with his theory of reflexivity in the market, and that is exactly how these players work in the market. That rather romantic tool of daily candlestick chart is useful because whenever some players start positioning to start or stop short-term moves in the Yen market, say several hundred pips, for whatever reasons, it reveals their intention to the market, more often than not. It sounds so weird to say tens of yards are spent relying on indicators so primitive like hand-drawn candlestick charts, but that is the truth in the Yen market. Same as millions of soldiers risking their lives depending on how their generals draw up the battle plan with their cheap red and blue pencils at their operation room desks. Crazy world, I would say, but that is the fact. And as you say, battle is a battle and those ones who make their first move with their candlestick may not always win, either. I happen to believe if a child can learn to trade with some simple signals he will do better than most traders, most of the time, making a good living. But then again, moving market is more than just following the signals. Good trades to you.

* * *

I guess if you are a day trader, 30-minute and 15-minute candle charts and line charts in combination with MACD and MA could be more useful than hourly charts or even daily charts. Especially watch out for the down-sign and up-sign with long tails in candle charts and confirmation of the change of short-term trend in line charts breaking accumulation area in these charts. If you are a nimble trader, even a candle sign is enough to start moving in with stops above or below the long tail end. For dollar/Yen trade, read Swiss/Yen, pound/Yen, and Euro/Yen together to confirm the top or bottom. For Euro/dollar or dollar/Swiss trade, read pound/Swiss and Euro/pound together to confirm the same. If you are a day trader, what matters is the flow of that particular day, not the bull or bear bias, so 30-min and 15-min candle charts and line charts are not bad tools to follow these flows. Good trades.

USING CROSSES AND GOLD

EUR/GBP and GBP/JPY have a value as the leading indicators of EUR/USD and USD/JPY moves. EUR/CHF is similar to EUR/GBP in forecasting value, but I stopped trading and looking at it a long ago after experiencing difficulties in running good-sized positions there.

In short, EUR/GBP and GBP/CHF are leading indicators for EUR/USD and USD/CHF, and GBP/JPY, EUR/JPY, and CHF/JPY are leading indicators for USD/JPY. EUR/JPY plays a very important role in EUR/USD direction, too, while GBP/JPY plays the same role for GBP/USD. For example, yesterday's EUR/USD weakness largely started from EUR/JPY sales keeping EUR/USD and USD/JPY downwards. As a rule of thumb, if EUR/USD does not move but EUR/GBP moves first, it is a good indicator that someone is maneuvering in EUR/USD front in the same direction later, and when EUR/USD moves but EUR/GBP does not move first or in tandem, then it is highly likely the EUR/USD move is countered by its opponent and the opposite move is highly likely soon. Same applies in USD/JPY and EUR/JPY, GBP/JPY front in the same fashion. IMHO. Good trades.

* * *

Good morning. EUR/USD, EUR/GBP, EUR/JPY, and GBP/CHF all have correlation to a certain degree affecting each other. It simply shows how the money moves around in these pairs. For daily candle studies, it is more accurate to read them all to see where the flow is going, and same for 4-hour or hourly or even 10-minute charts. In fact, GBP/CHF and EUR/GBP in many cases move a day or two before EUR/USD. Even by watching GBP/CHF and EUR/GBP charts, short-term or long-term as above, you can manage to move in front of EUR/USD moves in many cases. Same goes for GBP/JPY and EUR/JPY charts for USD/JPY moves. More study on these pairs moves will reveal some more interesting things, too. Good trades.

* * *

I have been using the USD index and EUR/GBP (or GBP/CHF) as my guide dogs since the late 1970s with reasonable accuracy for the medium-term trend. Never lost money on a medium-term bet relying on those guide dogs, in fact. But that cross does not work when the Pound is deliberately devalued.

AUD/JPY is one of the important pairs influencing AUD after the Dollar, Euro, and Pound. Usually a falling AUD/JPY is good for Yen bulls as well.

* * *

Good evening. Gold is the mirror of Dollar for hedging purposes and the correlation is excellent. Sometimes, when I am tired of double-checking too many "inside infos" rushing in every hour, I just watch Gold to confirm and go ahead with the moves. The Gold chart is one of the top charts you must always watch in FOREX trading. The EUR/GBP chart, along with the EUR/JPY chart, is an excellent mirror for EUR/USD directions most of the time, too. Gold, EUR/GBP, and EUR/JPY charts will tell most of the market story most of the time, with Gold and EUR/GBP leading the FOREX world most of the time. Good luck.

USING STOPS

Please always give a stop order per your risk profile when you open any new position.

For position traders, the basic bias of the market in their trading time frame, the liquidity situation of the market in that time frame, and the size of trading positions must be all taken into account when exercising stops, be they based on tech levels or a certain sum of money or a percentage of a total equity. It is a must but also it is form of art like trading itself. And every trader must develop his own unique style of using stops. But unfortunately, all this can be learned only by paying a certain amount of tuition fee to the market.

Yes, but as a position trader I never use tight stops. Same goes for trailing stops. I place them all very far away from the market so as not to be taken out by meaningless market noises. My initial stop is always 1 percent of my total equity, and I never commit the whole position at a go but always scale in and scale out.

* * *

Good morning. You can avoid your problem in most cases by leaving the market always by trailing stops (i.e., do not set the profit target). So, any winning trade must be held as long as the market does not tell you to leave by hitting your trailing stops. When you enter the market by market signals and leave by stops or trailing stops, it makes the most difficult part of the decision-making process rather easier for traders. Good trades.

USD/JPY HINTS

One of the silly rules of thumb in USD/JPY trading is it rarely moves 700 to 800 pips in a row without a 200 pips or more correction in the middle, and it almost always retraces back to 350 pips advance point from the start of its 700–800 pips move—all because of a liquidity problem in the Yen market.

The real battle of bulls and bears for the medium-term trend is always around the 20-day MA line in the Yen market. Daily option activities here and there are of no relevance as far as the medium-term trend is concerned.

Yen position traders sit on their positions gunning for several hundred pips at one go. For day trades, a much more nimble approach is required. As a Yen position trader, please never buy anything below falling daily 20 MA and never sell anything above rising daily 20 MA, no matter how attractive they look. So to start buying only when the daily 20 MA starts rising, from whatever level, is not only safe but also a proven way of making money, although it sounds so simple. IMHO. Good trades.

* * *

You can read how Yen traders make intraday moves by watching a 30-min USD/JPY candlestick chart (or line chart if you are not familiar with candle nuance). The 4, 8 hourlies are for positional moves. Good trades.

* * *

The Tokyo Fix is where the FX rate is established for the day by the banks for their customers. So even though the FX rate may change during the day, the customer gets the rate at the time of the fix. There is a fix in Tokyo, London, and Toronto (more I am sure).

Importers generally settle their accounts on the 5th, 10th, 15th, etc., of the month before and up until the fix (10:00 JST). Sometimes, if there is an excess dollar demand, USD/JPY will continue to climb slightly after the fix. USD bulls will also use this as a staging for extending a rally. USD bears (Yen bulls) will use this to establish better shorts.

REACTING TO NEWS

News or data are always read by the market along the prevailing market bias. Data can provide a good reading for the state of the market. If the data is bad but the price is still rising or not affected, it must be a bull market, which means a buy on dip strategy is a better one. Conversely, if the data is good but the price is not rising or even falling, it must be a bear market, which means a sell on bounce strategy is a better one. The inflexion point must be when bad news or good news no longer affects the prices as they have done before. Medium-/long-term bias changes are usually accompanied by such reactions to the news. For what it's worth.

It is not the numbers that count but how the market reacts to the numbers that counts. That gives some comfort to those who are not privy to the numbers already.

FAIR VALUE

The concept of fair value in any currency is largely that of CBers [central bankers] and economists and not much about trading. Almost always currencies overshoot from the fair value areas some 20 to 30 percent in their medium-term trend, and what makes all hard currencies range in reasonable areas over time since we had this floating regime in 1971 must the ability of relevant CBs to control the currency ranges and their real economy's weakness or strength to support those ranges. ECB [European Central Bank] folks were not joking when they said EUR/USD was some 25 percent undervalued from the fair value when EUR/USD was below parity levels two years ago. Same goes for BOJ [Bank of Japan] when they were saying Yen was some 10 to 20 percent overvalued when it was trading around 100 some three years ago, too. That is how these folks view the markets and try to guide the market. Of course, when U.S. Treasury folks say "The Dollar is still strong" when it is falling, they are begging the market to sell more Dollars.

DIFFERENT CENTERS

The first hour after opening in Tokyo tends to provide the best liquidity of the day, and that is when most heavyweight players try to position their way without having much difficulty for the day. The Sydney open is more often used as an ambush hour by certain players using the time window till the Tokyo open. One rule of thumb is when the Yen jumps at the Tokyo open, the chances are it will continue throughout the day and a few more days. On different point, learn to position trade Yen or any other currency if one is really going to make big money one day. For what it's worth.

* * *

One hour from the Tokyo open, London open, and New York open are the times where most liquidity of the market exists. And that is where market makers are busy setting the trend for the session or even the day. Your observation has merit because most of the session or daily moves are started either in the London open, Tokyo open, or NY open (especially the London open). Other markets are too thin for any good-sized traders to make their market views felt. Good luck.

* * *

London is just a marketplace where all sorts of FOREX folks flock to buy and sell. It does not have to be London, folks. It could be anyone from anywhere in the world with deep pockets who starts setting the market direction on a given day. Same goes for New York and Tokyo sessions markets. In any case, Tokyo and NY are still relatively small markets when compared to London as far as FOREX goes.

A WORD FOR NEW TRADERS

Traders that try to pick the tops and bottoms of the market throughout the day end up with mostly misery, because inexperienced fellows in FOREX departments—even in first-division clubs—try to pick the tops and bottoms, believing that is where the real big money is. And ego demonstration and bonus consideration come into play, too, for smart college graduates. The first thing I do when facing new recruits is to do my best to destroy their ego and fear in the market first. Once their ego and fear are reasonably cured, they become dutiful followers of the market like Pavlov's hounds and they can survive. And once they can survive, they can be taught how to put temporary tops and bottoms to the market at a much higher level of speculation school. Then, that may take at least a decade of training, too.

QUIPS FROM BC

- FOREX is all about how to hit the next ball correctly rather than worrying about something in the distant future. The next ball may be for 2 pips or 20 pips or 200 pips or 500 pips, depending on a trader's style.
- Anything is possible in FOREX.
- I am useless as a day trader. Corrections may take days or longer to complete.
- Good quality info is everything in this game.
- Bottom picking in the USD/JPY is the mother of all risky trades.
- We learn how to trade till we stop trading, and we learn from each other every day. That is the beauty of trading and life in general.
- Do not worry about what the market will do. Just worry about what you will do when the market reaches your "pain point" or "happy point." You will have an easier life as a trader that way.
- FOREX players can operate quietly, but they cannot hide their moves in those charts.
- No liquidity and no conviction by players make the market look like a vagrant loitering in his usual area.
- Good sleep is essential for good trading, but most of the traders I know of seem to sleep with one eye open.

CHAPTER 26

Introducing the Mundo—The Synthetic Global Spot Currency

T he Mundo is a synthetic global spot currency invented by FOREX trader Michael Archer in 2001. It is analogous to the Standard & Poor's 500 and Dow Jones Industrial Average in securities. (See Figure 26.1.)

To begin and for the sake of simplicity, we define the Mundo as the unweighted average of the four most heavily traded currency pairs:

EUR/USD
GBP/USD
USD/CHF
USD/JPY

The steps to calculate the present value of the Mundo are quite simple:

1. First, the USD must be the quote or second currency in the currency pair. Therefore, the reciprocals of both the USD/JPY and the USD/CHF must be calculated (divide the exchange rate into 1).

If USD/CHF = 1.2393, CHF/USD = 0.8069

If USD/JPY = 117.23, JPY/USD = 0.008530

This chapter is taken from Currency Codex (www.fxpraxis.com).

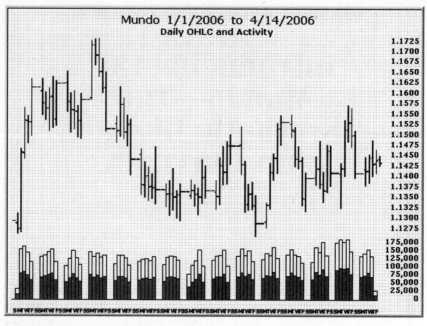

FIGURE 26.1 Mundo OHLC Bar Chart

2. Next, all pairs must be converted to their pip values. Multiply the EUR/USD, the GBP/USD, and the CHF/USD by 10,000:

$$EUR/USD \text{ pips} = 12,753$$
$$GBP/USD \text{ pips} = 18,872$$
$$CHF/USD \text{ pips} = 8,069$$

3. The JPY/USD currency pair is special because of its wide parity rate. Multiply it by 1,000,000:

$$JPY/USD \text{ pips} = 8,530$$

4. Now add the total number of pips:

$$12,753 + 18,872 + 8,069 + 8,530 = 48,224$$

5. Divide the sum of the pips by 4:

$$48,224 \div 4 = 12,056$$

6. To convert from the number of pips to the Mundo exchange rate, divide by 10,000:

$$12,056 \div 10,000 = 1.2056$$

TRANSITIVITY AND EQUILIBRIUM

The premise of the differential charts in Figures 26.2 to 26.5 is based on *transitivity*, the crucial element in arbitrage that relies on the equilibrium formula to keep all currency pairs in balance with each other. The simplest form of transitivity occurs in triangular arbitrage, which involves exactly three currencies:

$$EUR/USD = EUR/GBP \times GBP/USD$$

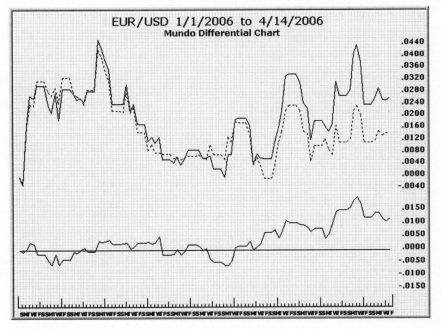

FIGURE 26.2 Mundo Differential Chart (EUR/USD)

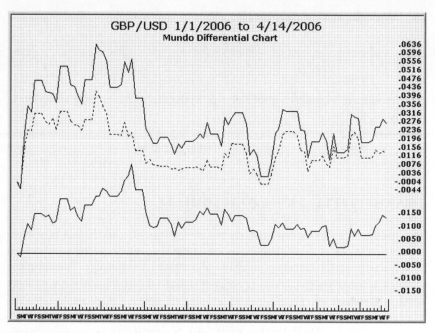

FIGURE 26.3 Mundo Differential Chart (GBP/USD)

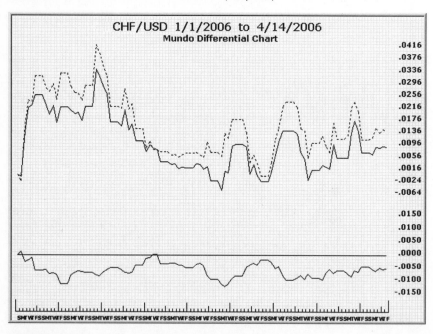

FIGURE 26.4 Mundo Differential Chart (CHF/USD)

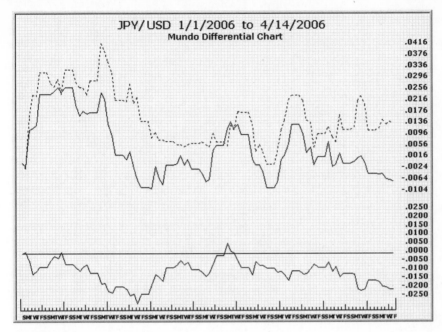

FIGURE 26.5 Mundo Differential Chart (JPY/USD)

An example of equilibrium involving all five major currencies is:

$$EUR/USD = (EUR/GBP \div GBP/CHF) \times (CHF/JPY \div USD/JPY)$$

Note that each single currency appears exactly twice in this formula.

USAGE

The differential chart is experimental and still requires thorough testing. One observation is that when the scaled major currency pair exceeds an arbitrary number of pips above the scaled Mundo currency, an upward trend is indicated. The converse appears true for a downward trend. There are substantial opportunities to use the Mundo as a forecasting tool with individual component pairs.

Leader/laggard relationships (also called dominance and dependence) may also be detected by the use of the Mundo differential charts. (See Figure 26.6.)

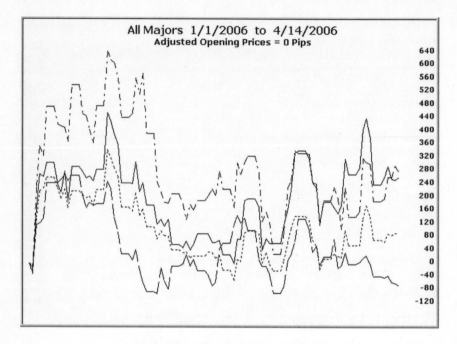

All Majors 1/1/2006 to 4/14/2006
Adjusted Opening Prices = 0 Pips

USD Major	Line Style	Close
GBP/USD	Dots and Dashes	275
EUR/USD	Solid Line	248
CHF/USD	Dots Only	81
JPY/USD	Dashes Only	−82

FIGURE 26.6 Composite Differential Oscillators

FOREX BETA

An important tool used by stock analysts is called the *beta coefficient*. A stock's beta is a measure of the performance of a single stock against the performance of the overall stock market. Mathematically, the beta coefficient of a stock called XYZ is a ratio and can be expressed as:

Beta(XYZ) = Slope of XYZ Stock ÷ Slope of Overall Market

The slope of the single stock and the slope of the overall market are determined by performing an ordinary least squares linear regression of each over the same period of time. If that stock increased in value by 12 percent while the overall market increased in value by only 10 percent during the same time period, then the stock's beta would be 1.2.

This statistic assists the investor in the selection of a security based on the investor's predilection to the risk/reward factor. Typically, stock beta values range from 0.5 to 1.5 or higher. High betas imply greater risk/reward, whereas low betas indicate that a particular stock is moving laterally and not keeping up with the fluctuations of the overall market.

For the purpose of this study, we arbitrarily define the prevailing price of the Mundo as the arithmetic average price of the 10 most frequently traded major and minor USD currency pairs:

Full Mundo Components

EUR/USD

AUD/USD

GBP/USD

NZD/USD

USD/CHF

USD/SEK

USD/JPY

USD/NOK

USD/CAD

USD/DKK

The four-component Mundo we began with may be henceforth labeled the Mini-Mundo.

All pairs are treated with equal weight, which means six of the pairs must be adjusted so that the USD is the quote currency. Then, using the same rules given earlier, we sum the most recent values of these 10 pairs and divide by 10 to calculate the current price of the Mundo.

We can now use an analogous coefficient to compare the volatility of a single currency pair to the volatility of the overall FOREX market as described in terms of the volatility of the Mundo.

Rather than using the ratio of the slope of a single currency pair and the slope of the Mundo, we will use the standard deviation of each. We can justify this change because of a major difference in the trading philosophies of stocks and spot currencies. Nearly all stock traders use a buy-and-hold strategy in which they hope that their investments will more than better the current inflation rate over long periods of time. Thus stock traders hold a long position in their trades and, in nonleveraged positions, they own the shares of stock outright.

Spot currency traders, in contrast, are not buying shares in a corporation or a mutual fund. They feel equally comfortable on either side of a currency trade, long or short. A FOREX trade is, in fact, the simultaneous buying of one currency while selling another currency. Spot currency traders (particularly scalpers) may initiate a long trade, follow a 5-minute rally, liquidate the long position at its peak, and then initiate a short position in the same currency pair and follow that security's decline to the next valley.

Therefore, spot currency traders are not particularly interested in the long-term slope of any currency pair. Instead they are more interested in the number of significant peaks and troughs that occur during their trading sessions. The standard deviation is therefore employed in our model for FOREX beta.

To calculate the FOREX beta of the EUR/USD pair, we use the following formula:

$$\text{Beta(EUR/USD)} = \text{StdDev(EUR/USD)} \div \text{StdDev(Mundo)}$$

A running calculation of this statistic using streaming data informs the FOREX day trader which currency pairs are showing the highest volatility relative to the whole spot currency market. This identifies the pairs with the highest risk/reward factor. The order of these pairs may change throughout the day as central banks around the world open and close.

Table 26.1 illustrates the current standard deviation and beta coefficient for each of the 10 currency pairs. During this period analyzed, the Mundo exhibited a standard deviation of 352.70 pips (or 3.53 U.S. cents).

TABLE 26.1 Mundo Standard Deviation

Currency	Standard Deviation	Beta
EUR/USD	802.61	2.28
GBP/USD	745.48	2.11
CHF/USD	570.65	1.62
JPY/USD	570.19	1.62
NZD/USD	506.27	1.44
AUD/USD	437.44	1.24
Mundo	352.70	1.00
CAD/USD	253.73	0.72
NOK/USD	124.65	0.35
DKK/USD	109.26	0.31
SEK/USD	94.43	0.27

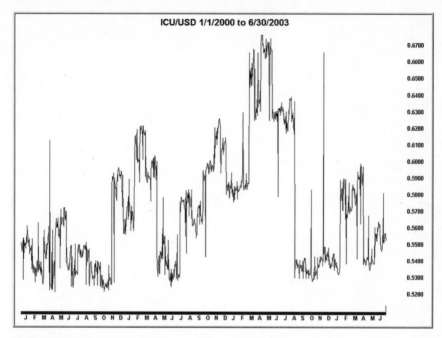

FIGURE 26.7   International Currency Unit (ICU)/USD

Thus, when compared to the Mundo's other components and to the Mundo itself, the EUR/USD showed the highest beta coefficient and therefore carries the greatest risk/reward factor. In other words, for the time period examined, the EUR/USD was 2.28 times more volatile than the average of all 10 spot currency pairs.

The first aspect to note is that the Mundo has a lower parity rate than the USD, roughly 53 to 67 U.S. cents. (See Figure 26.7.) Second, slight changes in the same price direction in the 10 underlying currency pairs may cause an exaggerated price change in the Mundo. This phenomenon is also partly due to the use of reciprocals in six of the currency pairs.

SUMMARY

The Mundo may have significant analytical and forecasting prospects for the trader. The author's web site at www.fxpraxis.com offers more information on the Mundo. He is hoping to encourage a FOREX broker-dealer to offer trading in the Mundo in the near future.

CHAPTER 27

A New Introduction to the Goodman Swing Count System

The Goodman Swing Count System (GSCS) is a method for analyzing and trading the markets based on the 50 Percent and Measured Move rules. It has similarities to Elliott Wave theory but is more systematically defined and objective. By *objective* I mean it is more of a predictive method whereas Elliott is a descriptive method. It is *not* a mechanical system; it requires study, effort, and subjective interpretation. I have spent 35 years studying and learning GSCS and am still finding new and useful nuances. Trading Goodman successfully is a feedback loop process of learning→trading→learning→trading.

The goal of the two GSCS volumes (Theory and Praxis) is to allow a new user to begin trading with the method quickly, learning as he or she goes, working from the most general ideas to the more specific ones. You should be able to at least dabble in Goodman after reading and studying GSCS-Theory.

The principles of Goodman's Swing Count System were informally set forth in a series of mostly annotated commodity futures charts from the late 1940s to early 1970s. These trading studies, simply titled "My System," were the work of Charles B. Goodman and were never published.

I met Charles Goodman at the Denver, Colorado, offices of Peavey & Company (later, Gelderman) in the fall of 1971. It was the occasion of my maiden voyage in the great sea of commodity trading (later, futures). In 1971 silver prices were finally forging ahead to the $2 per ounce level. A

This chapter is adapted from the www.fxpraxis.com Currency Codex feature.

10-cent limit move in soybeans elicited a full afternoon of postmortems by traders and brokers alike.

The Peavey office, managed by the late, great Pete Rednor, employed eight brokers (later, account representatives). The broker for both Mr. Goodman and me was the colorful—and patient—Ken Malo. Brokers, resident professional traders—including Mr. Goodman and the Feldman brothers, Stu and Reef—and a regular contingent of retail customers drew inspiration from a Trans-Lux ticker tape that wormed its way across a long, narrow library table in the back of the office. Most impressive was a large clacker board quote system covering almost the entire front office wall. This electromechanical quotation behemoth made loud clacking sounds (thus its name) each time an individual price flipped over to reveal an updated quote. Green and red lights flashed, denoting daily new highs and lows. Pete, apart from being an excellent office manager, was also a fine showman, using the various stimuli to encourage trading activity.

Almost everyone made frequent reference to Charlie's *huge* bar charts, posted on $2^{1}/_{2}$-by-4-foot sheets of graph paper, mounted on heavy particle board, and displayed on large easels. No one ever really knew what the numerous right-hand brackets (]) of varying lengths scattered throughout each chart meant. But there was always a great deal of speculation! The present work finally reveals the meaning of those mysterious trading hieroglyphics. (See Figure 27.1.)

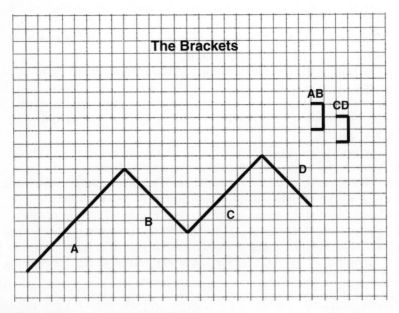

FIGURE 27.1 Those Mysterious Brackets

In the diagram, the brackets represent the price range projections for the two potential matrices AB and CD, in accordance with the Compensation-Carryover-Cancellation (3C) Rule. Where they overlap is said to be an Intersection.

The quiet but incessant chatter of the ticker tape, the load clacking of the quote board, the constant ringing of the telephones; the news ticker that buzzed *once* for standing reports, *twice* for opinions, and *three* times for hot news; the squawk boxes, and Pete Rednor's authoritative voice booming, "Merc! Merc!" What a spectacular scene it was! No wonder this author, then a 21-year-old trading neophyte, would soon make commodity futures and currency trading his life's work. Our broker, Ken Malo, was from a well-to-do Denver family. His pet market was Shell Eggs, a wild beast if ever there was one! Charlie tried to move him to quieter markets, Plywood and Iced Broilers—but Ken would have none of it. "Gentlemen don't trade Oats," or Plywood or Iced Broilers.

But nothing made a greater impression on me than the work of Charles B. (Charlie) Goodman. He instilled first some very simple ideas: "Avoid volatile markets when at all possible." "Trade only high-percentage short-term 'ducks.'" "Sit on your hands, dad, sit on your hands." It didn't take long for me to adopt the ultraconservative "Belgian Dentist" style of trading, that is, "Avoiding losing trades is more important than finding winning trades." (In Europe the term Belgian Dentist references an ultraconservative investor.)

The Belgian Dentist approach carried with me when I developed my artificial intelligence (AI) trading system in the 1980s—Jonathan's Wave. Even though it generated 48 percent annual returns with a zero expectation of a 50 percent drawdown (according to *Managed Account Reports*), it drove the brokers berserk because it could easily go a full month without making a single trade! At least some of Charlie's wisdom did not fall upon deaf ears—or microchips.

Charlie's trading advice, I am certain, allowed me to survive the financial baptism of fire that destroys most commodity and currency trading newcomers in a matter of months, if not weeks. Too many new traders hit the door trading with no comprehensive plan and with unrealistic expectations. It is the same door that hits them in the rear on the way out a few months or even a few weeks later.

Mr. Goodman was to be my one and only trading mentor. Over the decade that followed, he entrusted to me many, if not most, of his trading secrets. *To the best of my knowledge he shared this information on his work with no one else in such detail.*

Charlie's other major contribution to technical analysis was Market Environment (ME). A summary of this method is in Chapter 28. Charlie and I spent hundreds of hours together analyzing the trade studies from

"My System." We also analyzed hundreds of other commodity, currency, and securities charts. Charlie was happy with "My System" being organized in his mind. But as a new-generation technical analyst, I was anxious to see it formalized on paper and eventually in source code on a computer. To be honest, this created a small amount of friction between the two of us—Charlie was dead set against formalized systems and believed strongly in the psychological and money management elements of trading. A trading method was simply a tool to focus the mind—"like a psychic with a crystal ball," he would say.

Notwithstanding, by 1978 I was finally ready and able to formally state the principles of "My System." Because of its equal concern for price measurements (parameters) and price levels interacting together (matrices) I originally renamed "My System" ParaMatrix. My first investment management company in the late 1970s was ParaMatrix Investment Management, and I acted as both a Registered Investment Advisor (SEC) and a Commodity Trading Advisor (CFTC).

I am currently writing a program to identify the three primary Goodman trading opportunities: the Double Intersection, the Return, and Wave Propagation. However (and Charlie would certainly agree with me), I do not think it a good idea for this information to be used by anyone who is not firmly grounded in GSCS principles. There is too much temptation to use what should be a check on one's work as a decision-making tool. It is the fuzzy core of GSCS that can make you successful!

The systematic exposition of GSCS in rules and principles is one of the things that separates it from other market trading systems and methods and must always be emphasized.

Contrary to ongoing speculation, only two copies of my original 1979 "Principles of ParaMatrix" ever existed. I possess both of them. Charlie's original "My System" trade studies were mistakenly destroyed shortly after his death in 1984. What remains of them are the 200 or so examples I copied into "Principles of ParaMatrix." Most of these are commodity futures charts, although perhaps two dozen or so of them are securities charts.

The subsequent work, "Goodman's Swing Count System (GSCS)," is a substantially reorganized reissue of "Principles of ParaMatrix" with updated charts, much of what I have learned in the intervening years, and a simplified nomenclature that I am sure Charlie would have appreciated; "Keep it simple, dad!" he would always advise. I've also expanded on Charlie's ideas by filling in some less formed ideas such as his market notation, or calculus as he referred to it, and a method for charting which I have dubbed Goodman Charting.

The codification of Charlie's work has not been a simple task. As many of you know, it has been a work in progress for many years. For every word you see in this volume I have perhaps written two hundred more!

Charlie also had a Dependent Interfacing Rule he was working on at the time of his death. He wanted to fold it into the main GSCS rule base without interrupting the inner logic of the theory. I am currently working on this problem and, should I solve the problem of the Ninth Rule, I will provide an Addendum to GSCS-Theory to all purchasers.

My own direction in futures and currencies turned in the 1980s to artificial intelligence (Jonathan's Wave) and in the 1990s and today to artificial life and cellular automata (the Trend Machine). In spite of, or perhaps because of, these complicated, cutting-edge computer efforts, I continue to view Goodman's Swing Count System in a very positive light. To this day, the first thing I do when I see any chart is a quick Goodman analysis—*"Where are the Intersections?"* and *"How are the matrices propagating?"*

GSCS is a natural system for pursuing the conservative Belgian Dentist approach to trading, even without the aid of a computer. Charlie saw the oncoming computer revolution in trading and was neither impressed nor enthusiastic.

GSCS trade opportunities are as frequent today (perhaps more frequent, thanks to more liquidity and volatility in the markets) as they were 40 or 50 years ago. GSCS formations can be found at all chart levels, from FOREX tick charts to securities monthly charts. I believe the system's foundations have stood the test of time well. Patterns today are no different than they were decades ago, nor are the twin human emotions—fear and greed—and the underlying disequilibrium-equilibrium and thesis-antithesis-synthesis of buyers and sellers that create them. GSCS is an excellent method for finding support and resistance areas that no other method spots, and for locating *potential* turning points in any market. One of its best suits is that it can easily integrate into other trading techniques and methodologies. But I leave that part to you, dear reader.

The better you learn GSCS, the more opportunities you will find in your charts—and the better will be the trades you make off of them and the more high-percentage ducks will fill your basket.

Is it really a system? I have christened it the Goomdan Swing Count *System* because of the systematic way in which it is constructed. But because it requires study, effort, and judgment, it is perhaps more accurate to think of it as a *method*. Depending upon your perspective and knowledge of it, GSCS is between 70 percent and 90 percent mechanical and between 10 percent to 30 percent fuzzy core. By comparison, I rate Elliott Wave theory as 70 percent fuzzy core and 30 percent mechanical. Drummond Point and Line I rate 50 percent/50 percent. As you will learn in the

GSCS-Praxis workbook, it is the ability to anticipate the propagation of Goodman Waves that separates the men from the boys and Goodman from Elliott. And, such as life is, it is in wave propagation where much of the fuzzy core lurks.

The program demo provided with the two GSCS volumes represents the kernel idea of mechanizing perhaps 70 percent of the system. It is available as a learning tool, for additional perspective, and *not* as a trading tool. My G-Chart drawing tool I built for analyzing trends, matrices, and waves and conducting simple Goodman gedankenexperiments. I also make it available.

Mr. Goodman passed away in October of 1984 after a brief illness. I last saw Charlie at the hospital a few days before he passed; I'm sure he knew his remaining time on earth was short, but he managed to give me one of his terrific smiles of encouragement and a thumbs-up. It was always his desire to share with others—although, as is usually the case with true genius, few wanted to listen.

These days we are bombarded with ever more cryptic and computer-dependent software programs and black boxes. The irrational lust for success without effort is greater than anything Charlie knew in his heyday, I am certain. Perhaps now is the time for the simple yet theoretically well-grounded ideas of GSCS to populate.

The advent of computer analysis in the 1980s and computer trading in the 1990s has not borne fruit relative to the effort expended, much as Charlie anticipated. The majority of new traders are still shown the door quickly and it is the brokers who make most of the money.

The publication of GSCS-Theory and the GSCS-Praxis workbook would meet with Charlie's approval (especially the workbook!). His efforts in extracting an objective and almost geometrically precise (à la Spinoza) trading system out of a simple trading rule (the 50 Percent Rule) is most remarkable, and 35 years later simply leaves me in awe. It has certainly earned him the right to be included in the elite group of early scientific traders: Taylor, Elliott, Gann, and Pugh.

As previously mentioned, GSCS-Theory very closely follows the 1979 ParaMatrix book and to a large extent is my effort in systematizing GSCS from notes I took after sessions with Charlie in the 1970s. GSCS-Praxis more closely follows Charlie's approach to teaching by example but incorporates many more up-to-date examples from stocks, commodities, and FOREX. Since the first short paper on GSCS appeared on the Internet in 1998 I have received perhaps 2,000 inquiries about it. Both volumes attempt to incorporate what I have learned from explaining various aspects of it to others. Areas of GSCS that have received the most questions I have attempted to go into in greater depth.

THE GSCS RULES

Nine primary rules comprise the theoretical foundation of the Goodman Swing Count System.

The Nine Rules of GSCS

1. The 50 Percent Rule
2. The Measured Move Rule
3. The Rule of Buyer-Seller Equilibrium
4. The Rule of Recursion
5. The Wave Propagation Rule
6. The Return Rule
7. The Compensation-Carryover-Cancellation (3C) Rule
8. The Rule of Intersection
9. The Rule of Points

Charlie referred to them also as concepts or principles from time to time. Insofar as there are a number of secondary rules, I have assumed the nomenclature of labeling the primary ones "rules" and the secondary ones "principles." A tenth rule, clarifying the 3C Rule, is thought to exist, and I continue to search for it.

The 50 Percent Rule

The cornerstone of GSCS is the old 50 Percent retracement rule. This rule, familiar to most traders, is almost as old as the organized markets themselves. It has been traced to the times when insiders manipulated railroad stocks in the nineteenth century. (See Figure 27.2.)

The first systematic description of the rule was given in Burton Pugh's *The Great Wheat Secret*. This book was originally published in 1933. In 1973, Charles L. Lindsay published *Trident*. This book did much—some say too much!—to quantify and mathematically describe the rule. Nevertheless, it is must reading for anyone interested in this area of market methodology. Edward L. Dobson wrote *The Trading Rule That Can Make You Rich* in 1978. This is a good work with some nice examples.

But none of these, in my humble opinion, even scratch the surface relative to Goodman's work.

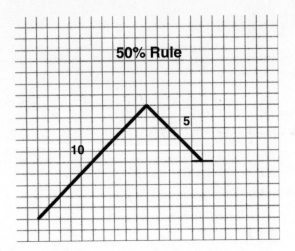

FIGURE 27.2 The 50 Percent Rule

There have been various formulations of the 50 Percent Rule, but the underlying idea is this:

> At the 50 percent retracement of any trend, prices will find either support or resistance. *This does not mean prices will always reverse from the 50 percent price point, only that prices will find support or resistance of some kind for some period of time.*

There is more to say on this in the Rule of Points.

Many traders have found the 50 Percent Rule to be a good rule of thumb, but observe that prices rarely stop right at the 50 percent point. The GSCS 3C Rule is a result of this important fact; it is perhaps the most interesting of the GSCS rules, although it is one of the last you should implement in your trading scheme.

The logic of the rule is quite simple. At a 50 percent retracement, both buyers and sellers of the previous trend (up or down) are, ceteris paribus, in balance. Half of each holds profits and half of each holds losses.

The 50 percent point moves with the trend. (See Figure 27.3.)

The Measured Move Rule

This rule is almost always associated with the 50 Percent Rule. It states that if prices do reverse from the 50 percent point, then they will carry to a distance equal to the price value of the first trend. (See Figure 27.4.) However, as explained in the Points Rule, it is not accurate to tie the Measured Move Rule always to the 50 Percent Rule.

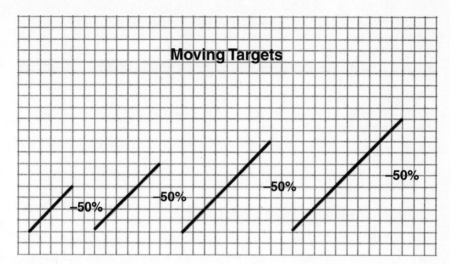

FIGURE 27.3 A Moving Target

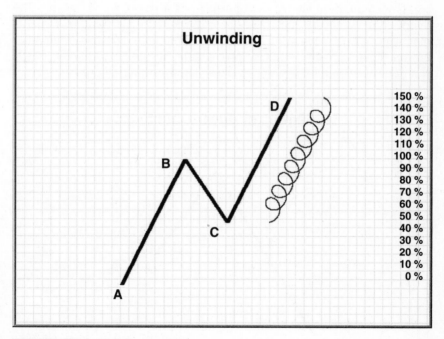

FIGURE 27.4 The Measured Move

Prices unwind to the measure move point when one side is a 100 percent winner and the other side is a 100 percent loser, on balance.

DEFINITIONS

A trend is the movement of prices in a given direction, up or down, without significant price correction. In Figure 27.4, AB, BC, and CD are all trends. A trend may also be called a swing.

A matrix is a measured move of three trends. In Figure 27.4, ABCD is a matrix.

The Rule of Buyer-Seller Equilibrium

Both the 50 Percent Rule and the Measured Move Rule imply equilibrium between buyers and sellers being established. Charlie considered equilibrium to be the primary market paradigm. It is the underlying force that moves all markets, in GSCS theory.

The equilibrium shown in Figure 27.5 is a tenuous one, indeed. The distribution of buyers and sellers over the initial price trend or swing is obviously not perfectly even: Some buyers hold more contracts than other buyers. They have also different propensities for taking profits or losses. Nor does it account for the buyers and sellers who have entered the market

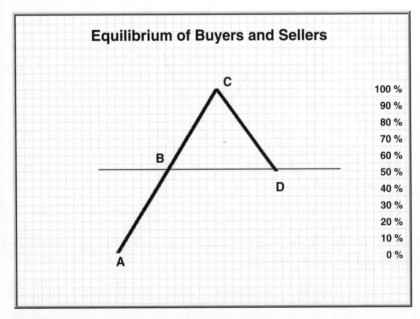

FIGURE 27.5 Equilibrium of the 50 Percent Rule

before the initial swing or during the reaction swing. Not all of the buyers and sellers from the original swing may be in the market any longer.

Remarkably, GSCS eventually takes all of this into account—especially the buyers and sellers at other price swing levels, called *matrices*.

Nevertheless, the 50 percent retracement point and measured move point are often powerful and very real points of equilibrium and are certainly known and defined hot spots of which one should be aware. Remember that both the futures markets and the currency markets are very close to a zero-sum game. It is only commissions, pips, and slippage that keep them from being zero-sum. At the 50 percent point, it doesn't take much to shift the balance of power for that particular swing matrix.

NOFRI'S TECHNIQUE

In 1975 a well-known Chicago grain floor trader, Eugene Nofri, published *The Congestion Phase System*. This small but power-packed volume detailed a short-term trading method using simple but effective congestion phases. While not precisely a work on the 50 Percent Rule, it touched—from a different angle—some of Charlie's ideas.

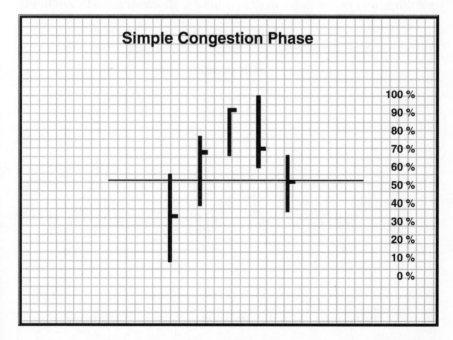

For my own theory of a market paradigm, please see my article "The Forex Propensity Index." It does not contradict the equilibrium paradigm, but rather expands on it in much greater detail and offers additional insights.

The Rule of Recursion

Rules occur and hold true at all price levels or matrices, and many are being worked simultaneously in any given ongoing market. This is a critical point. In modern terminology it would be said that price movements are recursive. Simply stated, this means that without labeling you could not tell the difference between a 10-minute chart and a daily or weekly chart—they all exhibit the same behavior and operate under the same rules.

The bar graphs in Figure 27.6 were taken from actual market data. It is functionally impossible to tell the time units apart with respect to the chart action.

The Rule of Recursion is critical to understanding the GSCS method for calculating wave and matrix price objectives, since matrices and waves at different levels are recursive and "talk" to each other.

The Wave Propagation Rule

Much of what Charlie was attempting to teach me didn't seem to fit until I understood the Wave Propagation Rule. I had studied Elliott Wave theory and thought of waves in series of five. In fact, all waves are series of three;

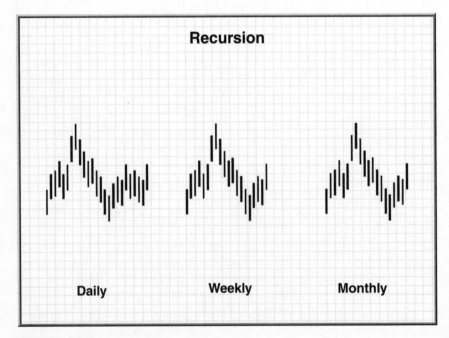

FIGURE 27.6 Recursion

it is their propagation (as Charlie first revealed) that erroneously makes them seem to be series of five.

In GSCS, waves propagate as matrices, the series of 1-2-3 or ABCD trends given in the earlier definitions. Once a matrix is completed, it becomes a trend for a larger matrix. In the context of the larger matrix, the secondary trend of the first matrix becomes insignificant with regard to the definition. (It remains important for other aspects of GSCS analysis.)

DEFINITION

A Goodman Wave is a matrix that has a smaller matrix as one of its trends.

DEFINITION

Waves propagate inward and outward from any point.

The formation in Figure 27.7 is not to be construed as a five-series-trend Elliott Wave, but a three-series-trend Goodman Wave in propagation.

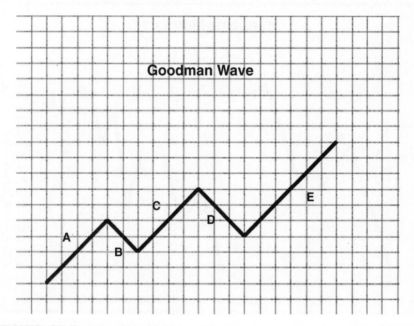

FIGURE 27.7 A Goodman Wave

The key is trend D, called the Return in GSCS theory. The difference is a critical.

In GSCS-Praxis, I try to show all the possible Goodman Wave forms. As a market unfolds, you can gradually eliminate many of them and eventually be able to home in on a limited number of possibilities with strong trading opportunities.

So, we have trends (or swings), matrices, and waves. I cannot emphasize strongly enough the importance of the Wave Propagation Rule. (See Figure 27.8.)

The Return Rule

It is the fourth trend or Return in a Goodman Wave that separates GSCS from Elliott. And it is a *very significant* difference.

The Return and the wave propagation it implies make GSCS substantially more predictive than Elliott, which is a descriptive theory. The fourth trend, D, in a five-series ABCDE is connected to ABC, not just C.

Of course, prices have minimum fluctuations and maximum movements, but it will help to think in the fashion of Figure 27.8. Charlie was

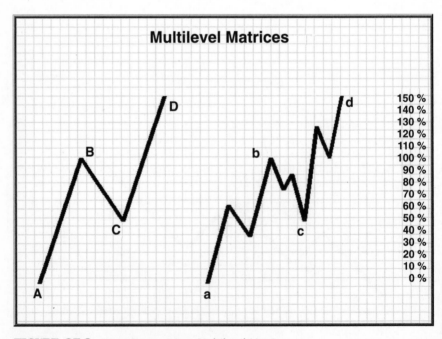

FIGURE 27.8 Wave Propagation: Multilevel Matrices

fond of referring to Zeno's Paradoxes when discussing this idea. Matrices and waves are propagating both inward and outward.

In theory:

- All price matrices (levels) in theory are part of a larger price matrix.
- All price matrices are composed of smaller price matrices.

The Compensation-Carryover-Cancellation (3C) Rule

The rules thus far Charlie called ordinal rules. They are not price-dependent, and require no calculation. The remaining rules he referred to as the cardinal rules, as they are price-specific and require calculation.

- By *ordinal* Charlie meant without a value and without reference to specific numbering.
- *Cardinal* meant with reference to specific numbering.

In teaching me to trade GSCS, Charlie suggested I work only with the ordinal rules before attempting to apply the cardinal rules. I believe this now to be an excellent idea.

You have perhaps made the observation yourself: The 50 Percent Rule and the Measured Move Rule aren't always (in fact aren't usually) exact. Prices rarely stop at exactly the 50 percent point and rarely run to exactly the measured move. Charlie wanted to know why. He confided in me that he had discovered the 3C Rule while doing what he called "bathtub analysis" in the early 1950s.

It is not enough to just keep a chart; you must actively work with it. By active analysis, Charlie basically meant the process of hypothesis testing. He felt unless you asked specific questions, made hypotheses, and sought answers, you wouldn't really see anything or learn much. If you don't look for it, you can't see it! Hypothesis testing is the correct way to look at a chart.

The human mind tends to want to draw conclusions and infer general rules quickly. We see a couple of examples of a phenomenon and assume it's a general rule. To avoid the temptation of this, always follow up your initial hypothesis testing with analysis of as many examples of the phenomenon as you can find.

Charlie called this "bathtub analysis" since he liked to take a book of charts into the bath with him, formulate hypotheses, and see how they played out on the charts. If, after a trend, prices move 60 percent instead of 50 percent, what can this mean vis-à-vis the Rule of Buyer-Seller Equilibrium? Are the sellers stronger than the buyers? Or are the buyers waiting for later to make their move?

(I always speak of buyers and sellers in the aggregate; obviously, individual decisions to buy and sell vary enormously.)

To the extent a price swing overshoots or undershoots its ideal 50 percent retracement, that price value will be made up on the next price swing within the matrix.

Now *this* is the trading rule that can make you rich!

For example, if prices fall only 40 percent of the initial trend and reverse, the measured move will actually be either 90 percent or 110 percent of the measured move point and value of the primary (initial) swing in the matrix. The 10 percent difference, GSCS holds, *must* be made up eventually. This is the subrule of Compensation. (See Figure 27.9.)

Furthermore: If the difference is not fully made up in the final price swing of a matrix, the cumulative "miss" value will carry over through each subsequent price matrix until it is made up. This is the subrule of Carryover. Charlie used a simple carryover table to add and subtract cumulative carryover values until they cancel. (See Figure 27.10.)

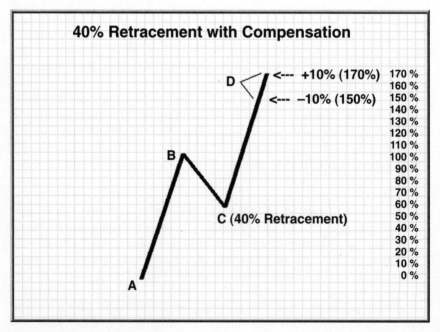

FIGURE 27.9 Compensation

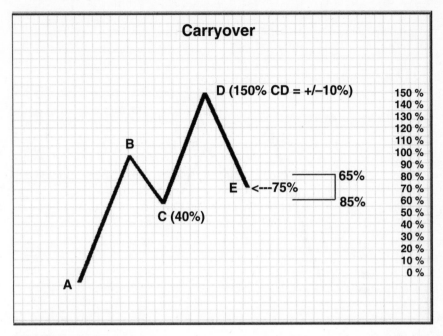

FIGURE 27.10 Carryover

When no carryover remains, the price matrix is said to have cleared or canceled. This is the GSCS concept of Cancellation. Cancellation is critical to finding GSCS support and resistance points and other chart hot spots where something *much less than random is likely to occur.* (See Figure 27.11.)

These calculations, intermatrix and intertrend, are not the easiest to keep, but practice does help. The chapter in "Goodman's Swing Count System (GSCS)" on the 3C Rule details how the calculations are managed, and GSCS-Praxis offers methods for doing them accurately.

One of the last discussions I had with Charlie was about the Over-Under component of the 3C Rule. Ever the mathematician seeking exactitude, he wanted to find a rule for when the carryover was over and when it was under. He felt strongly that such a rule—in harmony with all the other rules, of course!—existed. Such a rule would make the number of possible price outcomes considerably less and, consequently, prediction both easier and more exact.

I had suggested that finding the rule would require more chart samples than could be observed with even the longest bath. My idea was to run several thousand examples through a computer program in hopes of finding the new rule. Charlie had an enormous disdain for computers but

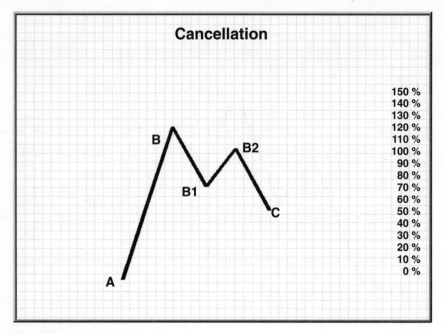

FIGURE 27.11   Cancellation

had given his blessing for such a study. As I write these words, a program has been written and I will soon run and tally the results from over 15,000 examples in pursuit of the new rule. Stay tuned!

Ever the optimists, we christened the new rule before we even found it, naming it the Rule of Dependent Interfacing.

The Rule of Intersection

I have always believed a trader could make a decent living trading the Return, an ordinal rule. Elliott traders think it is just another trend in a five-series wave, but as we have seen, it is much more important and useful.

The cardinal rule equivalent is the Rule of Intersection with respect to trading opportunities. If trading the Return could make you a decent living, correctly trading intersections could put you on easy street!

Solid, measured (cardinal) intersections aren't common. Double intersections are the most plentiful. Triple intersections are downright hard to find. Quadruple intersections are extremely rare—and finding them, with all the matrices involved, can make you downright dizzy.

An Intersection is a price range or point where the cancellations of two or more matrices or waves overlap. They are the hot spots of GSCS.

There is no analogous concept in Elliott, the best-known competitor to GSCS. Intersection makes GSCS much more objective and testable than other swing systems. A Double Intersection is the price conjunction of the measurement points of two connected matrices. For example, the measured move of a matrix is the same price point as the 50 percent move of a larger (connected) matrix in Figure 27.12. There are several Double Intersection templates in GSCS and many Intersection formations.

Since waves propagate both inward and outward, every trend can itself be a wave. Nonetheless, the number of possible wave permutations in Goodman is much smaller than the number in Elliott.

By definition, Intersections are cardinal. But watch your charts for the basic Intersection formations; they are often tradable ordinally.

Don't overemphasize the cardinal rules, at least while you are beginning to learn Goodman. Charlie taught me to be able to spot the basic rules ordinally, then overlay an understanding of the cardinal ideas later.

"Trading Goodman," as I often call it, centers around three techniques:

1. Trading the Return
2. Trading Intersections
3. Trading Wave Propagation

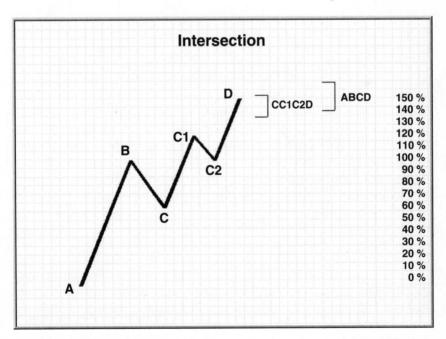

FIGURE 27.12 A Double Intersection

These often work as teams. For example, if you have a strong sense of how the wave is propagating, you will also have a good idea of which way prices will break out from an Intersection. When I look at an existing chart, I look for Intersections and the Return trend. When I am trading, I try to watch for how the matrices are propagating.

The Rule of Points

From a theoretical perspective, the five GSCS points, beginning with the 50 percent retracement, are simply prices where there should be additional support and resistance and where something predictable should occur. These points, in and of themselves, do not address price direction. (See Figure 27.13.)

Think of the markets as a pinball machine. The plunger is the Buyer-Seller Equilibrium. The pinballs are prices moving on a grid of price and time. The cushions are the GSCS price points. Physics is the science used for determining how the ball moves in the pinball machine from cushion to cushion; GSCS is the theory on how it moves from price to price in the market.

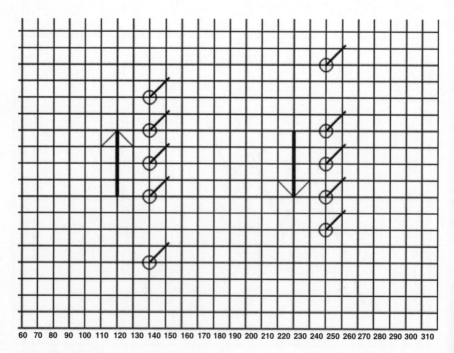

60 70 80 90 100 110 120 130 140 150 160 170 180 190 200 210 220 230 240 250 260 270 280 290 300 310

FIGURE 27.13 Points of a Trend

Remember—trends become matrices and matrices become waves, and in doing so become trends themselves. As a trend develops you can visualize how these points shift. (See Figure 27.14.)

The 50 percent point is indeed an equilibrium point. As such, the equilibrium must give way, but either side (buyers or sellers) in either a downtrend or an uptrend may prevail at any given matrix or price level.

Charlie realized the possibilities both for a *reversal* (as in the case of the completed measured move) and for a *continuation*. A continuation would be equivalent to the sellers (in an uptrend) and the buyers (in a downtrend) winning the tug-of-war within a matrix. In price action, this means that prices would fall or rise to at least the beginning point of the initial swing! Neither is either correct or wrong; they are both logical possibilities incorporated into GSCS theory.

In other words, the measured move is not a sure thing—the 50 percent retracement could also become a V or inverted V continuation. The 50 percent retracement is not a reversal point (necessarily) but should be considered as a point of interest where prices may be *more likely than randomly* to reverse with exceptional force or certitude. (See Figure 27.15.)

Watching and calculating points on the fly is an aid to determining wave propagation. If prices surge through a point, it may indicate that a

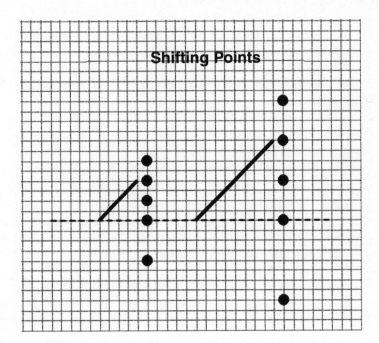

FIGURE 27.14 Shifting Point Values

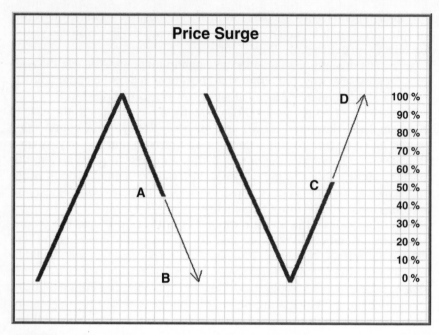

FIGURE 27.15 Reversal or Price Surge Continuation?

larger matrix is dominant and the currency matrix of 1-2-3 is simply a single wave of the larger matrix. See the Principle of Dominance in the following section for more detail.

In the context of GSCS, a continuation is *not* the failure of the Measured Move Rule.

GSCS PRINCIPLES

There are four GSCS principles. These are essentially lesser rules that help to apply the rules themselves to specific trading situations. These are most properly handled in GSCS-Praxis, but an overview of the most important are included in GSCS-Theory for completeness. The principles also help in the homing-in process, eliminating possibilities in order to get to a Belgian Dentist trading opportunity.

The Four GSCS Principles

1. The Flat/Complex Principle
2. The Principle of Dominance

3. The Breakaway Principle
4. The Principle of Doublets

The Flat/Complex Principle

Given a 1-2-3 matrix at any level of Goodman Wave propagation:

- If the 1 trend is composed of no other component trends (flat), then the 3 trend will be a matrix (complex).
- Conversely, given a 1-2-3 matrix (complex) and a 4 trend Return, the 5 trend of the Goodman Wave will be composed of no other component trends (flat). (See Figure 27.16.)

This chart shows that swings tend to be composed of two major components—one in which prices do not correct significantly and one in which a correction occurs. The swing that corrects is itself a matrix and the combination of a flat + complex swing is a Goodman Wave.

The Principle of Dominance

The Principle of Dominance is important to understanding and using wave propagation as a trading tool. Dominance is the big question in GSCS. What matrix is dominant? Is a given trend a secondary trend of Matrix A—or a primary trend of Matrix B?

The problem of dominance, in this writer's opinion, destroys any real predictive value of Elliott Wave theory—there are just too many possibilities at any given time to make useful trading decisions. (See Figure 27.17.)

It is true that GSCS has the same problem—though in a much smaller manner. There are multiple possibilities and many price junctures. Fortunately, there are fewer of them to start, and other rules, such as the Rule of Intersection, eliminate many of them. In GSCS you know in advance

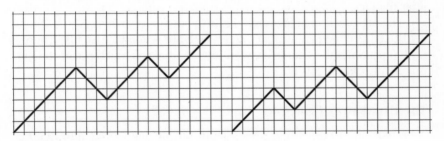

FIGURE 27.16 The Flat/Complex Principle

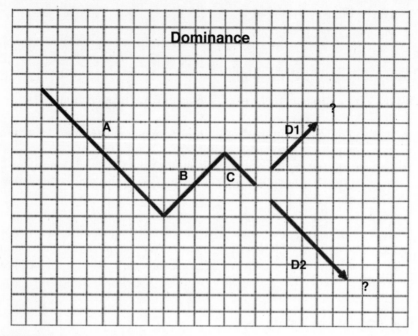

FIGURE 27.17   Dominance in GSCS

when the possibilities are limited and exactly where, pricewise, failure is determined.

These are just corrective waves (secondaries). The number of permutations in Elliott is astronomical. Trying to decide (in advance) which wave is primary and which wave is secondary at any given level seems fruitless to me. Remember that there are multiple waves building at the same time, also. Which belongs where? The three-series trend of a Goodman wave already prunes many of the permutations from the five-series trend of Elliott. GSCS has many other features that make it a much more predictive method than Elliott. I have always believed Elliott is good primarily for description after the fact.

The big question in Figure 27.17: Is the dominant matrix AB(CD2) or is it AB(CD1)? Which are primary and which are secondary trends? There is no 100 percent quantifiable answer, *but* Goodman is much easier to figure practically than Elliott is.

The Breakaway Principle

A breakaway occurs when prices jump out of one matrix into another. Breakaways are often easy to spot, and a breakaway is an excellent clue as to the dominant matrix. (See Figure 27.18.)

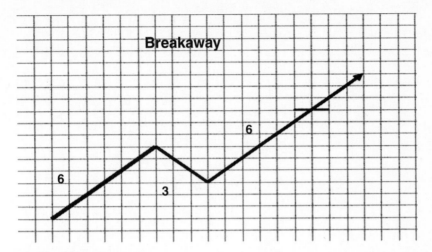

FIGURE 27.18 Breakaway

At the horizontal bar, prices have broken away from the matrix. This almost always indicates that the matrix is a secondary trend of a larger matrix. The 3 trend may turn out to be too small (less than 25 percent) to be considered a trend itself.

The Principle of Doublets

Prices may sometimes bounce between two GSCS points, creating a doublet trend. Doublets also are useful in finding dominance. Refer back the Rule of Points and the pinball analogy. (See Figure 27.19.)

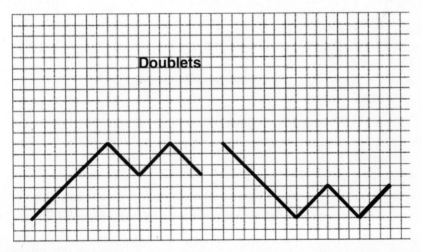

FIGURE 27.19 Doublets

CHAPTER 28

Market Environment (ME) Applications

I developed the market environment (ME) approach in the early 1980s after a discussion about the relative strength (RS) indicator with my then mentor, Charles B. Goodman, and have used it consistently within a wide range of applications. My Jonathan's Wave expert system succeeded in large part because it did not seek to make specific price predictions, but only sought forecasts of numeric-range market environments. *One does not need to forecast exact prices to make money in the markets!*

Market environment (ME) is a simple and useful method for quickly determining what type of market you are trading. Using market environments, you can also quickly and easily see a market's underlying structure; you can tell whether it is changing, and if so, how. Charlie said one could "tease out" indicator information directly off a chart. This is what ME does; and it has a wide range of applications for the trader—trading, money management, back-testing, and performance analysis and review. Primary information (from a chart) is always cleaner, easier to use, and less prone to information loss than secondary information (from an indicator).

Charlie was not a fan of indicators, but he loved charts. He felt you could see indicator information on charts and it was easier and more reliable to do so. In the relative strength conversation noted earlier, Charlie pointed out that RS was only a form of the old algebra slope-intercept formula ($y = mx + b$). It provided no new information you could not see on a chart *if you were looking for it*. But traders are fascinated by numbers

---

Reproduced from www.fpraxis.com, Currency Codex.

and the false sense of truth and certainty they provide. This faith in numbers now extends to the highest levels of the industry. Multibillion-dollar hedge funds are being run by 25-year-old quants—whiz-kid computer programmers with PhDs in mathematics but not a shred of real-world trading experience and often with only a rudimentary understanding of the markets. This is a formula for disaster, but that is another story for another time.

PRIMARY MARKET ENVIRONMENT ELEMENTS

There are six market environment elements. Taken together and used informally without a computer, they make up a technique that I call eye-balling a market. (See *Trader's Journal*, Volume 3, No. 2.) I believe you can learn more about a market in this manner than with a large battery of complex indicators.

You can see all the elements simply by looking at a bar chart. Gaining information about a market from a chart is always to be preferred over secondary methods such as indicators.

Directional Movement and Volatility

Every market you trade may be defined in terms of directional movement (DM) and volatility (V). These are the two primary components of market environment.

1. *Directional movement* is the net change in prices over a specified number of time units.
2. *Volatility* is the aggregate price movement over a specified number of time units given a minimum measured price fluctuation.

For example,

EUR/USD Weekly Average Price

117.5

116.9

117.7

118.0

117.4

117.5

117.0

118.1

DM = .9

V = 4.3

The volatility number (4.3) is a raw value and is typically used as the variable to compute a volatility index or moving average.

As mentioned, directional movement is the net price change over some period of time. Volatility is the gross or aggregate price movement as a function of some minimal price increment. The first denotes the basic trend of a market; the second, how active it is trading.

I use a simple computer program for market environment utilizing directional movement and volatility that creates a 16-combination matrix of directional movement and volatility. Each element is divided into four quadrants, yielding a continuum going from low directional movement and low volatility to high directional movement and high volatility. You can also subdivide by whether the basic market trend is up or down. This, then, gives 32 possible market environments. Eyeballing is almost as good. After you have studied enough charts, you can get a good estimate of both factors (DM and V) and where a market lies on the continuum just by looking.

The basic market environment uses just these two features of prices—directional movement and volatility. As stated earlier, directional movement is the net price change from one time unit to another. Volatility is the gross price movement between those two price points over a specified period of time. (See Figures 28.1 to 28.4.)

ME elements can be defined and grouped as either a matrix (see "ME Profiles" section later in this chapter) or as a continuum:

Directional Movement (DM)	Volatility (V)	Price Rhythm (PR)	Time Rhythm (TR)	Thickness (T)
3 and increasing	4 and decreasing	2 and decreasing	3 and decreasing	2 and steady

The Visual Basic 6.0 code will allow you to begin working with market environments more precisely, should you want to do so. If you are unable to use the code, you can simply eyeball the chart you are watching for the two factors of directional movement and volatility. Also watch for changes in both factors as prices develop. You can easily plot the movement of a

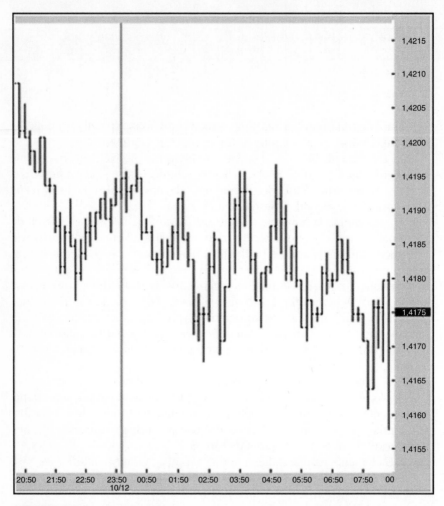

FIGURE 28.1   High DM, High V
Source: FXtrek IntelliChart™. Copyright 2001–2007 FXtrek.com, Inc.

market on the DM/V scale as it evolves over time. You will soon find patterns in the string of ME numbers.

SECONDARY ME ELEMENTS

These elements are secondary to Directional Movement and Volatility. Rhythm is the most important of them.

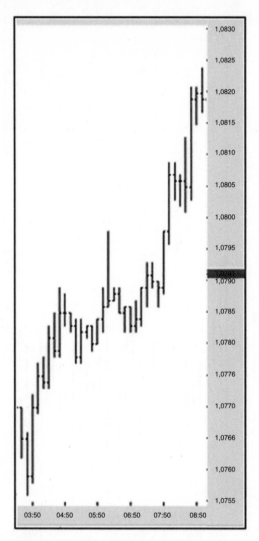

FIGURE 28.2 High DM, Low V
Source: FXtrek IntelliChart™. Copyright 2001–2007 FXtrek.com, Inc.

Thickness

Thickness is the third market environment factor. *Thickness* refers to how much overlay there is in prices, high to low, from one time unit to the next: $(H1 - L1) \div (H2 - L2)$, where H1 and H2 are the high prices of two consecutive units and L1 and L2 are the low prices of two consecutive units.

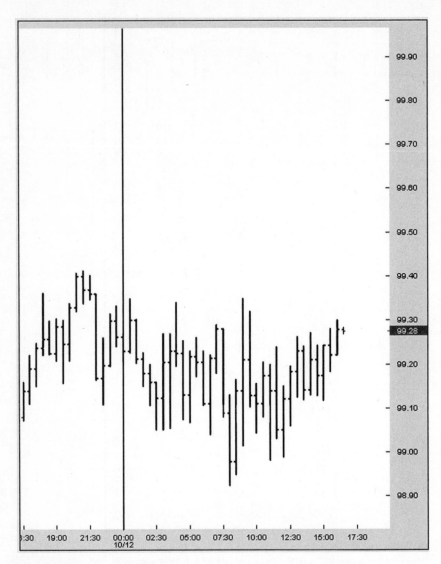

FIGURE 28.3 Low DM, High V
Source: FXtrek IntelliChart™. Copyright 2001–2007 FXtrek.com, Inc.

The lower the ratio in absolute value, the higher the thickness. Some FOREX pairs seem to be naturally thick. Thick markets tend to trade more slowly, even sluggishly. As a practitioner of the Belgian Dentist style of trading, thick markets appeal to me. In Europe, "Belgian Dentist" is used to refer to the most ultraconservative of traders.

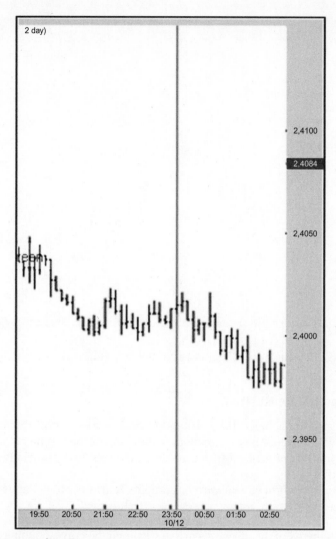

FIGURE 28.4   Low DM, Low V
Source: FXtrek IntelliChart™. Copyright 2001–2007 FXtrek.com, Inc.

An example of a thick chart is shown in Figure 28.5.

A note of caution: Thickness may also indicate that a pair is relatively illiquid. That is, there is not a great volume of trading involved and the thickness actually represents a wide bid/ask spread. Chart scale can also create illusory thickness and generally may alter the visual perception of ME elements.

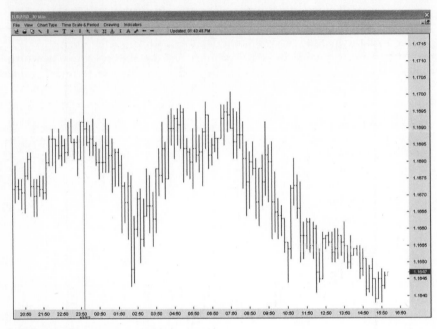

FIGURE 28.5 Example of a Thick Chart
Source: FXtrek IntelliChart™. Copyright 2001–2007 FXtrek.com, Inc.

Price and Time Rhythm

I've long ago concluded the markets do have some natural rhythms and cycles, which would be an excellent avenue for further technical analysis exploration. Surprisingly little has been done in this field, especially regarding FOREX.

But you don't need software or complex indicators to get an overview of a market's rhythm. Simply observe the following:

- The lengths of the upswings in a market and the corresponding lengths of the downswings—price rhythm.
- The time between peaks and valleys, peaks and peaks, and valleys and valleys—time rhythm.
- Primary price and time swings and secondary price and time swings. These often exhibit very regular rhythms. Counting units of price and time is sufficient to see the rhythm of a market. Using units instead of prices is a good idea for ME analysis.

A simple notation such as 10[primary or peak]/5[secondary or valley]-11/6-9/5-12/4 for primary/secondary price swings and time peaks/troughs will yield very good trading information. It is very hands-on. You can do it as you watch the markets; it requires no calculation but yields information just as good as complicated indicators. Doing things hands-on keeps you in touch with the market in a way an indicator cannot.

The ratios between the two (primary and secondary) are also worth observing. Of course you may use averages and oscillators to further massage the information.

You want to trade with the market's rhythm, not against it. If a market is having fairly regular 200-pip upswings and 100-pip downswings, you do not want to enter a sell order after a 50-pip upswing unless you have overwhelming evidence to the contrary. If a market is cresting an average of every 25 units (e.g., 22, 28, 21, 29, 25, 24, 26), you may not want to enter that sell order after only 17 units. (See Figure 28.6.)

For example,

Price rhythm (PR) = 10/5-9/6-10/5-9/[5 to 6]

Time rhythm (TR) = 4/2-5/3-5/2-6/[2 to 3]

The average down PR is 5.33 units. The average down TR is 2.33 units.

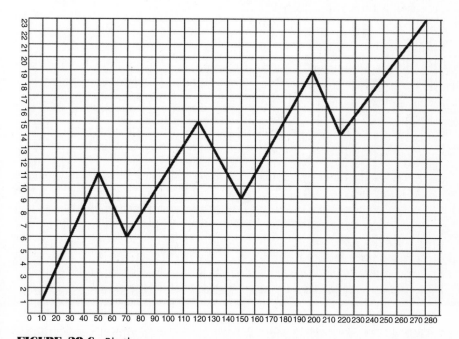

FIGURE 28.6 Rhythm

TERTIARY ME ELEMENTS

There are also two tertiary ME elements, shape and triangulation.

Shape

Consider the old indicator by which you take a moving average of the high and a moving average of the low, and plot them back half of the value of the moving average parameter.

In the old days this was called a semaphore. It gives you a channel in which price movements have occurred.

Shape is simply visualizing the channel or semaphore; forget the complexities of calculating various esoteric bands. Do it by simply looking for the price spikes over a period of time both up and down. It works best in thin, volatile markets, since the spikes tend to stand out.

There are many uncharted paths to using the various ME elements in combination.

I trade shape in this manner: Sell if the price spikes to the top of the channel when the market is over the average volatility—in other words, when the price hits the top of the channel at the end of the average volatility value; offset when the price declines deep into the channel. Buy in just the reverse fashion. (See Figure 28.7.)

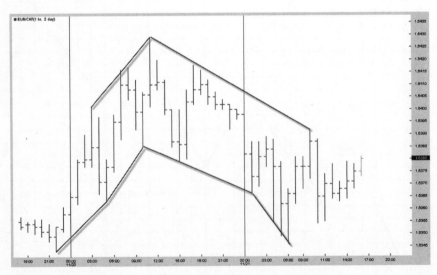

FIGURE 28.7 Shape

Source: FXtrek IntelliChart™. Copyright 2001–2007 FXtrek.com, Inc.

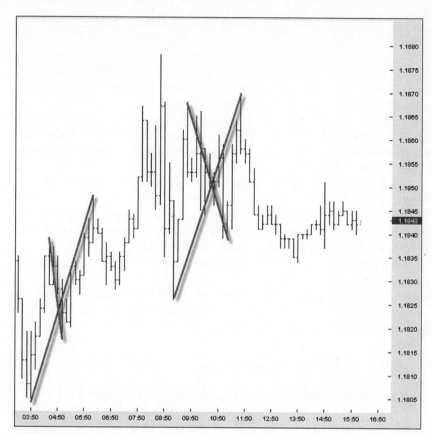

FIGURE 28.8 Triangulation
Source: FXtrek IntelliChart™. Copyright 2001–2007 FXtrek.com, Inc.

Triangulation

Triangulation is a derivative of pretzel charting, a technique (flag charts) developed first by commodity broker Eugene Hartnagle in the 1970s (see Currency Codex, www.fxpraxis.com). Lines connect alternating price highs and price lows. Interpretation of triangulation is beyond the scope of this chapter, but look for relative sizes of the upper and lower triangles, the types of triangles, and the slopes of the midlines. (See Figure 28.8.)

ME PROFILES

An ME profile is the set of primary and secondary market environments for any given chart—directional movement, volatility, thickness, price rhythm, and time rhythm. A cluster is a contiguous block on a profile matrix.

Figure 28.9 shows a profile matrix of directional movement (horizontal rows) to volatility (vertical columns). 1-1 indicates low DM and low V; 10-10 indicates high DM and high V. Again, there are many ways to record MEs—both informally and with a formal notation.

You may use this chart and track the DM/V profile for a market. Simply place a 1 in the appropriate square and, as the market evolves, place a 2 in another square, then a 3, and so forth. Yes, you may observe a geometric pattern in the 1-2-3-n sequence!

Again, there are many methods for tracking and recording ME elements, both informal and formal.

The combination of ME elements at any price-time point is an ME cluster. By utilizing identical scales for different ME elements, you may compare and manipulate different elements in a cluster.

Studying patterns of ME cluster sequences or chains offers fertile ground for serious research. For example, there is a strong tendency for a high DM/low V market to evolve into a low DM/high V pattern at tops and bottoms. ME element and cluster evolution is often in advance of a top or bottom—a leading indicator!

1	2	3	4	5	6	7	8	9	10
1	1	1	1	1	1	1	1	1	1
1	2	3	4	5	6	7	8	9	10
2	2	2	2	2	2	2	2	2	2
1	2	3	4	5	6	7	8	9	10
3	3	3	3	3	3	3	3	3	3
3	3	3	3	3	3	3	3	3	3
4	4	4	4	4	4	4	4	4	4
1	2	3	4	5	6	7	8	9	10
5	5	5	5	5	5	5	5	5	5
1	2	3	4	5	6	7	8	9	10
6	6	6	6	6	6	6	6	6	6
1	2	3	4	5	6	7	8	9	10
7	7	7	7	7	7	7	7	7	7
1	1	3	4	5	6	7	8	9	10
8	8	8	8	8	8	8	8	8	8
1	2	3	4	5	6	7	8	9	10
9	9	9	9	9	9	9	9	9	9
1	2	3	4	5	6	7	8	9	10
10	10	10	10	10	10	10	10	10	10

FIGURE 28.9 A 10×10 Directional Movement and Volatility Matrix

ME SYSTEM DEVELOPMENT

ME may also be used for system development. It is the backbone of the new expert system, JOSTAN FX, and is used for input, processing, and output. The ME syntax is perfect for the multiple iteration manipulation with a rule base, and—unlike in other expert systems—there is little or no information loss before, during, or after any manipulation.

Using ME input automatically smooths the data and allows diverse indicators to be compared (and manipulated) under a single syntax. A simple method for using DM would be to scale prices in a fan from 1 to 7. In this case, 1 would represent no price change (horizontal), while 7 would represent either infinite (vertical) price change or some scaled maximum price change.

As an example, instead of using price-date for input, a system developer could use a range or matrix of DM and/or V. The key factor to remember: One does not need to forecast exact prices to make money—forecasting DM is enough. Stops may be ME integrated, as well. For example, with an ME DM forecast of 6, a stop could be placed at the low-end price of 5 or the high-end price of 7 using the ME fan. A trailing stop could be used in similar fashion.

You may watch for and record MEs on multiple charts for the same pair or cross—for example, 5-minute, 1-hour, and 8-hour. I use this "3-D ME" to study how MEs and ME profiles evolve and interrelate.

In conjunction with 3-D ME, it is also possible to track and analyze the transition of ME profiles. My JOSTAN FX program has a continuously updated file of transitions in the knowledge base.

OTHER ME APPLICATIONS

ME has several other excellent applications:

- Analyze your trades on a regular basis, noting the MEs of each trade you made. You will almost certainly find ME profiles for which you had more success than others. Thereafter, when you are contemplating a trade, consider the ME profile in lieu of those statistics. Often eliminating just one or two bad trades a month is the difference between success and failure. Using this idea may keep you from making bad trades.
- If you are testing a new trading system, divide results into at least the primary MEs of DM and V. You can quickly see if it is predominantly a

trending system or a sideways trading system. Look for methods that do well in both—or at least do not collapse in the weaker of the two.

- Think about trades in terms of MEs. Remember you do not have to forecast exact prices to make money! If you can forecast the primary MEs, that is sufficient.
- Pairs and crosses have ME personalities. For long periods of time they will behave within ME profile zones I call clusters. Be cautious of trades that predict prices well out of the cluster, and have extra confidence in those that predict prices within the cluster.
- Hedge funds with multiple managers may analyze each manager by ME profiles to make sure the fund does not have a large preponderance of managers with the same ME profiles. It does no good to diversify if most managers do well in one type of market and poorly in another type. Money may be allocated to managers on the basis of predicted MEs once one determines the ME profiles of individual managers.

BATHTUB ANALYSIS

It is not enough to just keep a chart; your viewing of it must be an active process. You must work with it, live with it. By active analysis, Charlie basically meant the process of hypothesis testing. He felt that unless you asked specific questions, made hypotheses, and sought answers in a continuing *hypothesis→antithesis→synthesis* dialectic, you wouldn't really see anything or learn much. If you don't look for it, you can't see it! Hypothesis testing is the correct way to use a chart.

The human mind tends to want to draw conclusions and infer general rules quickly. We see two or three examples of a phenomenon and assume it's a general rule. To avoid this temptation, always follow up your initial hypothesis testing with analysis of as many examples of the phenomenon as possible. You may find the rule not worth pursuing or you may find it needs to be more general or more specific. In the latter case, avoid adding too many ad hoc rules in an attempt to make it work.

Charlie called this "bathtub analysis" since he liked to take a book of charts into the bath with him, formulate hypotheses, and see how it played out on the charts. I have perfected the technique by bringing along two or three fingers of a good single malt! He might ask, "What happens on the third bar after first an inside bar, then an outside bar?" You will find that answering such bathtub questions will give you an intimate feel for the chart—and lead you to other, potentially useful, questions and conclusions.

SUMMARY

Because ME is a hands-on technique, it will keep you in touch with and focused on the markets, working with them and actively looking, questioning, and participating. In this age of computer trading I cannot sufficiently emphasize the importance of this to successful trading.

Charlie's original concept was to use ME elements informally, perhaps with a shorthand notation. Obviously, ME can be (and has been) formalized for use with computerized trading methods. The potential for ME research, applications, and new discoveries is substantial.

APPENDIX: SAMPLE VISUAL BASIC SOURCE CODE FOR DM AND V

Over the years, I have written numerous trading programs and back-testing utilities for commodity futures and currencies. What follows is sample source code in Microsoft Visual Basic 6.0 to calculate moving directional movement and volatility indexes for market environments (ME). There are many ways to quantify these elements and the others of ME:

```
Public Type QUOTE_TYPE
  Date As Date
  Time As String
  O As Double
  H As Double
  L As Double
  C As Double
End Type
Public Q(MAXQUOTES) As QUOTE_TYPE
Public Sub CalculateDM(DMIdx%)
Dim i%
  For i = DMIdx + 1 To NumQuotes
    DM(i) = Q(i).C - Q(i - DMIDX).C
  Next i
End Sub
Public Sub CalculateVolatility(VolIdx%)
Dim i%, j%
Dim sum#, mean#
  sum = 0
  For i = VolIdx To NumQuotes
    sum = 0
```

```
    For j = i - VolIdx + 1 To i
      sum = sum + Q(j).C
    Next j
    mean = sum / VolIdx
    sum = 0
    For j = i - VolIdx + 1 To i
      sum = sum + Abs(Q(i).C - mean)
    Next j
    Vol(i) = sum / VolIdx
  Next i
End Sub
```

Common Sense Guidelines for the Average Trader

☐ **Look for a reputable broker:**
  ☐ Ability to trade effectively depends on consistent spreads and ample liquidity.
  ☐ Anyone can establish a position.
  ☐ Ability to close out a position at a fair market price is more important.
☐ **Live to trade another day:**
  ☐ Apply prudent money management skills.
  ☐ Avoid using excessive leverage that puts your investment capital at risk.
  ☐ Always trade with a stop!
☐ **Don't trade emotionally; stick to your plan and maintain discipline:**
  ☐ Establish a trading plan before initiating a trade.
  ☐ Set reasonable risk/reward parameters.
  ☐ Don't override your stops for emotional reasons.
  ☐ "Don't react to price action" means do not buy just because it looks cheap or sell because the price looks too high. Have supporting evidence to back up your trade.
☐ **Don't punt:**
  ☐ Punting is trading for trading's sake without a view.

☐ **Don't leave stops at obvious levels, such as round numbers (e.g., EUR/USD 1.20, USD/JPY 110):**
  ☐ Stops at obvious levels (called Jubbs stops) are more likely to be triggered.
☐ **Don't add to a losing position unless it is part of a strategy to scale into a position:**
  ☐ In other words, don't double up just in the hope of recouping losses; do so only if it is part of a broader trading strategy.
☐ **Trading with or against the trend:**
  ☐ When trading with a trend, consider the use of trailing stops.
  ☐ When trading against the trend, be disciplined taking profits and don't hold out for the last pip.
☐ **Treat trading as a continuum:**
  ☐ Don't base success on one trade.
  ☐ Avoid emotional highs or lows on individual trades.
  ☐ Consistency should be an objective.
☐ **FOREX trading is multicurrency:**
  ☐ Watch crosses, as they are key influences on spot trading.
  ☐ Crosses are one foreign currency versus another, such as EUR/JPY (euro versus yen) or EUR/GBP (euro versus pound).
  ☐ Crosses can be used as clues for direction for spot currencies even if you are not trading them.
☐ **Be cognizant of what news is coming out each day so you don't get blindsided:**
  ☐ Beware of trading just ahead of an economic number and be wary of volatility following key releases.
☐ **Beware of illiquid markets:**
  ☐ Adjust strategies during holiday or preholiday periods to take into account thin liquidity.
  ☐ Beware of central bank intervention in illiquid markets.

Jay Meisler, a partner in Global-View.com, says one problem of trading with too-high leverage is that one piece of surprise news can wipe out one's capital. "Those who treat FOREX trading as if they were in a casino will see the same long-term results as when they go to Las Vegas," he says, adding: "If you treat FOREX trading like a business, including proper money management, you have a better chance of success" (*Newsweek International*, March 15, 2004).

Treat this business as a marathon and not a sprint so you avoid burnout and maintain stamina for the long haul.

Resources for the FOREX Trader

PERIODICALS

Though the following monthly (unless otherwise specified) magazines focus on very specific material, each frequently prints very informative and timely articles on the FOREX marketplace:

Active Trader (TechInfo, Inc.)—www.activetradermag.com

Futures (Futures Magazine, Inc.)—www.futuresmag.com

Technical Analysis of Stocks & Commodities (Technical Analysis, Inc.)—www.traders.com

Currency Trader (online)—www.currencytradermag.com

FX Week—www.fxweek.com

E-FOREX (quarterly)—www.e-forex.net

BOOKS

The following list, though in no way complete, provides traders with FOREX library essentials:

Archer, Michael, *Getting Started in Forex Trading Strategies* (John Wiley & Sons, 2007).

Archer, Michael D., *The Goodman Swing Count System Codex* (FX-Praxis, 2007).

Archer, Michael D., and James Lauren Bickford, *The FOREX Chartist Companion* (John Wiley & Sons, 2006).

Booker, Rob, *Adventures of a Currency Trader* (John Wiley & Sons, 2007).

Evans, Lewis, and Olga Sheean, *Left Brain Thinking: The Right Mindset and Technique for Success in Forex* (Inside Out Media, 2006).

Henderson, Callum, *Currency Strategy* (John Wiley & Sons, 2002).

Horner, Raghee, *Thirty Days of Forex Trading* (John Wiley & Sons, 2005).

Klopfenstein, Gary, *Trading Currency Cross Rates* (John Wiley & Sons, 1993).

Lein, Kathy, *Day Trading the Currency Market* (John Wiley & Sons, 2005).

Louw, G. N., *Begin Forex* (FXTrader, 2003).

Luca, Cornelius, *Technical Analysis Applications in the Global Currency Markets* (Prentice Hall, 2000).

Luca, Cornelius, *Trading in the Global Currency Markets* (Prentice Hall, 2000).

Murphy, John, *Intermarket Financial Analysis* (John Wiley & Sons, 1999).

Murphy, John, *Technical Analysis of the Financial Markets* (Prentice Hall, 1999).

Person, John L., *Forex Conquered* (John Wiley & Sons, 2007).

Reuters Limited, *An Introduction to Foreign Exchange and Money Markets* (Reuters Financial Training, 1999).

Shamah, Shani, *A Foreign Exchange Primer* (John Wiley & Sons, 2003).

There are hundreds (if not thousands) of books pertaining specifically to technical analysis. A few of the best-known are:

Aby, Carroll D., Jr., *Point and Figure Charting* (Traders Press, 1996).

Aronson, David R., *Evidence-Based Technical Analysis* (John Wiley & Sons, 2007).

Bickford, Jim, *Chart Plotting Algorithms for Technical Analysts* (Syzygy, 2002).

Bulkowski, Thomas N., *Encyclopedia of Chart Patterns* (John Wiley & Sons, 2005).

DiNapoli, Joe, *Trading with DiNapoli Levels* (Coast Investment, 1998).

Kaufman, Perry J., *New Trading Systems and Methods* (John Wiley & Sons, 2005).

McGee, John, *Technical Analysis of Stock Trends* (American Management Association, 2001).

Nison, Steve, *Japanese Candlestick Charting Techniques* (Prentice Hall, 2001).

Wilder, J. Welles, Jr., *New Concepts in Technical Trading Systems* (Trend Research, 1978).

A fine resource for finding more titles is www.traderspress.com.

ONLINE BROKERS AND DEALERS

www.gftforex.com

www.forex.com

www.fxcm.com

www.fxdd.com

www.gcitrading.com

www.dbfx.com

www.mbtrading.com

www.saxobank.com

www.fxsolutions.com

www.cmcmarkets.com

www.migfx,com

www.cmsfx.com

www.odls.com

World Currencies and Symbols

able C.1 is a list of global currencies and the three-character currency codes that we have found are generally used to represent them. Often, but not always, this code is the same as the ISO 4217 standard. (The ISO, or International Organization for Standardization, is a worldwide federation of national standards.)

In most cases, the currency code is composed of the country's two-character Internet country code plus an extra character to denote the currency unit. For example, the code for Canadian dollars is simply Canada's two-character Internet code ("CA") plus a one-character currency designator ("D").

We have endeavored to list the codes that, in our experience, are actually in general industry use to represent the currencies. Currency names are given in the plural form. This list does not contain obsolete Eurozone currencies.

Reprinted with permission of John Wiley & Sons, Inc. *Getting Started in Currency Trading: Winning in Today's Hottest Marketplace, 2nd Edition* by Michael Duane Archer (Wiley, 2008).

TABLE C.1	Symbol, Place, Currency Name	
AED	United Arab Emirates	Dirhams
AFA	Afghanistan	Afghanis
ALL	Albania	Leke
AMD	Armenia	Drams
ANG	Netherlands Antilles	Guilders
AOA	Angola	Kwanza
ARS	Argentina	Pesos
AUD	Australia	Dollars
AWG	Aruba	Guilders
AZM	Azerbaijan	Manats
BAM	Bosnia and Herzegovina	Convertible Marka
BBD	Barbados	Dollars
BDT	Bangladesh	Taka
BGN	Bulgaria	Leva
BHD	Bahrain	Dinars
BIF	Burundi	Francs
BMD	Bermuda	Dollars
BND	Brunei Darussalam	Dollars
BOB	Bolivia	Bolivianos
BRL	Brazil	Brazil Real
BSD	Bahamas	Dollars
BTN	Bhutan	Ngultrum
BWP	Botswana	Pulas
BYR	Belarus	Rubles
BZD	Belize	Dollars
CAD	Canada	Dollars
CDF	Congo/Kinshasa	Congolese Francs
CHF	Switzerland	Francs
CLP	Chile	Pesos
CNY	China	Renminbi
COP	Colombia	Pesos
CRC	Costa Rica	Colones
CUP	Cuba	Pesos
CVE	Cape Verde	Escudos
CYP	Cyprus	Pounds
CZK	Czech Republic	Koruny
DJF	Djibouti	Francs
DKK	Denmark	Kroner
DOP	Dominican Republic	Pesos
DZD	Algeria	Algeria Dinars
EEK	Estonia	Krooni
EGP	Egypt	Pounds
ERN	Eritrea	Nakfa
ETB	Ethiopia	Birr
EUR	Euro Member Countries	Euros

TABLE C.1 *(Continued)*

FJD	Fiji	Dollars
FKP	Falkland Islands	Pounds
GBP	United Kingdom	Pounds
GEL	Georgia	Lari
GGP	Guernsey	Pounds
GHC	Ghana	Cedis
GIP	Gibraltar	Pounds
GMD	Gambia	Dalasi
GNF	Guinea	Francs
GTQ	Guatemala	Quetzales
GYD	Guyana	Dollars
HKD	Hong Kong	Dollars
HNL	Honduras	Lempiras
HRK	Croatia	Kuna
HTG	Haiti	Gourdes
HUF	Hungary	Forint
IDR	Indonesia	Rupiahs
ILS	Israel	New Shekels
IMP	Isle of Man	Pounds
INR	India	Rupees
IQD	Iraq	Dinars
IRR	Iran	Rials
ISK	Iceland	Kronur
JEP	Jersey	Pounds
JMD	Jamaica	Dollars
JOD	Jordan	Dinars
JPY	Japan	Yen
KES	Kenya	Shillings
KGS	Kyrgyzstan	Soms
KHR	Cambodia	Riels
KMF	Comoros	Francs
KPW	Korea (North)	Won
KRW	Korea (South)	Won
KWD	Kuwait	Dinars
KYD	Cayman Islands	Dollars
KZT	Kazakstan	Tenge
LAK	Laos	Kips
LBP	Lebanon	Pounds
LKR	Sri Lanka	Rupees
LRD	Liberia	Dollars
LSL	Lesotho	Maloti
LTL	Lithuania	Litai
LVL	Latvia	Lati

(Continued)

TABLE C.1 (*Continued*)

LYD	Libya	Dinars
MAD	Morocco	Dirhams
MDL	Moldova	Lei
MGA	Madagascar	Ariary
MKD	Macedonia	Denars
MMK	Myanmar (Burma)	Kyats
MNT	Mongolia	Tugriks
MOP	Macau	Patacas
MRO	Mauritania	Ouguiyas
MTL	Malta	Liri
MUR	Mauritius	Rupees
MVR	Maldives	Rufiyaa
MWK	Malawi	Kwachas
MXN	Mexico	Pesos
MYR	Malaysia	Ringgits
MZM	Mozambique	Meticais
NAD	Namibia	Dollars
NGN	Nigeria	Nairas
NIO	Nicaragua	Gold Cordobas
NOK	Norway	Krone
NPR	Nepal	Nepal Rupees
NZD	New Zealand	Dollars
OMR	Oman	Rials
PAB	Panama	Balboa
PEN	Peru	Nuevos Soles
PGK	Papua New Guinea	Kina
PHP	Philippines	Pesos
PKR	Pakistan	Rupees
PLN	Poland	Zlotych
PYG	Paraguay	Guarani
QAR	Qatar	Rials
ROL	Romania	Lei
RUR	Russia	Rubles
RWF	Rwanda	Rwanda Francs
SAR	Saudi Arabia	Riyals
SBD	Solomon Islands	Dollars
SCR	Seychelles	Rupees
SDD	Sudan	Dinars
SEK	Sweden	Kronor
SGD	Singapore	Dollars
SHP	Saint Helena	Pounds
SIT	Slovenia	Tolars
SKK	Slovakia	Koruny
SLL	Sierra Leone	Leones
SOS	Somalia	Shillings

TABLE C.1	*(Continued)*	
SPL	Seborga	Luigini
SRG	Suriname	Guilders
STD	São Tome and Principe	Dobras
SVC	El Salvador	Colones
SYP	Syria	Pounds
SZL	Swaziland	Emalangeni
THB	Thailand	Baht
TJS	Tajikistan	Somoni
TMM	Turkmenistan	Manats
TND	Tunisia	Dinars
TOP	Tonga	Pa'anga
TRL	Turkey	Liras
TTD	Trinidad and Tobago	Dollars
TVD	Tuvalu	Tuvalu Dollars
TWD	Taiwan	New Dollars
TZS	Tanzania	Shillings
UAH	Ukraine	Hryvnia
UGX	Uganda	Shillings
USD	United States of America	Dollars
UYU	Uruguay	Pesos
UZS	Uzbekistan	Sums
VEB	Venezuela	Bolivares
VND	Vietnam	Dong
VUV	Vanuatu	Vatu
WST	Samoa	Tala
XAF	Communauté Financière Africaine	Francs
XAG	Silver	Ounces
XAU	Gold	Ounces
XCD	East Caribbean	Dollars
XDR	International Monetary Fund	Special Drawing Rights
XOF	Communauté Financière Africaine	Francs
XPD	Palladium	Ounces
XPF	Comptoirs Français du Pacifique	Francs
XPT	Platinum	Ounces
YER	Yemen	Rials
YUM	Yugoslavia	New Dinars
ZAR	South Africa	Rand
ZMK	Zambia	Kwacha
ZWD	Zimbabwe	Zimbabwe Dollars

Time Zones and Global Banking Hours

The chart shown in Figure D.1 emphasizes the importance of the effect of time of day on FOREX market activity and volatility based on hours of operation around the globe. The top row is Greenwich Mean Time expressed in 24-hour military format. Banking hours are arbitrarily assumed to be 9:00 A.M. to 4:00 P.M. around the globe.

Examples of chart usage are:

- Locate Denver (row 6, or GMT less 7 hours). The first darkened cell in this row indicates when Denver banks open relative to other world banks.
- Move upward to the top row to see that the concurrent time in London is 16:00 or 4:00 P.M., when British banks are now closed.
- A FOREX trader in New York must trade between 3:00 A.M. and 11:00 A.M. Eastern Standard Time in order to follow the heightened activity in central European markets (GMT+1: Zurich, Frankfurt, Vienna, Copenhagen).
- San Francisco banks are closing while Sydney banks are opening, and so on.

Reprinted with permission of John Wiley & Sons, Inc. *Getting Started in Currency Trading: Winning in Today's Hottest Marketplace, 2nd Edition* by Michael Duane Archer (Wiley, 2008).

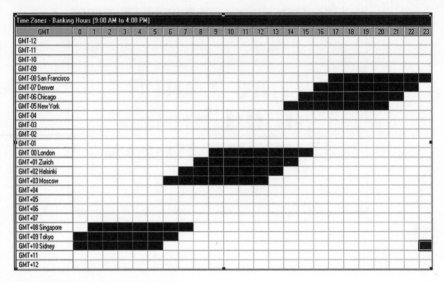

FIGURE D.1   Global Banking Hours

The darkened areas in Figure D.1 accentuate the major banking centers. FOREX is a 24-hour market, so you can trade 24 hours a day during the week. Time of day (TOD) can strongly influence trading volume, liquidity, and volatility.

Glossary

algorithmic trading Trading by means of an automated computer program. Sometimes called program trading.

application program interface (API) Computer code or routines for integrating trading programs to a broker-dealer's trading platform. Most commonly used to allow a proprietary trading program to read and process a broker-dealer's data feed.

appreciation The strengthening of a currency in price in response to market demand.

arbitrage The purchase or sale of an instrument and simultaneous taking of an equal and opposite position in a related market, in order to take advantage of small price differentials between markets.

ask price The price at which the market is prepared to sell a specific currency in a foreign exchange contract or cross currency contract. At this price, the trader can buy the base currency. In the quotation, the ask price is shown on the right side of the quotation. For example, in the quote USD/CHF 1.4527/32, the ask price is 1.4532, meaning you can buy one U.S. dollar for 1.4532 Swiss francs.

at best An instruction given to a dealer to buy or sell at the best rate that can be obtained.

at or better An order to deal at a specific rate or better.

balance of trade The value of a country's exports minus its imports.

ballooning The practice by market makers of increasing pip spreads during fast or illiquid markets.

bar chart A type of chart that consists of four significant points: the high and the low prices, which form the vertical bar; the opening price, which is marked with a little horizontal line to the left of the bar; and the closing price, which is marked with a little horizontal line of the right of the bar.

base currency The first currency in a currency pair. It shows how much the base currency is worth as measured against the second currency. For example, if the USD/CHF rate equals 1.6215, then one USD is worth CHF 1.6215. In the foreign exchange markets, the U.S. dollar is normally considered the base currency for quotes, meaning that quotes are expressed as a unit of $1 USD per the other currency quoted in the pair. The primary exceptions to this rule are the British pound, the Eurozone euro, and the Australian dollar.

bear market   A market characterized by declining prices.

bid price   The price at which the market is prepared to buy a specific currency in a foreign exchange contract or cross currency contract. At this price, the trader can sell the base currency. It is shown on the left side of the quotation. For example, in the quote USD/CHF 1.4527/32, the bid price is 1.4527, meaning you can sell one U.S. dollar for 1.4527 Swiss francs.

bid/ask spread   The difference between the bid and ask price.

big figure quote   Dealer expression referring to the first few digits of an exchange rate. These digits are often omitted in dealer quotes. For example, a USD/JPY rate might be 117.30/117.35, but would be quoted verbally without the first three digits—that is, as 30/35.

BLS   Bureau of Labor Statistics.

book   In a professional trading environment, the summary of a trader's or desk's total positions.

Bretton Woods Agreement of 1944   An agreement that established fixed foreign exchange rates for major currencies, provided for central bank intervention in the currency markets, and pegged the price of gold at U.S. $35 per ounce. The agreement lasted until 1971, when President Nixon overturned the Bretton Woods Agreement and established a floating exchange rate for the major currencies.

broker   An individual or firm that acts as an intermediary, putting together buyers and sellers for a fee or commission. In contrast, a dealer commits capital and takes one side of a position, hoping to earn a spread (profit) by closing out the position in a subsequent trade with another party.

bull market   A market distinguished by rising prices.

Bundesbank   Germany's central bank.

cable   Trader jargon referring to the British sterling/U.S. dollar exchange rate. So called because the rate was originally transmitted via a transatlantic cable beginning in the mid-1800s.

call   An option to purchase a currency.

cambist   An expert trader who rapidly buys and sells currency throughout the day.

candlestick chart   A chart that indicates the trading range for the day as well as the opening and closing prices. If the opening price is higher than the closing price, the rectangle between the open and close is shaded. If the closing price is higher than the opening price, that area of the chart is not shaded.

cash market   The market in the actual financial instrument on which a futures or options contract is based.

central bank   A government or quasi-governmental organization that manages a country's monetary policy. For example, the U.S. central bank is the Federal Reserve, and the German central bank is the Bundesbank.

centralized market   Any market where all orders are routed to one central exchange. FOREX is not a centralized market.

CFTC   Commodity Futures Trading Commission.

chartist   An individual who uses charts and graphs and interprets historical data to find trends and predict future movements. Also referred to as a technical trader.

cleared funds   Funds that are freely available, sent in to settle a trade.

clearing   The process of settling a trade.

closed position   Exposure in foreign currencies that no longer exists. The process to close a position is to sell or buy a certain amount of currency to offset an equal amount of the open position. This will square the position.

CME   Chicago Mercantile Exchange.

collateral   Something given to secure a loan or as a guarantee of performance.

commission   A transaction fee charged by a broker.

confirmation   A document exchanged by counterparties to a transaction that states the terms of said transaction.

consumer price index (CPI)   A weighted average of prices of a basket of consumer goods and services, such as food, medicine, and transportation. The CPI is calculated by taking price changes for each item in a specified basket of goods and averaging them according to their estimated importance.

contagion   The tendency of an economic crisis to spread from one market to another. In 1997, political instability in Indonesia caused high volatility in its domestic currency, the rupiah. From there, the contagion spread to other Asian emerging currencies, and then to Latin America, and is now referred to as the Asian contagion.

contract   The standard unit of trading in futures and options.

counter currency   The second listed currency in a currency pair. See also quote currency.

counterparty   One of the participants in a financial transaction.

country risk   Risk associated with a cross-border transaction, including but not limited to legal and political conditions.

cross currency pair   A foreign exchange transaction in which one foreign currency is traded against a second foreign currency, for example, EUR/GBP.

cross rate   Same as cross currency pair.

currency   Any form of money issued by a government or central bank and used as legal tender and a basis for trade.

currency pair   The two currencies that make up a foreign exchange rate, for example, EUR/USD.

currency risk   The probability of an adverse change in exchange rates.

day trader   Speculator who takes positions in currencies, which are then liquidated prior to the close of the same trading session or day.

dealer   An individual or firm that acts as a principal or counterparty to a transaction. Principals take one side of a position, hoping to earn a spread (profit) by closing out the position in a subsequent trade with another party. In contrast, a broker is an individual or firm that acts as an intermediary, putting together buyers and sellers for a fee or commission.

deficit   A negative balance of trade or payments.

delivery   A FOREX trade where both sides make and take actual delivery of the currencies traded.

depreciation   A fall in the value of a currency due to market forces.

derivative   A contract that changes in value in relation to the price movements of a related or underlying security, futures contract, or other physical instrument. An option is the most common derivative instrument.

devaluation   The deliberate downward adjustment of a currency's price, normally by official announcement.

directional movement (DM)   In technical analysis, the net price change from one specified time unit to another specified time unit.

downtick   A new price quote at a price lower than the preceding quote.

econometric analysis   Using mathematical formulas or models to make trading decisions with fundamental information and data.

economic indicator   A government-issued statistic that indicates level of current economic growth and stability. Common indicators are employment rates, gross domestic product (GDP), inflation, retail sales, and so forth.

ECU   European Currency Unit; see European Monetary Union (EMU).

electronic communications network (ECN)   A system wherein orders to buy and sell are matched through a network of banks and/or dealers. See market maker, the other widely used method of order execution, and no dealing desk (NDD) broker, a hybrid.

end of day (EOD) order   An order to buy or sell at a specified price. This order remains open until the end of the trading day, which is typically 5:00 P.M. EST.

euro   The currency of the European Economic and Monetary Union (EMU); a replacement for the European Currency Unit (ECU).

European Central Bank (ECB)   The central bank for the European Economic and Monetary Union.

European Economic and Monetary Union (EMU)   The principal goal of the EMU is the establishment of a single European currency called the euro, which officially replaces the national currencies of the member countries. The 15 current members of the EMU are Germany, France, Belgium, Luxembourg, Austria, Finland, Ireland, the Netherlands, Italy, Spain, Portugal, Greece, Slovenia, Cyprus, and Malta.

exotics   A currency pair with the USD and a less traded currency such as the Thai baht or the Chilean peso. Considered riskier to trade than the majors and minors.

fast market   A market is fast when it is hit with a large volume of orders over a short period of time. Markets are often fast after an unexpected news announcement.

Federal Deposit Insurance Corporation (FDIC)   The regulatory agency responsible for administering bank depository insurance in the United States.

Federal Reserve (Fed)   The central bank for the United States.

first in, first out (FIFO)   Accounting rule according to which open positions are closed. All positions opened within a particular currency pair are liquidated in the order in which they were originally opened.

flat/square   Refers to a trader on the sidelines with no position.

floating stop   An automated trailing stop.

foreign exchange (FOREX, FX)   The simultaneous buying of one currency and selling of another.

FOREX futures   FOREX traded as a futures contract.

forward   The prespecified exchange rate for a foreign exchange contract settling at some agreed future date, based on the interest rate differential between the two currencies involved.

forward points   The pips added to or subtracted from the current exchange rate to calculate a forward price.

fundamental analysis   Analysis of economic and political information with the objective of determining future movements in a financial market.

futures contract   An obligation to exchange a good or an instrument at a set price on a future date. The primary difference between a futures contract and a forward is that futures are typically traded over an exchange (exchange-traded contracts or ETCs), versus forwards, which are considered over-the-counter (OTC) contracts. An OTC contract is any contract *not* traded on an exchange.

FX   See foreign exchange.

G-8   The eight leading industrial countries, being the United States, Germany, Japan, France, United Kingdom, Canada, Italy, and Russia.

going long   The purchase of a stock, commodity, or currency for investment or speculation.

going short The selling of a currency or instrument not owned by the seller.

gold standard A monetary system whereby a country allows its monetary unit to be freely converted into fixed amounts of gold and vice versa.

good till canceled (GTC) order An order to buy or sell at a specified price. This order remains open until filled or until the client cancels.

gross domestic product (GDP) Total value of a country's output, income, or expenditures produced within the country's physical borders.

gross national product (GNP) Gross domestic product plus income earned from investment or work abroad.

Guerrilla trader Similar to a scalper, but trades in bursts of several trades, then recedes to the sidelines. Sometimes called a sniper.

hedge A position or combination of positions that reduces the risk of a trader's primary position.

high-frequency trading Trading very frequently; scalping. A high-frequency trader uses tick data. See also ultra-high-frequency trading.

"hit the bid" Acceptance of purchasing at the offer or selling at the bid.

IMM International Monetary Market.

inflation An economic condition whereby prices for consumer goods rise, eroding purchasing power.

initial margin The initial deposit of collateral required to enter into a position as a guarantee on future performance.

interbank rate The foreign exchange rates at which large international banks quote other large international banks.

intervention Action by a central bank to affect the value of its currency by entering the market. Concerted intervention refers to action by a number of central banks to control exchange rates.

introducing broker (IB) Generally a small broker who relies on a larger broker-dealer to execute his trades and hold fiduciary responsibility for client funds.

King Kong Syndrome The emotional high that overtakes traders when they do exceptionally well for a period of time, such as making a dozen consecutive winning trades. Usually followed by a large losing trade and a reality check.

kiwi Slang for the New Zealand dollar.

landing area A "box" with the price objectives defined as the vertical lines and the time objectives defined as the horizontal lines.

leading indicator One of the statistics that are considered to predict future economic activity.

leverage   Also called margin. The ratio of the amount used in a transaction to the required security deposit.

LIBOR   The London Interbank Offered Rate. Banks use LIBOR when borrowing from another bank.

limit order   An order with restrictions on the maximum price to be paid or the minimum price to be received.

liquidation   The closing of an existing position through the execution of an offsetting transaction.

liquidity   The ability of a market to accept large transactions with minimal or no impact on price stability; also, the ability to enter and exit a market quickly.

long position   A position that appreciates in value if market prices increase. When the base currency in the pair is bought, the position is said to be long.

loonie   Slang for the Canadian dollar.

lot   A unit to measure the amount of the deal. The value of the deal always corresponds to an integer number of lots.

major currency   Any of the following: euro, pound sterling, Australian dollar, New Zealand dollar, U.S. dollar, Canadian dollar, Swiss franc, Japanese yen. See also minor currency.

managed account   Having a third party such as a professional money manager make trading decisions for you. Also called a discretionary account.

margin   The required equity that an investor must deposit to collateralize a position.

margin call   A request from a broker or dealer for additional funds or other collateral to guarantee performance on a position that has moved against the customer.

market maker   A dealer who regularly quotes both bid and ask prices and is ready to make a two-sided market for any financial instrument. Most retail FOREX dealers are market makers. A market maker is said to have a dealing desk.

market risk   Exposure to changes in market prices.

mark-to-market   Process of reevaluating all open positions with the current market prices. These new values then determine margin requirements.

maturity   The date for settlement or expiry of a financial instrument.

mercury chart   A modified bar chart used in commodity futures. Each bar shows the price range for a time unit and changes in open interest and volume from the previous time unit.

minor currency   Any one of the currencies between a major currency and an exotic. The Italian lira and Swedish krona are minor currencies.

money management   The techniques traders utilize to manage their money both in the aggregate and for specific trades.

money supply   The aggregate quantity of coins, bills, loans, credit, and any other liquid monetary instruments or equivalents within a given country's economy.

Mundo   A synthetic global currency calculated as the average of multiple currency pairs. See Michael Archer and James Bickford, *Forex Chartist Companion* (John Wiley & Sons, 2006).

net position   The amount of currency bought or sold that has not yet been offset by opposite transactions.

NFA   National Futures Association.

no dealing desk (NDD) broker   Broker that provides a platform where liquidity providers such as banks can offer prices to the NDD platform. Incoming orders are routed to the best available bid or offer. See also market maker and electronic communications network (ECN).

offer   The rate at which a dealer is willing to sell a currency. See ask price.

offsetting transaction   A trade that serves to cancel or offset some or all of the market risk of an open position.

one cancels the other (OCO) order   A designation for two orders whereby when one of the two orders is executed the other is automatically canceled.

open order   An order that will be executed when a market moves to its designated price. Normally associated with good till canceled (GTC) orders.

open position   An active trade with corresponding unrealized P/L, which has not been offset by an equal and opposite deal.

option   A FOREX option is the right to purchase or sell a currency at a specified price for a specified time period.

order   An instruction to execute a trade at a specified rate.

over the counter (OTC)   Used to describe any transaction that is not conducted over an exchange.

overnight position   A trade that remains open until the next business day.

pip   The smallest unit of price for any foreign currency. Digits added to or subtracted from the fourth decimal place, that is, 0.0001. Also called point.

point   100 pips.

point and figure chart   Similar to a swing chart but uses Xs to denote upward-moving prices and Os to denote downward-moving prices.

political risk   Exposure to changes in governmental policy that may have an adverse effect on an investor's position.

position   The netted total holdings of a given currency.

position trader   A trader who holds positions over multiple trading sessions.

premium   In the currency markets, describes the amount by which the forward or futures price exceeds the spot price.

pretzel chart   A price chart connecting the open, high, low, and close in such a fashion that it resembles a pretzel with two closed three-sided spaces connected through a center point.

price transparency   Describes quotes to which every market participant has equal access.

profit/loss (P/L)   The actual realized gain or loss resulting from trading activities on closed positions, plus the theoretical unrealized gain or loss on open positions that have been marked to market. Same as gain/loss.

programmed trading   See algorithmic trading.

put   An option to sell a currency.

pyramiding   Adding to a position as the market moves up or down. Pyramiding a winning position is risky; pyramiding a losing position is suicide.

quote   An indicative market price, normally used for information purposes only.

quote currency   The second currency quoted in a FOREX currency pair. In a direct quote, the quote currency is the foreign currency itself. In an indirect quote, the quote currency is the domestic currency. See also base currency and counter currency.

rally   A recovery in price after a period of decline.

range   The difference between the highest and lowest price of a futures contract recorded during a given trading session.

rate   The price of one currency in terms of another, typically used for dealing purposes.

requoting   The practice of a broker-dealer filling an order at a price not seen on the public price feed. Like ballooning and running stops, most typical of market makers and frowned upon by traders.

resistance level   A term used in technical analysis indicating a specific price level at which analysis concludes people will sell.

revaluation   An increase in the exchange rate for a currency as a result of central bank intervention. Opposite of devaluation.

risk   Exposure to uncertain change, most often used with a negative connotation of adverse change.

risk management   The employment of financial analysis and trading techniques to reduce and control exposure to various types of risk.

rollover   Process whereby the settlement of a deal is rolled forward to another value date. The cost of this process is based on the interest rate differential of the two currencies.

round trip   Buying and selling of a specified amount of currency.

running stops   The practice of market makers entering orders for the purpose of hitting customer stop loss orders. Also called harvesting stops. Like ballooning, considered a negative practice by traders.

scalper   Someone who trades very often. Trades are typically measured in minutes but sometimes seconds.

SEC   Securities and Exchange Commission.

settlement   The process by which a trade is entered into the books and records of the counterparties to a transaction. The settlement of currency trades may or may not involve the actual physical exchange of one currency for another.

short position   An investment position that benefits from a decline in market price. When the base currency in the pair is sold, the position is said to be short.

slippage   The difference in pips between the order price approved by the client and the price at which the order is actually executed.

spot price   The current market price. Settlement of spot transactions usually occurs within two business days.

spread   The difference between the bid and ask prices.

sterling   Refers to British pound.

stop loss order   Order type whereby an open position is automatically liquidated at a specific price. Often used to minimize exposure to losses if the market moves against an investor's position. As an example, an investor who is long USD at 156.27 might wish to put in a stop loss order for 155.49, which would limit losses should the dollar depreciate, possibly below 155.49.

support level   A technique used in technical analysis that indicates a specific price floor at which a given exchange rate will automatically correct itself. Opposite of resistance level.

swap   In currency trading, the simultaneous sale and purchase of the same amount of a given currency at a forward exchange rate.

swing chart   A form of charting connecting prices filtered by a minimum increment; similar to point and figure charts. Pugh swing charts use vertical lines connected by short horizontal lines. Line swing charts use angular lines connecting price to price. Swing charts are said to be price-functional; the time frame is not a parameter.

Swissy   Market slang for Swiss franc.

technical analysis   An effort to forecast prices by analyzing market data—that is, historical price trends and averages, volumes, open interest, and so forth.

tick   A minimum change in time required for the price to change, up or down.

trading session   Most commonly means one of the three eight-hour sessions for trading FOREX over a 24-hour period—Asian, European, and North American. Technically, there are five sessions between Sunday evening and Friday evening: The New York exchange trades from 7:30 A.M. to 5:00 P.M. EST. The Sydney, Auckland, and Wellington exchanges trade from 3:00 P.M. to 11:00 P.M. EST. The Tokyo exchange trades from 6:00 P.M. to 11:00 P.M., stopping for an hour-long lunch break, then trading again until 4:00 A.M. EST. The Hong Kong and Singapore exchanges trade from 7:00 P.M. to 3:00 A.M. EST. The last exchanges trading are the Munich, Zurich, Paris, Frankfurt, Brussels, Amsterdam, and London exchanges. These all trade from 2:30 A.M. to 11:30 A.M. EST.

trailing stop   The practice of moving a stop loss in the direction of the market's movement. Used primarily to protect profits. See also floating stop.

transaction cost   The cost of buying or selling a financial instrument.

transaction date   The date on which a trade occurs.

turnover   The total money value of all executed transactions in a given time period; volume.

two-way price   When both a bid and an ask are quoted for a FOREX transaction.

ultra-high-frequency trading   Trading extremely frequently, limited only by how fast you can click the mouse. Called "churning the customer's account" in the old days.

unrealized gain/loss   The theoretical gain or loss on an open position valued at current market rates, as determined by the broker in its sole discretion. Unrealized gain/loss becomes profit/loss when the position is closed.

uptick   A new price quote at a price higher than the preceding quote.

uptick rule   In the United States, a regulation whereby a security may not be sold short unless the last trade prior to the short sale was at a price lower than the price at which the short sale is executed.

U.S. prime rate   The interest rate at which U.S. banks will lend to their prime corporate customers.

value date   The date on which counterparties to a financial transaction agree to settle their respective obligations—that is, exchange payments. For spot currency transactions, the value date is normally two business days forward. Also known as maturity date.

variation margin   Funds a broker must request from the client to have the required margin deposited. The term usually refers to additional funds that must be deposited as a result of unfavorable price movements.

volatility   A statistical measure of a market's price movements over time characterized by deviations from a predetermined central value (usually the arithmetic mean). Also, the gross price movement over a specified period of time given a minimum value unit. See also directional movement (DM) for net price movement.

whipsaw Generally a sideways market ("trading market" as opposed to "trending market") with high volatility in which prices move with you for a short time, then against you.

yard Slang for a billion.

About the Authors

John M. Bland (GVI John) is a co-founder of Global-View.com and a principal and co-manager of the web site. Prior to Global-View, John was a fund manager, independent trader, and consultant. As a vice president and senior dealer, he created and co-managed with Jay Meisler a FOREX interbank and futures trading operation before going out on his own.

Jay M. Meisler (GVI Jay) is a co-founder of Global-View.com and a principal and co-manager of the web site. Jay developed his trading skills at Bankers Trust Company. In addition to trading in New York City and London, Jay spent three years in Singapore as chief foreign exchange and money market dealer.

Michael D. Archer (FXP Mike) is the founder of FXPraxis.com, a research and learning web site for currency traders. He has traded futures and FOREX since the early 1970s and has written numerous books and articles on the subject. His special interest is in applying complexity theory (especially cellular automata) to market forecasting.

Index